An American Triptych

An American Triptych

Anne Bradstreet, Emily Dickinson, Adrienne Rich

BY WENDY MARTIN

The University of North Carolina Press
Chapel Hill and London

© 1984 The University of North Carolina Press
All rights reserved
Manufactured in the United States of America
Set in Sabon by G & S Typesetters
Design by Naomi P. Slifkin

First printing, January 1984
Second printing, June 1984

Library of Congress Cataloging in Publication Data

Martin, Wendy.
An American triptych.

Includes bibliographical references and index.
1. American poetry—Women authors—History and criticism.
2. Feminism in literature.
3. Theology, Puritan, in literature.
4. Bradstreet, Anne, 1612?–1672—Criticism and interpretation.
5. Dickinson, Emily, 1830–1886—Criticism and interpretation.
6. Rich, Adrienne Cecile, 1929– —Criticism and interpretation.

I. Title.
PS310.F45M3   1983   811'.009'9287   83-6864

ISBN 0-8078-1573-X
ISBN 0-8078-4112-9 (pbk.)

For my daughter,
Laurel Martin-Harris,
and my parents,
Earl and Teresa Martin

Contents

Preface

In the 1960s, I was trained as a specialist in early American literature; at that time, I became convinced that Puritanism had had a dramatic influence on subsequent national, social, and political developments. But it was not until the 1970s, when I expanded the range of my scholarship to include American women writers from the seventeenth century to the present, that I recognized the interconnection between Puritan values and American feminist thought. In this book, I have explored the lives of three major American women writers whose work constitutes a female counter-poetic, and I have tried to demonstrate the continuing influence of early American thought on contemporary feminism. It is my hope that scholars and students of American literature, American culture, and feminist criticism will find this study valuable.

I would like to thank Doris Betts, Albert Gelpi, Sandra Gilbert, Alicia Ostriker, and Elaine Showalter, and my colleagues, Michael Kowal, Joseph McElroy, and Donald Stone, for their thoughtful readings of this book in manuscript form. Adrienne Rich has given me considerable help during the many years it took to write this book; in addition to permitting me to tape a lengthy conversation with her, she has sent me her poems in advance of publication, and I very much appreciate her support. I am very much indebted to Sacvan Bercovitch, whose incisive suggestions deepened my understanding of the religious and political tensions of Anne Bradstreet's life and whose extraordinary scholarship has illuminated the currents of American thought.

The astute comments of Iris Tillman Hill and the expert editing of Sandra Eisdorfer helped me to pull the manuscript together in the final stages. I am grateful to them and to Nell Irvin Painter, who devoted long hours to proofreading galleys with me. During the two decades that I have been a student and scholar of American literature and culture, I have benefited from the insight and example of Brom Weber and Jim Woodress.

Finally, I would like to express my gratitude to Jed Harris, my husband, who has never known me when I was not working on this book.

While working full time, he has taken care of our daughter, Laurel, cleaned the house, cooked the meals, typed much of the manuscript, and provided editorial assistance. Without his insight, his patience, and his consistent encouragement, this book would not have been written.

Chapel Hill, North Carolina
January 1983

An American Triptych

Introduction

This is a book about three American poets who were women. As Americans, as women, as poets, they shared nationality, gender, an aesthetic tradition, but each expressed this experience in the context of her particular historical moment. Anne Bradstreet was the first woman poet in the New World; Emily Dickinson, in the nineteenth century, became a model for all women poets who followed, a model of eccentricity and isolation; Adrienne Rich, our contemporary, has consciously confronted not only the meaning of the American female poetic career but also the political responsibilities the woman poet owes her country, her sex, her time.

American literary scholarship has investigated the origins of our national traditions, and many studies have explored the connection between American literature and religion, but few have applied these concepts to women writers to discover how the American experience has been transformed and transfigured in their work.[1] And none of these studies has concentrated on the evolution of female culture from Puritans to the present to determine how these American women poets have created an alternative vision grounded in the reality of their daily lives—a reality that has been ignored or distorted by the prevailing ethos.

From the severe demands of Puritanism on Anne Bradstreet through the personalized Romanticism that simultaneously inspired and restricted Emily Dickinson to the private and public feminism that has liberated and challenged Adrienne Rich, these poets have created a female aesthetic-ethic. Their poetry celebrates the life of this earth and demonstrates their commitment to nurturance rather than dominance. Their lives bear witness to their resistance to "the fathers" earthly and heavenly, and their work elaborates their vision of a loving community of women that forms the basis of a countertradition to the androcentric society in which they lived.

In the past decade, feminist criticism has been concerned with the special issues of the female imagination and the profession of the woman writer; several feminist studies have concentrated on British women writers or on novelists.[2] Recently a few studies have concentrated on American women poets, but none has explored their relationship to early American thought.[3] Although there are many parallels in American and

British experience, there were major differences, especially for those women who chose to write poetry. Emily Dickinson and Adrienne Rich both read *Jane Eyre*, but the world they inhabited was not Charlotte Brontë's.

Anne Bradstreet, Emily Dickinson, and Adrienne Rich have spanned important phases in the development of American history and culture from Puritanism to transcendentalism to modern feminism. This study attempts to create a full portrait of each poet as she lived or is living in her own time; for, by placing these poets in a specific social and historical context, from colonial to romantic to contemporary American, it is possible to appreciate better their growth as artists and as individuals. In addition, it is necessary to understand the work of these poets as part of a web of American experience. Their personal and artistic conflicts and challenges are clarified by the understanding of the larger cultural context of their lives.

Bradstreet, Dickinson, and Rich lived most of their adult lives in the Northeastern United States—Bradstreet in Andover, Massachusetts; Dickinson in Amherst, Massachusetts; Rich in Boston, New York City, and most recently, Montague, Massachusetts. Anne Bradstreet's family left the security of their familiar lives in England to encounter the unknown conditions of the "vast wilderness" of the New World. In addition to coping with the harsh and life-threatening conditions in the Massachusetts Bay Colony, Bradstreet had a demanding existence as the mother of eight children and wife of a Puritan governor. In spite of her burdensome domestic responsibilities in a relatively primitive environment, she managed to publish the first volume of poems written by a woman in the New World.

Bradstreet lived in a society that needed its cohesive religious ideals to survive the New World rigors. Faith in God's providential plan sustained the "errand into the wilderness" and enabled the Puritans to endure the harsh conditions of New England. Bradstreet's world was absolute—God was at its center. As the sermons of John Cotton, John Winthrop, Cotton and Increase Mather, and Jonathan Edwards reveal, the Puritans thought of themselves as destined to carry out a divine mission. In spite of the eschatological framework that supported Bradstreet's daily life, she sometimes questioned the validity of the Puritan voyage and doubted the existence of God. But she ultimately learned to control her agonizing skepticism by committing herself to the religious values of her culture.

Emily Dickinson was much less committed to the morals of nineteenth-century congregational Amherst than was Bradstreet to the Puritan church. As a rebellious adolescent, Dickinson took a vow to stand apart from the conventional world—to listen to her inner voice. As a young woman, she wrestled with her fears of impiety and damnation as well as with her anxiety about being a disobedient daughter; she emerged from the struggle committed to poetry. In the age of the economic individualism of the robber barons and the rapid industrialization of the Northeastern cities, Dickinson, like Thoreau, Hawthorne, and Melville, rejected commercial values. Writing in relative isolation and obscurity during the American Renaissance, she remained in her parents' home where she created a haven for herself and her friends. Subverting the role of the Victorian lady, Dickinson used her leisure and privacy to gain time to write poetry.

Adrienne Rich has had a many-faceted life: she has been a student, wife, mother, teacher, radical feminist and lesbian, political activist, and public speaker as well as an internationally known poet. Each of these dimensions of her experience has contributed to her vision. As a contemporary poet who is active in the public sphere, Rich has not accepted the choices necessitated by Bradstreet's piety and Dickinson's privatism. As a modern woman, she has insisted on a fusion of her private and public experience. Her poetry is concerned with war, urban poverty, sexism, and racism as well as with private emotion and the appreciation of nature.

There are many common threads of experience in the biographies of these three poets. Each of them had prominent, powerful fathers who were leaders of their respective communities: Thomas Dudley was a Puritan magistrate; Edward Dickinson was a much respected lawyer and trustee of Amherst College; Arnold Rich was a brilliant pathologist at Johns Hopkins University. These dominant men inspired their daughters to become poets, while resisting their personal and artistic autonomy. The mothers of these poets—Dorothy Dudley, Emily Norcross, and Helen Jones—chose traditional lives, subordinating their individual interests to those of their husbands. These daughters of submissive women and stern, demanding men experienced considerable conflict in shaping the circumstances of their lives, but, ultimately, this conflict was the crucible of their identities as poets who have insisted on creating their own aesthetic and ethical priorities.

All three poets have resisted the prevailing ethos of their time. For example, Anne Bradstreet resisted the seventeenth-century ideal of providential destiny, which spurred and sustained the Puritan colonization of the New World. Her father and brothers were leaders of the Puritan expedition of 1630, but Bradstreet confessed that her "heart rose" in protest. Emily Dickinson resented the industrial development of New England and was critical of the ideal of manifest destiny, which was the nineteenth-century version of the Puritan mission. Her father and brother were Amherst lawyers, community leaders, and apologists for commerce.

In the twentieth century, Adrienne Rich has been an articulate critic of American technological materialism and expansionism, which constitute yet a further extension of manifest destiny and the Puritan errand into the wilderness.

The work of Bradstreet, Dickinson, and Rich creates an alternative response to the patriarchal tradition in art and politics. Each of these poets has evolved a deeply personal vision that affirms her experience in a society that has often denied women a voice. Adrienne Rich has been the most conscious of her need to create a poetic and social vision that honors life in its diverse forms. Emily Dickinson's garden was her private paradise, all the more precious because she accepted its transience. In contrast to Dickinson and Rich, who celebrate temporal concerns, Bradstreet rejected her love of the world as vanity and feared the satanic lure of carnality. Yet in spite of her powerful religious perspective, she too was deeply affected by nature's beauty and loved her earthly life. Her poetry demonstrates that her belief in heaven was actually a sublimated expression of her love of life on earth.

While the lives of Bradstreet, Dickinson, and Rich chronicle the shifts in the status of American women from private companion to participant in a wider public life, their poetry records their deeply felt personal responses to their worlds, responses ranging from resigned acceptance of traditional religion and private rebellion to public criticism of the culture that shapes and limits their experience. Bradstreet, Dickinson, and Rich have much to tell us about the evolution of feminist and patriarchal perspectives. The work of these three poets is part of a larger cultural process, and it is illuminating to trace out the historical shifts that have resulted in the evolution from Bradstreet's religious meditations to Dickinson's fierce privatism to Rich's public discourse. All men are not patriarchs, nor are all women feminists, but these two poles define an important dimension in our culture that this book explores.

In the theocentric universe of Anne Bradstreet, human beings were divided into the categories of unregenerate and regenerate; those who were saved by God were promised eternal life and those who were not were damned forever. Bradstreet chose life. Emily Dickinson's cosmos was private, gynecocentric; life on earth was the focus of her nurturing, protective energy, and attention. Finally, Adrienne Rich extends Dickinson's woman-centered vision beyond the private sphere to encompass the public world. All three women understand and appreciate the intricate balance of "this great household upon the earth," as Anne Bradstreet wrote. Reverence for life—generativity—is the central theme of their poetry, a generativity that radically challenges patriarchal ideology and politics.

Because Rich and Dickinson are American poets, the form of their poetic vision sometimes parallels the Puritan eschatology of Bradstreet's work. Friends replace the saints in Dickinson's world, and Rich substitutes the international community of women for the elect. But unlike Bradstreet, Dickinson and Rich do not place God in the center of a hierarchically ordered universe; instead, theirs is an ecological perspective in which all life—animal, vegetable, and mineral—is revered as an essential part of the awesome cosmos. For Dickinson and Rich, life is intrinsically sacred while Bradstreet believed God imparted divine meaning to existence.

Although Puritanism was monotheistic and more concerned with eternal life than with mortal experience, Anne Bradstreet felt earth's pull. The city on a hill was a womanless ideal, but as the mother of eight children, Bradstreet knew that women gave birth to the army of saints. And she so deeply loved life on earth that she committed herself to God in the hope that the joy she felt in this life would be perpetuated eternally in heaven. Unlike Anne Bradstreet, Emily Dickinson did not repress her understanding of cyclic time, earth's fecundity, or mortality. Committing her life and her art to the celebration of nature's powers, she became mother earth's high priestess while her father guarded the law. Dickinson's sister and women friends were also celebrants of the cycle of growth and decay; their custom of sending baskets of flowers or fruits and vegetables to acknowledge a birth or to mourn a death is a domestic version of the rituals of ancient nature worship that still survives today. Adrienne Rich shares the generative vision of Dickinson. Reviving the power of the furies in her later poetry, she decries the phallic technological city that prizes profit and prowess while denying the importance of nurturing and reverence toward life. Her recent poetry affirms the cycle of nature in contrast to the abuse of nature by the fathers in their need for transcendence. In both her poetry and prose, Rich has repeatedly observed that modern life has been greatly impoverished by the loss of female vision.

Although there is a dramatic contrast between the content of the feminist vision and the Puritan vision, it is instructive to understand that there are striking parallels in form and that these shared patterns are an important part of American culture. Although the ideals of the community of women are based on feminist/lesbian values, the conceptual framework that forged the community has its roots in early American history. Both Puritan reformation and feminist transformation are structurally similar: both envision the creation of a new world whether it be the city upon a hill or the community of women. The Puritan heart prepared to receive God's grace has its parallel in the feminist process of consciousness raising, and both Puritans and feminists accept struggle as an essential part of their lives as pilgrims or pioneers. Just as the Puritan errand into the wilderness was grounded in the conviction that the New World colony was a redemptive mission, so Rich's feminist vision is based on a belief that communities concerned with honoring and protecting life—a nurturing ethos—can help to reverse the destructive effects of patriarchal culture. Like the commonwealth of saints, the concept of the community of women is a profoundly political phenomenon involving an evolution from an acceptance of traditional values to the questioning of these values to rebellion and finally to separation from the dominant culture in order to form a new social order. This pattern of protest and reform and this belief in regeneration and renewal—of the possibility of beginning again—is a prominent characteristic of much American psychological and social life.

There is an evolution from Puritanism to prophecy in the work of Bradstreet, Dickinson, and Rich—prophecy, not in the sense of foretelling events or assuring a bright future for the saints, as the Puritans used it, but in the preclassical sense of the utterance of truths that well up from the depths of awareness deeper and more complete than that afforded by reason or faith. Bradstreet tried to be dutiful to her fathers, divine and mortal; Dickinson rejected male authorities and created a "covered vision"; Rich has translated Dickinson's private cosmology into a public discourse that predates Judeo-Christian mythology for metaphors to affirm female experience. Like many feminists, Rich has observed that patriarchal religious and social systems have had a negative effect on our civilization by emphasizing the importance of transcendence, power, and control. Urging that the city upon a hill open its gates to everyone regardless of gender, race, or class, Adrienne Rich hopes that the feminist vision of the community of women will be the beginning of a new chapter in American history. This millennial ideal recalls the desire of the Puritan settlers to establish a new social order more than three centuries ago.

Anne Bradstreet's world was essentially Aristotelian: her world consisted of ordered spheres—earth, the heavens, and the underworld—each having its characteristic form. Individual choices were foreordained and occurred in a ritualized, linear order; a saint progressed from temporal to eternal life. Influenced by Newtonian physics, Dickinson's world consisted of a stable earth in the whirling heavens. No longer a fixed point, God was disappearing and eternal life was problematic. Almost as if to counteract this essential instability, Dickinson remained at home to explore the spinning heavens; no longer an inexorable orderly progression, the changing seasons became cycles of growth and decay. Home, for Dickinson, then, was a fixed point in the flux. However, all space is relative in Adrienne Rich's world; her relationship to it is dynamic and characterized by an exhilarating mutuality and variability; unlike Bradstreet or Dickinson, she frequently shifts her social and psychic ground and creates new personal and poetic forms to explore her experience.

After much confusion and self-doubt, Bradstreet accepted her inevitable journey from earth to heaven. Dickinson stayed at home, in her garden and with her network of friends; to the extent that she withdrew from linear time, she created an eternity in art. Dickinson insured stability by renouncing the larger world. Home was her personal, fixed center. In contrast, Rich celebrates changeability, variety, movement. Her life is more dynamic than either Bradstreet's or Dickinson's; it has consisted of many points of view, many perspectives. Hers is a stochastic universe, shaped by Einsteinian physics, in which there is neither center nor circumference; her experience is open-ended, and her work responds to contemporary social conditions and problems. Like her episodic life, Rich's work is many-directional, turning on possibility, variation, and change.

Religious values gave meaning to Bradstreet's life at a time when it was dangerous to perceive the world as anything but a reflection of God's glory. It was sometimes painful for her to accept the Puritan values, and she ultimately chose heaven as an affirmation of this life. When Emily Dickinson rejected the certainties of patriarchal religion, she accepted the risk of independence and the burden of being in charge of her life. In relinquishing the comforting assurances of heaven, she accepted her personal mortality and the loss of her loved ones at death. By giving up the illusion of a foreordained life, Dickinson gained the power of her senses; what she could see, taste, or feel imparted meaning to Dickinson's world. She used her autonomy to bend religious and social structures to meet her needs—whether it was to parody Watts's hymns or the ideal of the Victorian lady. Adrienne Rich, as a modern woman, has used history, psychology, and science to understand the world in which she lives, and she has allowed her own feelings and experience to guide her in shaping her reality. Bradstreet risked heresy if she interpreted her experience for herself, Dickinson chose to take that risk, and Rich insists on the right of all women to create the conditions of their lives.

Bradstreet struggled to write poetry in a society that was hostile to the imagination. Her voice was sometimes subdued by religious concerns; nevertheless, she was able to express the range of her feelings. Dickinson exercised extraordinary emotional and aesthetic freedom in her poems, but she did not actively or persistently seek publication. Building on the Bradstreet-Dickinson legacy, Rich has given artistic form to her personal and political convictions, and her poetry is internationally known and read. There is an evolution from Bradstreet's ultimate submission to Dickinson's quasi-rebellion to Rich's rejection of patriarchal culture that parallels a metaphysical evolution—from Bradstreet's hierarchical universe to Dickinson's cyclic world in which home is the fixed point to Rich's acceptance of flux in a universe in which there is no stability.

In the work of these poets there is a continuum from acceptance of traditional patriarchal values to passive resistance against convention to a deep alienation that has inspired the vision of a new society. All three poets have protested, to varying degrees, the disjunction of mind and nature that characterizes Judeo-Christian thought.[4] The work of Bradstreet, Dickinson, and Rich suggests a female poetic in which nature is not subordinate to reason and in which genius, literary or otherwise, is not perceived as male energy uncontaminated by female matter. Replacing androcentric metaphors that define nature as a woman whose mysteries must be penetrated and whose body must be dominated by the male mind, or transcended by the male poet, the poetry of Dickinson and Rich often depicts the male principle as an intrusion on female process. In a reformulation of masculine hierarchies that create stratified order according to the principles of graduated power, or dominance and submission, the female countertradition postulates the coexistence of mutability—the disorderly, the unpredictable—with logos—the accountable, the knowable. With each of these poets, communal reciprocity and intersubjectivity increasingly take the place of hierarchical authority.

Traditionally, women's history and literature have not been monumental in scope and do not lend themselves to heroic declamation. The jeremiad, political speech, and literary epic are male forms requiring a command of public space that women have not had. The images of women's experience more often come from daily life—the sampler, the quilt, and the photograph album. Because these women poets reject the male hierarchies that accord more importance to public than to private life, their poetry is not a narrative of sublime moments but a chronicle of the quotidian. Anne Bradstreet admitted that she grew weary of the heroic couplets that she laboriously penned to please her father; Emily Dickinson adapted Watts's leaden meters to suit her own playful, ironic perceptions; Adrienne Rich has used a variety of literary styles from prose narrative to sustained lyric in an effort to break down rigid genre hierarchies.

It is not my intention to provide a comprehensive account of American women poets but to examine three representative women poets against the background of their historical time and place. There are no other Puritan women poets of Anne Bradstreet's stature; certainly there are no nineteenth-century women poets who approach Emily Dickinson's position in the canon. Although H. D., Edna St. Vincent Millay, Marianne Moore, Sylvia Plath, and many other twentieth-century American women poets could have been included in this study, I have chosen to concentrate on Adrienne Rich as the contemporary poet whose work most completely represents an extension of the concerns of Bradstreet and Dickinson.[5] This book is an effort not only to understand the experience of three major women poets whose art spans the period of our nation's history but also to suggest the outlines of an American female poetic. It portrays three faces of feminism, three phases of poetic form. Each frame holds a portrait that examines in detail the life and work of the Puritan wife of a colonial magistrate, the white-robed, reclusive New England seer, and the modern feminist and lesbian activist—together, they compose the panels of an American triptych.

PART ONE

Anne Bradstreet

"As weary pilgrim"

As weary pilgrim, now at rest,
  Hugs with delight his silent nest
His wasted limbes, now lye full soft
  That myrie steps, have troden oft
Blesses himself, to think upon
  his dangers past, and travailes done

The Works of Anne Bradstreet
in Prose and Verse, 42

Introduction

When Anne Bradstreet (1612–72) dedicated her "Meditations Divine and Morall" to her son, Simon, on March 20, 1664, she told him that because this material was deeply personal, it contained no references to the work of other writers: these reflections, she confided to the fourth of her eight children, contain "nothing but myne owne." This is a declaration of strength by a seasoned writer who felt less dependent on literary and religious authorities to buttress her ideas or substantiate her perceptions than she had in her youth. In contrast to her earliest poetry, which closely followed male poetic models, Bradstreet's later work was rooted in her actual experience as a wife, as a mother, and as a woman in seventeenth-century New England.

Much of the material in the first edition of *The Tenth Muse*, published in 1650 when Bradstreet was thirty-eight, was formulaic and divorced from her personal observations and feelings. The often wooden lines and forced rhymes of her early poems reveal Bradstreet's grim determination to prove that she could write in the lofty style of the established male poets, but her deeper emotions are obviously not engaged in the project. After the publication of her first volume, Bradstreet gained confidence in her own responses as a source and subject for her poetry, and as she began to write of her desire for artistic achievement, her love for her family and temporal life, as well as her ambivalence about the religious issues of faith, grace, and salvation, her poetry became more finely honed and emotionally powerful.

As a child, Bradstreet was bedridden with rheumatic fever; as an adolescent she almost died from smallpox. As a young woman she endured a three-month ocean crossing from England to the New World, the dangers of starvation, disease, and Indian attacks, and the hazards of eight pregnancies and deliveries. As a mature woman, she mourned the deaths of her parents and would live to grieve deeply over the untimely loss of three grandchildren and a beloved daughter-in-law. Bradstreet left the comforts of an aristocratic manor house in the English countryside to accompany her father and husband to the Massachusetts Bay Colony where they hoped to better their estates as well as find religious freedom. Once in New England, she uprooted her household several times to move to increasingly more distant, uncivilized, and dangerous outposts so that her father and husband could increase their property as well as their political power in the colony.

Although she played the role of a dedicated Puritan and a dutiful daughter and wife, Bradstreet often expressed ambivalence about the male authorities in her life, including God, her father and husband, and the literary critics and authors whose models she initially copied. On one hand, she very much wanted their approval and, on the other, she was angered by their denial of the value of her experience and abilities. In her dedication of *The Tenth Muse* to her father Thomas Dudley, Bradstreet assumes the persona of the obedient daughter: "From her that to your self, more duty owes / Then water in the boundless Ocean flows," and she describes her work as "lowly," "meanly clad," "poor," and "ragged" in contrast to the soaring strength of her male mentors.[1] In the "Prologue" to the volume, Bradstreet persists in her strategy of self-deprecation, describing her muse as "foolish, broken, blemished" in her effort to conceal her ambition. In dramatic contrast to her declarations of weakness is Bradstreet's eulogy honoring the "Happy Memory" of Queen Elizabeth, the only poem in *The Tenth Muse* that contains no apologies. Here she expresses her unqualified admiration for the queen as an exemplar of female prowess:

> Who was so good, so just, so learn'd so wise
> From all the Kings on earth she won the prize.
> Nor say I more then duly is her due,
> Millions will testifie that this is true.
> She hath wip'd off th' aspersion of her Sex,
> That women wisdome lack to play the Rex
> (*Works*, 358–59)

These assertive lines claim for Elizabeth what Bradstreet dared not claim for herself—power, judgment, wisdom, achievement. Certainly it was less stressful and less dangerous to make this bold declaration praising female abilities in a historical context than it would have been for Bradstreet to publicly proclaim the worth of her own work. Although Bradstreet was an educated woman, a child of one colonial governor and the wife of another, this privileged status alone could not protect her against the scorn and persecution visited upon women who stepped beyond their deferential role in Puritan society. Only by careful execution of her pre-scribed responsibilities could she escape the fate of Anne Hutchinson and her own sister Sarah Keayne who had both been excommunicated from the church and ostracized by the community for speaking their minds in public. Certainly Bradstreet's life and work illuminate the conflict that American women writers have traditionally experienced between a need for intellectual and emotional autonomy and a desire for recognition and acceptance from male authorities.

The second edition of *The Tenth Muse* published posthumously in Boston in 1678 contains several superbly crafted poems that provide a sense of Bradstreet's potential achievement had she not felt constrained to adopt a dutiful and deferential stance. These love poems, elegies, and meditations are considerably more candid about her spiritual crises, her deep attachment to her family, and her love of mortal life than was her earlier work; perhaps her father's death in 1653 as well as the publication of her work in 1650 gave her the psychological freedom necessary to ex-press herself more openly. The more honestly she wrote of her emotional and religious tensions and her desire for recognition and her love of life on earth, the more accomplished her poetry became, and the imitative and often strained poems of the first edition were superseded by the ex-pertly crafted lines of the second edition.

Puritans accepted doubt and confusion about faith and conversion as part of the arduous process of weaning the affections from earthly at-tachments, but Anne Bradstreet's resolute efforts to be worthy of God's grace intensified her uncertainty about the promise of eternal life. Her mixed emotions are articulated in "Contemplations," published in the second edition of *The Tenth Muse*, which most critics consider to be her best poem:

> Then higher on the glistering Sun I gaz'd,
> Whose beams was shaded by the leavie Tree,
> The more I look'd, the more I grew amaz'd,
> And softly said, what glory's like to thee?
> Soul of this world, this Universes Eye,
> No wonder, some made thee a Deity:
> Had I not better Known, (alas) the same had I.
> (*Works*, 371)

Bradstreet's faith is paradoxically achieved by immersing herself in the beauty and strength of nature, and her hope for heaven is an expression of a desire to live forever—a prolongation of earthly joy rather than a renunciation of life's pleasures. Male critics such as Robert Richardson,

William Irvin, and Robert Daly interpret this poem as a document of Bradstreet's moral triumph over earthly attachments,[2] while Bradstreet's recent biographers, Elizabeth Wade White and Ann Stanford, observe that she was often distressed by the conflicting demands of poetry and religious faith.[3]

Near the end of her life, weakened by chronic illness and saddened by the deaths of her loved ones and the destruction of her home, her library, unpublished manuscripts, and most of her household effects by fire, Anne Bradstreet finally appeared to take genuine comfort in the promise of an afterlife. Nevertheless, her penultimate poem, an elegy for her month-old grandson written three years before her own death, reveals deep reservations about the wisdom of God's decisions:

> With dreadful awe before him let's be mute,
> Such was his will, but why, let's not dispute,
> With humble hearts and mouths put in the dust,
> Let's say he's merciful as well as just.
>
> (*Works*, 406)

Bradstreet's forced resignation barely conceals her anguished rage about a death that seems to be arbitrary and unfair. Unlike some of her male contemporaries—John Winthrop, Samuel Sewall, and Thomas Shepard—who accepted the deaths of their family members as afflictions intended to correct their own sins, Anne Bradstreet's response was not so self-centered. For example, when his son dies at four months, Thomas Shepard does not grieve for the infant but laments the fact that his sinfulness caused "the Lord to strike at innocent children for my own sake." And even his wife's death is subsumed by his devouring conscience: "[H]e took away my dear, precious, meek and loving wife in childbed. . . . this affliction was very heavy to me, for in it the Lord seemed to withdraw his tender care for me and mine which he graciously manifested by my dear wife."[4] In contrast to Shepard's egocentric conviction that God has singled him out for punishment, Bradstreet is shocked by the apparently wanton demonstration of divine power. These polarized responses of mastery and nurturance mirror the masculine and feminine patterns prescribed by their society.

Anne Bradstreet ultimately represented her life as a pilgrimage toward heaven, but her work reveals that it was actually a journey from artistic ambition to resolute piety. In spite of her intensely religious society, much of Bradstreet's work is occupied with secular concerns; in spite of the dangers of public assertion by a woman, she longed for recognition; and in spite of her concerted efforts to be devout, she was finally unable to fully accept the Puritan God. Although Bradstreet never renounced her religious faith, she observed that if it were not for the unfortunate fact of dissolution and decay, she would not seek salvation, "for were earthly comforts permanent, who would look for heavenly?" (*Works*, 69).

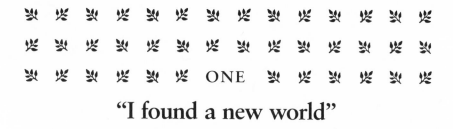

"I found a new world"

When Anne Dudley Bradstreet arrived in the New World after a three-month journey aboard the *Arbella*, which with the *Talbot*, the *Ambrose*, and the *Jewell* had sailed from England in April 1630, she admitted that her "heart rose" against the Puritan mission. She was eighteen and unhappy about being forced to leave her comfortable life in the mansion of the earl of Lincolnshire where her father, Thomas Dudley, had been steward of the earl's estate and her husband, Simon Bradstreet, had been her father's assistant. Life at Theophilus Lincoln's manor in Sempringham had been gracious and stimulating, and Anne Bradstreet reluctantly left the amenities of this aristocratic household to face the dangers of an unknown land.[1] The three-month voyage across the Atlantic was arduous, and the Charlestown records describe the suffering of the newly arrived colonists:

> Many people arrived sick of the scurvy, which also increased after
> their arrival, for want of houses, and by reason of wet lodging in
> their cottages, etc. Other distempers also prevailed; and although
> [the] people were generally very loving and pitiful, yet the sickness
> did so prevail, that the whole were not able to tend the sick, as
> they should be tended; upon which many perished and died, and
> were buried about the Town Hill.[2]

The grievances that brought the Puritan expedition to New England were not Anne Bradstreet's but belonged to the two men she loved. Whatever degree of pride or self-preservation Bradstreet possessed caused her to rebel against her part in the destiny of the Puritan tribe: " [I] came into this Country, where I found a new world and new manners, at which my heart rose. But after I was convinced it was the way of God, I submitted to it and joined the church at Boston" (*Works*, 5). This was not *her* mission to the New World and its bleak reality. Although she joined the Boston congregation, Bradstreet remained ambivalent about the Puritan enterprise. Although she never overtly rejected the authority of the church, her faith was often troubled. Unlike Anne Hutchinson, Anne Bradstreet did not risk censure and exile, but her poetry reveals that she continued to have doubts about salvation and eternal life for much of her life.

Anne Bradstreet's earliest years in Northamptonshire where her father, Thomas Dudley, was a clerk to Judge Nicolls, as well as her life in the manor at Lincolnshire from the time she was seven until her departure from England at eighteen, provide a dramatic contrast to the harsh conditions of seventeenth-century Massachusetts. Living among educated and leisured aristocrats, she learned to read and write and to enjoy literature, the study of languages, and music. Having access to the wide variety of books in Theophilus Lincoln's large library, she was probably familiar with Spenser, Marlowe, Jonson, and Bacon as well as Milton, Herbert, and Shakespeare.[3] It is also likely that she read those poets who were sympathetic to the New England effort—Quarles, who contributed translations to the *Bay Psalm Book*, and Sidney and Donne, who considered emigration to the New World.[4]

Anne Bradstreet's father was a thoughtful and well-informed man who taught his daughter Greek, Latin, French, and Hebrew and encouraged her to read and write poetry. Although Thomas Dudley did not have a university education, he was tutored by an Oxford graduate in Latin language and literature at a "free school" in Northampton and was described by Cotton Mather as "a devourer of books."[5] In general, Bradstreet lived among people who were highly educated and widely read. Most of the men in the earl's immediate family and household had degrees from Oxford or Cambridge as did Anne's brother Samuel. Although Anne Bradstreet did not attend the university with her brother— Cambridge was a male institution—she was educated in the Elizabethan tradition that valued female intelligence.[6]

Anne Bradstreet's family background is representative of those Puritans who, as Raymond Williams and Larzer Ziff suggest, embraced religious nonconformity in an effort to gain control over their lives.[7] Deprived of land by the sixteenth- and seventeenth-century British primogeniture laws, younger sons usually entered professions—law, estate management, the army, or the clergy—but they no longer exercised the social or economic power of their fathers and eldest brothers. The doctrine of grace central to Puritanism offered this disenfranchised group an opportunity to assert their inner worth as individuals, and nonconformist religion provided a rationale for resisting the entrenched social structure.

Apparently, Thomas Dudley came from a family of considerable social standing, and Elizabeth Wade White speculates that he was the younger son of a baron.[8] After serving as captain in Queen Elizabeth's army, he returned to Faxton, Northampton and improved his financial condition by marrying Dorothy Yorke, the daughter of a yeoman whose "Estate" according to Cotton Mather was "Considerable." When the Dudleys joined the earl of Lincoln's Puritan household in Sempringham, they experienced no shift in religious values. The manor house was only eighteen miles from the nonconformist center of Boston, where John Cotton was vicar; and as members of the Lincolnshire congregation, Thomas Dudley and his assistant Simon Bradstreet, who became his son-in-law, were actively involved in the religious and political struggles with King Charles I and Archbishop Laud, who were hostile to the nonconformist emphasis on covenantal theology and Augustinian piety.

Anne Bradstreet's description of the moral training that she and her sisters, Patience, Sarah, Mercy, and Dorothy, and her brother Samuel, received at Sempringham demonstrates the Puritan emphasis on moral purity and the cleansed conscience:

> In my young years, about 6 or 7 as I take it, I began to make
> conscience of my wayes, and what I knew was sinfull, as lying,
> disobedience to Parents, etc. I avoided it. If at any time I was over-
> taken with the like evills, it was a great Trouble. I could not be at
> rest 'till by prayer I had confest it unto God. I was also troubled at
> the neglect of Private Dutyes, tho: too often tardy that way. I also
> found much comfort in reading the Scriptures, especially those
> places I thought most concerned my Condition, and as I grew to
> have more understanding, so the more Solace I took in them.[9]

This habit of intensive self-scrutiny provided the psychological scaffolding for nonconformist protest against the royal sacerdotalism and the elaborate rituals of Anglicanism and Royal Catholicism that culminated in the the mass exodus to the New World. The moral outrage that fueled the "great migration" is expressed in the scornful lines of Anne Bradstreet's poem "The Dialogue between Old England and New" written during the English civil war—twelve years after she and her family landed on the Massachusetts shore:

> These are the dayes the Churches foes to crush,
> To root out Popelings head, tail, branch and rush;
> Let's bring *Baals* vestments forth to make a fire,
> Their Mytires, Surplices, and all their Tire,
> Copes, Rotchets, Crossiers, and such empty trash,
> And let their Names consume, but let the flash

Light Christendome, and all the world to see
We hate *Romes* whore, with all her trumpery.
(*Works*, 340–41)

Enraged by the abridgment of religious and civil rights and illegal taxes
levied by Charles I, a group of beleaguered Puritans, including Anne
Bradstreet's father and new husband, formed the New England Company
with the intention of emigrating. This group was granted a charter in
1628 in the name of the Massachusetts Bay Company to administer their
New World settlement; Thomas Dudley was listed as one of the founders
and Simon Bradstreet was designated as deputy secretary. Grounded in
economic necessity and spiritual consensus, this messianic enterprise
bound the Puritan tribe with legal and financial requirements that were
as stringent as the exacting moral obligations of covenant theology.
Strengthened by a conviction of providential destiny as prophesied in the
Bible, the founders of the joint stock company and their families in 1630
undertook the three-month ocean crossing that was described by Samuel
Danforth as "the errand into the wilderness." [10]

Once on board the *Arbella*, John Winthrop elaborated the duties and
responsibilities of the colonists, emphasizing the binding obligations of
their covenant with God. Although Winthrop's clarification of this contract helped to reduce the extreme anxiety of the passengers on a crowded
ship sailing an unpredictable sea toward an unknown land, his assurances
did not mitigate the seasickness, scurvy, and malnutrition that afflicted
many of the voyagers. In the midst of these travails, Winthrop reminded
his constituents that they were like the tribe of Moses in search of the
promised land—their mission was to build the Holy City in the New
World. As the ships approached the Massachusetts shore, Winthrop observed: "We had now faire sunneshine weather, and so *pleasant* a *sweet*
ayre as did much refreshe us, and there came a *smell off the shore* like the
smell of a garden." [11] But the sunshine and sweet air were not harbingers
of a comfortable life. After the four ships landed, there was no respite
from hardship as Thomas Dudley's letter to the countess of Lincoln indicates: "We found the Colony in a sad and unexpected condition, above
eighty of them being dead the winter before; and many of those alive
weak and sick; all the corn and bread amongst them all hardly sufficient
to feed them a fortnight." [12]

Among those who died of fever in the first months after their landing
were Theophilus Lincoln's sister, Lady Arbella, and her husband Isaac
Johnson. Some of the colonists were killed while exploring the terrain in
search of food and appropriate housing sites; John Winthrop's son Henry
drowned in sight of the shore while swimming across an inlet to get a

better view of Indian wigwams. Dudley estimated that from their arrival in Massachusetts to the following December, "there died by estimation about two hundred at least." [13] Attributing the high mortality rate to "want of warm lodging and good diet, to which Englishmen are habituated at home," he lamented, "there is not one house where there is not one dead and in some houses many." [14] In addition to scurvy, fever, uncertain food supplies, and inadequate housing, Indian attacks were an ever-present danger.

Although Thomas Dudley and Simon Bradstreet were founders of the Massachusetts Bay Company and leaders of the colony, they had few amenities. Their families lived in the same house in Salem for many months and their cramped quarters offered little protection from the winter cold. In his letter to the countess of Lincoln, Thomas Dudley complained that there was "no table" on which he could work or write and that the two families were confined to the room in which there was a fireplace: "They break good manners, and make me many times forget what I would say and say what I would not." [15]

When the Puritan expedition left Southampton for the unknown shores of New England in 1630, John Cotton used a text from 2 Sam. 1 : 7 – 10 of the Geneva Bible as the basis of his parting message—"God's Promise to His Plantation"—to his parishioners: "Also I will appoint a place for my people Israel, and will plant it, that they may dwell in a place of their own, and move no more." But the biblical promise of a permanent dwelling did not prove to be true for Anne Bradstreet. Once in the New World she was obliged to uproot her household several times in order to follow her father and husband from Salem to Charlestown, to Cambridge, to Ipswich, and finally to Andover in their search for more favorable living conditions. Because the circumstances in Salem were so oppressive, the Bradstreets and Dudleys joined with the families of John Winthrop, Isaac Johnson, and John Wilson in the move to Charlestown in the summer of 1630. But the situation did not improve, and during the harsh winter that followed, the group had an extremely difficult time getting enough to eat. They managed to survive on "clams, and muscles, and ground-nuts, and acorns, and these got with much difficulty." [16] After several months of this rudimentary diet, Anne Bradstreet must have longed for the sumptuous meals she had eaten in the spacious dining hall of the manor house.

In the spring of 1631, the Dudleys and Bradstreets moved again, this time to Newtown, later called Cambridge. A year later the nineteen-year-old Anne Bradstreet "fell into a lingering sicknes like a consumption, together with a lamenesse" (*Works*, 5). Undoubtedly her ill health was aggravated by the repeated dislocations as well as poor living conditions, but her first extant poem "Upon a Fit of Sicknes, Anno 1632" indicates that she interpreted this episode as a reminder of her mortality. In her letter "To My Dear Children," in effect a spiritual autobiography probably written in her final years, Bradstreet explains that she was making an effort to submit to the circumstances of her new life and accepted this illness as a spiritual lesson "which correction I saw the Lord sent to humble and try me and doe mee Good: and it was not altogether ineffectual" (*Works*, 5). In the same letter she observes that she felt that her attempts to subdue her pride were rewarded by the birth of her first child, Samuel, two years later: "It pleased God to keep me a long time without a child, which was a great greif [sic] to me, and cost mee many prayers and tears before I obtain one, and after him gave mee many more" (*Works*, 5).

In 1635, perhaps in an effort to achieve autonomy from Winthrop, who had accused Dudley of "usury" in the sale of corn and "ostentation" in the decoration of his house,[17] the Bradstreets and the Dudleys moved to Ipswich, also known as Aggawam, forty miles north of Newtown. In this outpost, which was constantly in danger of Indian attacks, the Bradstreets who now had two children, Samuel and Dorothy, were granted a parcel adjoining the nine-acre Dudley homestead. Here Anne Bradstreet began to write in earnest, composing most of the poems that appeared in the first edition of *The Tenth Muse*. She was not the only writer in this frontier town; Nathaniel Ward, the pastor of the Ipswich congregation from 1634 to 1636, was the author of "The Simple Cobbler of Aggawam in America," which was immensely successful in London where it was published in 1647.

Sarah and the younger Simon Bradstreet were born in 1638 and 1640 during the period when Simon Bradstreet was most active as a member of the Court of Assistants, which required him to be away from Ipswich for several weeks at a time. Some of Bradstreet's best poetry was written to her husband during his prolonged absences. Her lyric love poems are artful and passionate; they are an admirable fusion of deep personal feeling and the craft of the Elizabethan sonnet:

> O strange effect! now thou art *Southward* gone,
> I weary grow, the tedious day so long;
> But when thou *Northward* to me shall return,
> I wish my Sun may never set, but burn
> Within the Cancer of my glowing breast,
> The welcome house of him my dearest guest.
> Where ever, ever stay, and go not thence,
> Till natures sad decree shall call thee hence;

Flesh of my flesh, bone of my bone,
I here, thou there, yet both but one.
(*Works*, 395)

Here Bradstreet uses the metaphysical conceit that equates the sun with male agency and earth with female receptivity to describe her traditional marriage. In this paradigm, men have vitality and active energy while women respond to the male animating force. In spite of the fact that Bradstreet portrays herself as forlorn and dispirited while her husband was attending to his responsibilities in the public sphere, she actually had much to do in the private realm. Because her household was one of the more prosperous in Ipswich, Anne Bradstreet had servants to help her with the cooking, preserving, spinning and weaving cloth, gardening, livestock tending, and the many other tasks of raising a large family. Some of the servants were indentured from England; others were Negro and occasionally Indian.

Many families had large gardens and orchards as well as some live-stock and poultry, which enabled them to eat simply but well.[18] Of course, not all settlers were sufficiently wealthy to afford large homesteads and servants, and many had very simple diets indeed. For example, an apprentice stonemason observed that he found it difficult to digest "his master's food, viz. meate and milk, or drink beer . . . because he was not used to eat such victualls, but to eate bread and water porridge and to drink water."[19] For the more affluent, household furnishings were simple but reasonably comfortable and even included such amenities as feather-beds and silver bowls.[20] Although clothing was regulated by sumptuary laws—embroidered or needlework caps, ornamental laces, bands and sashes, short sleeves, and long hair were prohibited in the Massachusetts Bay Colony—there was a considerable range of fabric from calico and cambric to silk and velvet and a variety of clothing styles, including bonnets and ruffs, available to the settlers who could afford them.[21] Because the Dudleys and Bradstreets were socially prominent and reasonably wealthy, their houses and wardrobes were probably as substantial as any in the colonies.

Both Thomas Dudley and Simon Bradstreet took advantage of opportunities to increase their estates as well as their personal power whenever possible. Each move in the New World brought them more prosperity and prestige; their houses became larger and more comfortable, and their social and political influence more extensive. Although Dudley and his son-in-law combined personal gain with social service, others simply moved to improve their worldly estates. There was considerable discussion about moving for "outward advantages," indicating an underlying tension in the colony between individual liberty and community welfare that became increasingly apparent as the years passed. Winthrop asked his constituency to take active responsibility for the social contract that he had outlined on the *Arbella*:

> Ask thy conscience, if thou wouldst have plucked up thy stakes, and brought thy family 3000 miles, if thou hadst expected that all, or most, would have forsaken thee there. Ask again, what liberty thou hast towards others, which thou likest not to allow others towards thyself; for if one may go, another may, and so the greater part, and so church and commonwealth may be left destitute in a wilderness, exposed to misery and reproach, and all for thy ease and pleasure.[22]

Although Dudley's moves invariably improved his worldly estates, he could not be accused of ignoring the community welfare. For example, after serving as deputy governor of the colony in 1638 and 1639, he decided to leave Ipswich for Roxbury, which was only two miles from Boston, in order to be closer to the center of colonial government. A few years after the move to Roxbury, Dorothy Yorke Dudley died at the age of sixty-one, and her daughter's "Epitaph on my dear and ever honoured Mother" depicting Dorothy Dudley as pious, efficient, just, and charitable—a model of traditional female virtue—provides most of what little information there is about her:

Here lyes,
A Worthy Matron of unspotted life,
A loving Mother and obedient wife,
A friendly Neighbor, pitiful to poor,
Whom oft she fed, and clothed with her store;
To Servants wisely aweful, but yet kind,
And as they did, so they reward did find:
A true Instructor of her Family,
The which she ordered with dexterity.
The publick meetings ever did frequent,
And in her Closet constant hours she spent;
Religious in all her words and wayes,
Preparing still for death, till end of dayes:
Of all her Children, Children, liv'd to see,
Then dying, left a blessed memory.
(*Works*, 369)

Only four months after his wife's death, Thomas Dudley married the widow Catherine Hackburne and continued to assume major responsibilities in the governing of the colony: in 1644, he served as sergeant major general of the military forces; in 1645, he was once again elected governor; from 1646 to 1650, he served as deputy governor, and in 1650, he was appointed to the Board of Overseers at Harvard College.

In 1645, the Bradstreets relocated once again. This time they moved to Andover, another frontier town about fifteen miles inland from Ipswich that exempted its settlers from all taxes and levies. Here Simon Bradstreet served as a magistrate and John Woodbridge, who was married to Anne Bradstreet's sister, Mercy, was the minister. The move brought not only increased prestige to Simon Bradstreet but also a large, comfortable house and a twenty-acre homestead. By this time, there were five Bradstreet children: Samuel, Dorothy, Sarah, Simon, and Hannah. Mercy was born a few months after the move to Andover; Dudley was born in 1648 and John in 1652.

During the years in Ipswich, Anne Bradstreet had written enough poems to complete the first edition of *The Tenth Muse*. In spite of her exhausting domestic responsibilities, Bradstreet wrote very little about her experience of pregnancy, childbirth, and parenthood, but a brief description of "Childhood" in her lengthy poem "The Four Ages of Man" provides a glimpse of her ethos of sacrificial womanhood:

> With tears into the world I did arrive,
> My mother still did waste as I did thrive,
> Who yet with love and all alacrity,
> Spending, was willing to be spent for me.
> With wayward cryes I did disturb her rest,
> Who sought still to appease me with the breast:
> With weary arms she danc'd and *By By* sung,
> When wretched I ingrate had done the wrong.
> (*Works*, 150)

When John Woodbridge was dispatched in December 1647 to the Isle of Wight to negotiate with King Charles, who had taken refuge there in Carisbroke castle during the English civil war, he brought Bradstreet's manuscript with him and arranged to have it published in London, where it appeared in 1650 and sold for sixpence. The title page summarized the contents of the volume:

> *The Tenth Muse* Lately sprung up in *America Or* Severall Poems, compiled with great variety of Wit and Learning, full of delight.

Wherein expecially is contained a compleat discourse and description of The Four *Elements, Constitutions, Ages of Man, Seasons of
the Year.* Together with an Exact Epitomie of the Four Monarchies,
viz. The *Assyrian, Persian, Grecian, Roman.* Also a Dialogue, between Old *England* and New, concerning the late troubles. With
divers other pleasant and serious Poems. By a Gentlewoman in
those parts. (*Works*, 79)

Bradstreet's volume proved to be very popular, as indicated by its listing
in William London's *Catalogue of the Most Vendible Books in England*
(1658). Her poetry was well received, and she was praised for her wit and
craft as well as her comprehensive grasp of history and politics.

Three years after the publication of *The Tenth Muse*, Thomas Dudley
died at the age of seventy-seven. His daughter was forty-one and had
given birth to her last child, John, a year earlier in July 1652. Mourning
her father's death in a lengthy elegy, Bradstreet praised his patriotism,
stern morality, and lack of pretentiousness:

One of thy Founders, him *New-England* know,
Who staid thy feeble sides when thou wast low,
Who spent his state, his strength, & years with care
That After-comers in them might have share.
True patriot of this little Commonweal,
Who is't can tax thee ought, but for thy zeal?
Truths friend thou wert, to errors still a foe,
Which caus'd Apostates to maligne so.
Thy love to true Religion e're shall shine,
My Fathers God, be God of me and mine.
Upon the earth he did not build his nest,
But as a Pilgrim what he had, possest.
High thoughts he gave no harbour in his heart,
Nor honours pufft him up, when he had part:
Those titles loath'd, which some too much do love
For truly his ambition lay above.

(*Works*, 366)

Dudley's own epitaph for himself recorded by Cotton Mather in the
Magnalia reveals hatred of "Heresie and Vice" and concludes, I DY'D NO
LIBERTINE.[23] The contrasts between Bradstreet's elegies for her mother
and her father dramatize the differences in roles that Puritan women and
men were expected to play in their society. Dorothy Yorke Dudley is
praised for being loving, charitable, long-suffering, and a good moral ex-

ample to her children while Thomas Dudley was revered for being forthright, determined, patriotic, and principled. Men were the civil and moral
leaders of the larger community while women, who were expected to
be virtuous and modest, for the most part remained at home to govern
the family.

Anne Bradstreet tried to be a dutiful wife and mother as well as an
obedient daughter and made every effort to meet the expectations of her
family and community. But she also wanted to be recognized as a poet.
Much of Bradstreet's early poetry, most of which is found in the first edition of *The Tenth Muse*, expresses this conflict between the roles of
writer and conventional woman. Acknowledging the influence of Sidney
and Du Bartas, Bradstreet makes a determined effort to establish herself
as being worthy of attention. In her "Elegie upon that Honourable and
renowned Knight, Sir *Philip Sidney*," written eight years after Anne Bradstreet arrived in the New World, she pays tribute to the power of Sidney's
poetry. At the same time, she makes clear her wish to be accepted by the
community of poets on her own merits, and asserting her right to join the
male poets on Parnassus, she advances toward the sacrosanct mountaintop. But as she approaches her longed-for destination, she is overwhelmed
by feelings of inadequacy and unworthiness and abandons her goal:

> So proudly foolish I, with *Phaeton* strive,
> Fame's flaming Chariot for to drive.
> Till terrour-struck for my too weighty charge,
> I leave't in brief, *Apollo* do't at large.
> (*Works*, 350)

Simultaneously ambitious and fearful, the fledgling poet longs for acclaim
yet is startled by her own aggression. It is important to note that here, as
in most of her early poems, Bradstreet's concerns are primarily aesthetic
and political, not discernibly spiritual.

In the poem dedicating the *The Tenth Muse* to her father, who encouraged his daughter's poetry writing, Bradstreet admits that her style is not
as skillful as she would wish. Referring to his own poem on the four parts
of the world (which is not extant), she modestly says that her efforts are
not worthy of his lofty, forceful work:

> Their paralels to finde I scarcely know
> To climbe their Climes, I have nor strength nor skill,
> To mount so high requires an Eagles quill;
> Yet view thereof did cause my thoughts to soar;
> My lowly pen might wait upon these four

I bring my four times four, now meanly clad
To do their homage, unto yours, full glad
(*Works*, 97–98)

In general, she is careful to defer to the men she admires, and she attempts to gain their acceptance by subordinating her work to theirs. By
making herself small in contrast to their masculine grandeur and by emphasizing the modesty of her literary accomplishments, she hopes to convince them that she is not straying beyond the sphere assigned to women.
In this way, Bradstreet tries to establish her place as a poet in a community of male writers whether it be Sidney, her father, or hostile critics.
This strategy of self-diminution to conceal ambition is later used by
Emily Dickinson, who depicts herself as small and meek when requesting
advice about her work from the literary critic Thomas Higginson.

Although the lines in the prologue of *The Tenth Muse* reveal Bradstreet's anxiety about whether or not she will be accepted by these men,
they also express her anger about being vulnerable to their criticism and
demonstrate her fierce pride in her intelligence and poetic craft:

I am obnoxious to each carping tongue
Who says my hand a needle better fits,
A Poets pen all scorn I should thus wrong,
For such despite they cast on Female wits:
If what I do prove well, it won't advance,
They'l say it's stoln, or else it was by chance.
(*Works*, 101)

Bradstreet does not entirely repress her resentment that her work does
not receive the attention it deserves; here, as in other poems in this volume, she makes only a modest claim on art, as befits a proper woman:

Let Greeks be Greeks, and women what they are
Men have precedency and still excell,
It is but vain unjustly to wage warre;
Men can do best, and women know it well
Preheminence in all and each is yours;
Yet grant some small acknowledgement of ours.
(*Works*, 102)

Clearly, Bradstreet is disturbed that female accomplishments are deval-
ued, but she is careful to pay homage to male critics and readers in an
attempt to circumvent their attacks. Only the deliberate ambiguity of the

third line resulting from the pun on "vain" belies Bradstreet's abject humility.

Masking both her fear and rage, Bradstreet concludes the prologue by asking for a thyme or parsley wreath rather than the bay laurel, which is the traditional prize for poetic excellence, military victory, or athletic prowess:

> And oh ye high flown quills that soar the Skies,
> And ever with your prey still catch your praise,
> If e're you daigne these lowly lines your eyes
> Give Thyme or Parsley wreath, I ask no bayes,
> This mean and unrefined ure of mine
> Will make you glistering gold, but more to shine.
>
> (*Works*, 102)

This request for domestic herbs rather than the time-honored crown indicates Bradstreet's effort to stay within boundaries allotted to women. However, these deliberately diminutive stanzas that Bradstreet hopes will make her skill and accomplishments less threatening to men are not without irony. In addition to pointing out that the nine muses are female as is "poesy," which is "*Calliope's* own Child," she slyly chides her critics for having an inflated opinion of themselves. By underscoring her modesty and humility, she mocks their self-importance. In both versions of the poem, her ironic use of "Bayes" camouflages Bradstreet's fear of antagonizing male critics who, like barking dogs, would mark her as their prey; in addition, by likening male poets to plundering eagles, she suggests that they compel praise rather than earn it freely. Because "Bayes" is capitalized in the first edition, the pun is less obvious. By claiming her work is crude and unpolished, she appears to accept an inferior position. However, in the first edition of the poem, Bradstreet equates public acclaim with an unhealthy pride and makes it clear that the "Parsley wreath" is more "wholesome" than the crown of bay laurel granted to conquering heroes. Not only is Bradstreet's irony a protective masque designed to conceal her vulnerability, it exposes, however obliquely, the pomposity and cruelty of those male writers and critics who disdain women.

The second phase of Bradstreet's poetic evolution is characterized by subjects drawn from her own experience rather than from the British literary models used in her early work. After her father's death in 1653, her poetry is deeply personal, even sensuous. She writes of her intense love for her husband and children, her grief at the loss of her parents and grandchildren, her joy in nature. Religious and secular concerns are intertwined as Bradstreet plays out her personal drama between the flesh and the spirit. Her love poems to her husband express an aspect of this struggle:

> And if I see not half my days that's due,
> What nature would, God grant to yours and you;
> The many faults that well you know I have,
> Let be interr'd in my oblivions grave;
> If any worth or virtue were in me,
> Let that live freshly in thy memory
> And when thou feel'st no grief, as I no harms,
> Yet love thy dead, who long lay in thine arms:
> And when thy loss shall be repaid with gains
> Look to my little babes my dear remains.
> And if thou love thy self, or loved'st me
> These O protect from step Dames injury.
> And if chance to thine eyes shall bring this verse,
> With some sad sighs honour my absent Herse;
> And kiss this paper for thy loves dear sake,
> Who with salt tears this last Farewel did take.
>
> (Works, 393–94)

In these couplets, there is an acceptance of death as inevitable, but the emphasis is on *this* life. The poet wants to be remembered by her husband and loved beyond the grave: "Yet love thy dead, who long lay in thine arms." Her concerns are not of her spiritual fate, but for the well-being of her children as well as the continued devotion of Simon Bradstreet. She also confesses her fear that his new wife will not be kind to their children—any illusions she may have had about her husband's exclusive devotion to her were probably dispelled by her father's hasty remarriage. Clearly, her passion for her husband and her love for her children supersede her considerations of eternal life.

The conflict between personal feelings and religious duty is again expressed in her poem, "Upon my Son Samuel his goeing for England," dated November 6, 1657:

> Preserve, O Lord from stormes and wrack,
> Protect him there, and bring him back;
> And if thou shalt spare me a space,
> That I again may see his face,
> Then shall I celebrate thy Praise,
> And Blesse thee for't even all my Dayes.

If otherwise I goe to Rest,
Thy Will be done, for that is best;
Perswade my heart I shall him see
Forever happefy'd with Thee.
(*Works*, 25)

The emphasis here is on the potential loss of her son; her prayer begs for
his return while indicating resigned submission to fate. However, the tone
of the poem reveals that the poet's devotion to God is actually condi-
tional on Samuel's well-being. The prayer is a bargain with God: "If my
son returns safely, then I shall celebrate and bless you." This deep feeling
and intense concern for the safety of her loved ones is again seen in the
poem, "Upon my dear and loving husband his goeing into England,"
dated January 16, 1661:

Lord let my eyes see once Again
    Him whom thou gavest me,
That wee together may sing Praise
    For ever unto Thee.
(*Works*, 34)

Once more, the poet requests a quid pro quo from God: "If my husband
returns to me safely, together we will sing your praise." The poet pleads
for continued happiness on earth; secular concerns take precedence over
spiritual ends.

In her final years, Bradstreet's emotions are more disciplined, enabling
her to focus more clearly on religious matters. Her spiritual autobiography begun on March 20, 1664, documents her efforts to subdue her
earthly desires. She no longer bargains with God but struggles to accept
his will:

All men are truly sayd to be tenants at will, and it may be as truly
sayd, that all have a lease of their lives,—some longer, some
shorter,—as it pleases our great landlord to let. All have their
bounds set, over which they cannot passe, and till the expiration of
that time, no dangers, no sicknes, no paines nor troubles, shall put
a period to our dayes; the certainty that that time will come, together with the uncertainty, how, where, and when, should make
us so to number our dayes as to apply our hearts to wisedome, that
when wee are put out of these houses of clay, we may be sure of an
everlasting habitation that fades not away. (*Works*, 69−70)

Again, the emphasis is on the joys of earthly life that are regrettably temporal; however, this passage demonstrates Bradstreet's effort to accept her mortality and to prepare for death, heaven, and eternity. Now Bradstreet uses the metaphor of the pilgrimage to characterize her experience.

Although the metaphors and analogies of Bradstreet's *Meditations* are drawn from her own experience, the form is that of the ritual discipline of emotions intended to help the sinner take stock of moral shortcomings in order to be prepared to receive God's grace. Many Puritans believed that through constant scrutiny of the emotions and self-denial, the heart is gradually weaned from earthly desire. Resistance to God is slowly overcome until finally the unregenerate person is broken in spirit and ready to serve the Lord.[24] In the battle against human depravity, the heart had to be "bruised" and ultimately broken in order to create an awareness of the hopelessness of the human condition; once humbled, the sinner was prepared to accept God's irresistible grace. William Perkins elaborates the phases of salvation in an early Puritan treatise, *A Golden Chaine* (1612–13):

> There are for the bruising of this stony heart, foure principall hammers. The first, is the knowledge of the Law of God. The second, is the knowledge of sinne, both original and actuall, and what punishment is due unto them. The third, is compunction, or pricking of the heart, namely, a sense and feeling of the wrath of God for the same sinnes. The forth, is an holy desperation of a man's own power, in the obtaining of eternall life.[25]

This pattern of humiliation, acceptance of grace, and hope for regeneration can be seen in the work of such seventeenth-century British poets as Donne, Herbert, and Traherne as well as in their American counterparts Bradstreet and Taylor. For example, Donne's Sonnet XIV vividly describes the conversion experience:

> Batter my heart, three person'd God; for, you
> As yet but knocke, breathe, shine, and seeke to mend;
> That I may rise, and stand, o'erthrow mee, and bend
> Your force, to breake, blowe, burn and make me new.[26]

And George Herbert's poem, "Perseverance," portrays the helplessness and total dependence of the broken spirit on God's grace:

> Onely my Soul hangs on thy promises
> With face and hands clinging into thy brest,

Clinging and crying, crying without cease,
Thou art my rock, thou art my rest.[27]

Although Bradstreet never matched Donne's exaltation or Herbert's abject depths, her meditations demonstrate her efforts to discipline her straying thoughts and to channel her energy, which she feared would otherwise lead her astray. But her spiritual reflections remain at the level of obligatory exercises rather than passionate expressions of regeneration: "That which now I chiefly labour for is a contented, thankfull heart under my affliction and weaknes, seeing it is the will of God it should bee thus" (*Works*, 21).

Since heaven was not a palpable place but a state of mind, Bradstreet used the meditation form to direct her attention to God, to prepare for death, and to control her anxiety about her spiritual fate. Initially, Bradstreet's models for poetry were British, and there was little that was religious in her work. In her middle years, she wrote deeply personal and even sensuous poems celebrating her love for her family and nature. After struggling with the antithetical demands of literary ambition and religious dogma, Bradstreet finally managed to combine piety and art by viewing her writing as a chronicle of preparation for eternal union with God. This fusion of aesthetics and theology allowed her to perceive her frustrations and disappointments as necessary for the tempering of her soul. Although she continued to have deep reservations about the wisdom of God's divine plan, Bradstreet ultimately capitulated to her fathers—earthly and heavenly.

TWO

The Tenth Muse

In spite of the many disruptions in her life and her demanding responsibilities as a wife and mother, Anne Bradstreet persisted in her poetry
until she had enough material for *The Tenth Muse Lately Sprung Up In
America*, which was published in 1650. Her brother-in-law, Reverend
John Woodbridge, who had taken her manuscript with him to London
and had arranged for its publication there without Bradstreet's knowledge, insists in the introduction to the volume that he "presumed to bring
to publick view, what she resolved in such a manner should never see the
Sun" (*Works*, 84). The fact that Anne Bradstreet did not seek publication
directly but did so by proxy was interpreted as a sign of her modesty and
piety and, in addition, that indirect approach was a practical way to circumvent the accusation of excessive ambition.

In the preface, John Woodbridge proclaims that *The Tenth Muse* is the
"Work of a Woman, honoured, and esteemed where she lives, for her gracious demeanour, her eminent parts, her pious conversation, her cour-
teous disposition, her exact diligence in her place, and discreet managing
of her Family occasions" (*Works*, 83–84). Woodbridge also assured
readers that Bradstreet took no time from her family obligations to write
her book: "[T]hese Poems are the fruit but of some few houres, curtailed
from her sleep and other refreshments" (*Works*, 84). Statements of praise
for Bradstreet by Nathaniel Ward, the author of the lengthy popular
poem, "The Simple Cobbler of Aggawam in America," and Reverend
Benjamin Woodbridge, brother of John Woodbridge, were also included
in the volume. These encomiums emphasizing Bradstreet's virtue helped
to defend her from attacks by those reviewers and readers at home and
abroad who might have been shocked by the impropriety of a female
author.

The first edition of *The Tenth Muse* contains poetry that is overwhelm-
ingly secular in content. In the first section are four long poems, known
as the quaternions: "The Four Elements," "The Four Humors of Man,"

"The Four Ages of Man," and "The Four Seasons"; these consist of orations by characters representing each of the subjects. The next section of the volume, "The Four Monarchies," is also composed of four parallel subjects—Assyrian, Persian, Greek, and Roman societies—but here the emphasis is somewhat more religious in that the dissolution of these civilizations is presented as evidence of God's divine plan for the world. This grandiose production is followed by "A Dialogue between Old England and New," elegies to Sir Philip Sidney, Du Bartas, and Queen Elizabeth, "David's Lamentation for Saul and Jonathan," and "The Vanity of All Worldly Creatures."

The issue of power and powerlessness is the central concern of Bradstreet's first volume of poetry. Each of the poems explores an aspect of dominance and subordination ranging from the internecine struggle among the elements to civil wars and conflict between the sexes. In the final poem of the collection, "The Vanity of All Worldly Creatures," God is depicted as the supreme ruler because he is not subject to the political and historical vicissitudes that are at the core of the quaternions. For Bradstreet, God is the all-powerful Supreme Being who dominates the cosmic power struggle. In contrast to this patriarchal structure that Bradstreet characterizes as a competitive struggle for dominance and territorial hegemony at all levels of life from the physical to the personal and political, she evolves a gynecocratic vision that is based on nurturance, cooperation, and relationship. In "The Four Elements," for example, the four sisters, representing Earth, Air, Fire, and Water, find a cooperative solution to their conflicts. "The Dialogue between Old England and New" laments the devastating effect of male territoriality. The conversation between two women—Mother England and her daughter, New England—reveals Bradstreet's distress about the waste and loss caused by the battles to demonstrate moral superiority. As Old England's lament indicates, the destructive impact of civil strife on human life was more disturbing to Bradstreet than the political substance of the conflict:

> Oh pity me in this sad perturbation,
> My plundred towns, my houses devastation,
> My weeping Virgins and my young men slain;
> My wealthy trading fall'n, my dearth of grain
> (Works, 339)

The emphasis is not on the differences between the Puritans and the king as the cause of the social upheaval but on the tragic loss of life and destruction of a nation's well-being resulting from what Bradstreet depicts as a profligate male power struggle.

In contrast to her gynecocratic vision that provides a thematic counterpoint throughout *The Tenth Muse*, Bradstreet articulates the traditional female response to male power in her poems honoring Sir Philip Sidney and Guillaume Du Bartas. Acknowledging her debt to her poetic mentors, Bradstreet depicts herself as insignificant in contrast to their greatness. They live on the peak of Parnassus while she grovels at the bottom of the mountain modestly disclaiming any effort to equal them. To Sidney she writes: "But to say truth, thy worth I shall but staine, / Thy fame, and praise, is farre beyond my straine" (*Works*, 346). In her tribute to Du Bartas, she reiterates her self-effacing stance, describing herself as unfruitful, dull, and unattractive, venerating his work as sacred, and belittling hers as profane:

> But barren I my Dasey here do bring,
> A homely flour in this my latter Spring,
> If Summer, or my Autumn age do yield,
> Flours, fruits, in Garden, Orchard, or in Field,
> Thy shall be consecrated in my Verse,
> And prostrate offered at great *Bartas* Herse
> (*Works*, 353)

In her admiration of Du Bartas, she assumes a diminutive role: "My muse unto a Child I may compare." Referring to herself as a "silly pratler," "weak brain'd," she begs him to "Pardon if I adore, when I admire" (*Works*, 354, 355). She concludes her praise by asking permission to bring her "Mite" to honor him. This self-effacement and lack of confidence in her artistic abilities was the obverse of her desire to be worthy of public acknowledgment. Using the mask of child, "dim wit," and "pauper," she conceals her ambition to be as accomplished as those she admires.

As a woman poet, Bradstreet was in a double bind. Unlike Sidney, Spenser, or Du Bartas, she could not consecrate her work to a female muse—a traditional male ritual to express ambition in a socially acceptable manner. By dedicating his work to Calliope, or Stella, or the dark lady, the male artist could achieve the stance of selflessness. Since the women who were the recipients of this devotion and adoration were essentially passive and functioned primarily to inspire men, they were not competing for the same accolades. Not surprisingly, Bradstreet dedicated her work to male figures—her father, admired poets, God—who unlike their female counterparts were powerful and accomplished, and in the case of God, omnipotent. In order not to appear presumptuous or competitive, Bradstreet had to solicit their protection, defer to their superior abilities, and assume a deferential pose. In addition, Bradstreet's self-deprecation was a strategy to ward off attacks from hostile critics. By presenting herself as insecure, insignificant, and inept, she hoped to disarm her potential opponents and thereby avoid their negative commentary or rejection. This is a tactic traditionally used by women to conceal their socially unacceptable aggression and anger. Two hundred years later Emily Dickinson employed this same strategy and, like Bradstreet, depicted herself as a compliant daisy content to follow the sun's orbit.

Although these poems are outwardly self-deprecating, Bradstreet again uses irony to deflate male arrogance. For example, in her elegy on Sidney, she seems to say that his work is too complex and intricate—too sublime—for her to follow or emulate; however, Bradstreet actually implies that his labyrinthine lines are excessively ornate:

> Fain would I shew, how thou fame's path did tread,
> But now into such Lab'rinths am I led
> With endless turnes, the way I find not out,
> For to persist, my muse is more in doubt:
> Calls me ambitious fool, that durst aspire,
> Enough for me to look, and so admire.
> And makes me now with *Sylvester* confesse,
> But *Sydney's* Muse, can sing his worthinesse.
>   (*Works*, 350)

It is interesting to note that in the second edition of *The Tenth Muse*, Bradstreet extensively revised her elegy in order to put herself on a more equal footing with Sidney. The reference to Sidney as "thou" becomes "he"; "led" is replaced by the pun "lead"; her lowercase muse is capitalized in the second version giving her parity with Sidney; and she omits the lines "Call her ambitious fool, that durst aspire, / Enough for me to look, and so admire." By eliminating most of the phrases and adjectives that emphasize her subordinate position, the second edition of this poem demonstrates Bradstreet's growing self-confidence.

Although Anne Bradstreet was careful to observe Puritan restrictions on female behavior in her domestic life and appeared to accept her powerlessness, her poem "In Honor of that High and Mighty Princess Queen Elizabeth *Of Happy Memory*," written in 1643, makes it quite clear that she was angered by her culture's devaluation of women. Praising Elizabeth as a model of female prowess, the thirty-one-year-old Bradstreet chides her male readers for trivializing women. In a personal caveat underscoring her dislike of patriarchal arrogance, Bradstreet recalls a time when prevailing patterns of power were reversed:

Nay Masculines, you have thus taxt us long,
But she, though dead, will vindicate our wrong.
Let such as say our Sex is void of Reason,
Know tis a Slander now, but once was Treason.

(*Works*, 361)

These boldly assertive lines provide a dramatic contrast to the self-effacing stanzas of "The Prologue" in which Anne Bradstreet appears to subordinate herself to male critics and readers.

In contrast to earlier Puritan portraits of Queen Elizabeth in the poetry of Spenser and the histories of John Speed and William Camden, which depict Elizabeth and her court as a microcosm of universal order, Bradstreet shifts the emphasis to the queen's personal attributes—her magnetism, intelligence, and political acumen, dramatizing Elizabeth's prowess as an individual woman, not as God's representative on earth. The powerful queen is portrayed as replacing the authority of the male rulers, whether kings or Puritan magistrates:

Full fraught with honour, riches and with dayes
She set, she set, like *Titan* in his rayes.
No more shall rise or set so glorious sun
Untill the heavens great revolution,
If then new things their old forms shall retain,
Eliza shall rule *Albion* once again.

(*Works*, 361)

Here Elizabeth embodies the sun's power, which is attributed to men in the other poems of *The Tenth Muse*, indicating that Bradstreet perceived supremacy as an arbitrary rather than inherently natural phenomenon. In addition, in this portrait Bradstreet expresses the hope that if history is cyclical, women may well have power again.

Bradstreet's apotheosis of Elizabeth I is daring because Bradstreet openly takes pride in the queen's temporal glory. In a society that considered that art best which praised God and celebrated the wonders of his ways, poetry that elaborated the splendor of a queen was suspect. In contrast, Cotton Mather's use of the sun as an emblem of Christian radiance in the "Life of Sir William Phips" indicates that God, and no mere mortal, governed the universe: "We have by a plain and true history secured the story of our successes from falling under the disguises of mythology. . . . No, 'tis our Lord Jesus Christ, worshipped according to the rules of his blessed gospel, who is the great Phoebus, that '*SUN* of righteousness,' who hath so saved his churches from the designs of the 'generations of the dragon.'"[1] Women played no part in Puritan religious structure; the heavenly host, like church hierarchy, was dominated by men.

Because she won back the throne from Bloody Mary, a Catholic queen, Elizabeth was often praised by Protestant writers: John Foxe's *Book of Martyrs*, as well as Sidney and Spenser, commend her courage. However, Bradstreet's identification with the queen was unusual and might have seemed idolatrous had Elizabeth not been a heroine of the Protestant cause. The Puritans depicted Elizabeth as a new Judith or Deborah, but in her panegyric of the queen, Bradstreet uses secular rather than religious images.

In contrast to Bradstreet, who focuses on Elizabeth's military victory in Spain and her mastery of domestic and international politics, other poets of the period praised their ruler as the representative of the divinely ordered universe. For example, in the "April Eclogue" of *The Shepherd's Calendar*, Spenser uses the conventions of pastoral and allegorical poetry to portray the queen as the manifestation of sacred harmony:

> See, where she sits upon the grassy green,
>   (O seemly sight!)
> Yclad in scarlet, like a maiden queen,
>   And ermines white:
> Upon her head a cremosin coronet,
> With damask roses and daffadillies set:
>   Bay leaves between,
>   And primroses green,
> Embellish the sweet violet.[2]

Bradstreet's Elizabeth is mighty—a "dread virago," "Protectrix," and "Amazon"—not the "flower of virgins" of the "April Eclogue." In another portrait of Elizabeth in "The Hymn of Love," Spenser again articulates the seventeenth-century correlation of cosmic order and the royal court as the apex of the flourishing commonwealth. Whereas the Elizabeth of Spenser is praised by muses and graces, Bradstreet's royal heroine surpasses the accomplishments of Minerva, Dido, Cleopatra, and Zenobia. Bradstreet's queen is active, proud, and commanding, not a passive reflection of a divine plan.

> *Here lyes the pride of Queens, Pattern of Kings,*
> *So blaze it Fame, here's feathers for thy wings.*
> *Here lyes the envi'd, yet unparalled Prince,*
> *Whose living virtues speak, (though dead long since)*

If many worlds, as that Fantastick fram'd
In every one be her great glory fam'd.
(*Works*, 362)

This coda italicizes Bradstreet's forthright pride in female power: reveling in Elizabeth's glory, Anne Bradstreet unabashedly proclaims the queen as triumphant over all men, even kings. Queen Elizabeth's royal edicts provide a healthy corrective for the passivity of the Puritan woman who was compelled to attend church meetings three times a week but forbidden to take part in the interpretation of Scripture. Elizabeth's radiant splendor and life-affirming qualities provide a dramatic constrast to the repressive style of the New England patriarchs. *The Tenth Muse* reveals Bradstreet's interest in a gynecocentric universe. As we have seen, her elegy on Queen Elizabeth is a tribute to female abilities that are not regulated and controlled by men; the queen eclipses the authority of the New England divines, and her regal self-assertion is a dramatic contrast to the fallen Christian woman whose only possibility for redemption lies in self-abnegation.

Bradstreet's lengthy poems on the four elements—humors, ages, seasons, and monarchies—in *The Tenth Muse* draw on Hooker's *Laws of Ecclesiastical Polity*, Raleigh's *History of the World*, Joshua Sylvester's translation of Du Bartas's *Devine Weeks and Workes* as well as the work of Spenser and Sidney. Like other Renaissance poets, Shakespeare, Donne, Davies, and Jonson, these writers perceived the cosmos as unified by elaborate correspondences that express God's architecture. However, Bradstreet diverges from her male models in eliminating the hierarchy, or the great chain of being, that gave structure to the Elizabethan world. For example, Spenser's "An Hymn in Honor of Love" sets forth the stratified, territorial vision:

The earth, the air, the water, and the fire,
Then gan to range themselves in huge array,
And with contrary forces to conspire
Each against the other by all means they may,
Threat'ning their own confusion and decay:
Air hated earth, and water hated fire,
Till Love relented their rebellious ire.

He then them took, and, tempering goodly well
Their contrary dislikes with loved means,
Did place them all in order and compel

To keep themselves within their sundry reigns,
Together linkt with adamantine chains;
Yet so, as that in every living wight
They mis themselves, and show their kindly might.

So ever since they firmly have remained,
And duly well observed his behest;
Through which now all these things that are contained
Within this goodly cope, both most and least,
Their being have, and daily are increased
Through secret sparks of his infused fire,
Which in the barren cold he doth inspire.[3]

By using the language of aggression—arrayed forces, conspiracy, threat, enmity—Spenser creates an embattled cosmos in which territorial lines are drawn and campaigns are waged. The solution to the turbulence caused by conflict and struggle for hegemony is to create an arbitrary order through carefully defined boundaries; adamantine chains restrain the warring elements, and control is achieved not through self-imposed restraint but through external constraint.

The opening stanzas of Bradstreet's *The Four Elements* parallel Spenser's emphasis on dominance and submission:

The Fire, Air, Earth and water did contest
Which was the strongest, noblest and the best,
Who was of greatest use and might'est force;
In placide Terms they thought now to discourse,
That in due order each her turn should speak;
But enmity this amity did break
All would be chief, and all scorn'd to be under
Whence issu'd winds & rains, lightning & thunder
The quaking earth did groan, the Sky lookt black
The Fire, the forced Air, in sunder crack;
The sea did threat the heav'ns, the heavn's the earth,
All looked like a Chaos or new birth
(*Works*, 103)

In Spenser's poem, this conflict is resolved when "Love" unites the rebellious elements by establishing territories for each of them, but Bradstreet's poems replace the stratified Elizabethan cosmos with an essentially female universe in which balance is ultimately achieved by mutuality and cooperation. Relationship—as represented by sisters who share a com-

mon heritage—replaces hierarchy. Interdependence rather than dominance and subordinance is the ordering principle of Bradstreet's vision.
This vision of harmony in *The Tenth Muse* provides a contrast to an established chain of order and graduated differences of rank.

In both "The Four Elements" and "The Four Humours," the protago-
nists are initially depicted as antagonistic sisters whose quarrels threaten
to disrupt the universe. Each sister is so intent on achieving dominance
that the floods, fires, storms, and earthquakes resulting from their wran-
gling threaten to destroy the cosmos. The Puritans and the Elizabethans
viewed such disruption as the harbinger of chaos that was to be feared. In
Bradstreet's poems, the sisters' struggle for dominance is resolved by their
collective realization that each of them has an essential part in the functioning of the cosmos, that the interplay of the elements and the humors
creates balance. The feared confusion is a prelude to the birth of a new
world view in which process takes precedence over product and dominance gives way to mutuality. This need for collaboration is articulated
by the sisters who represent the four humors of the body:

> Unless we agree, all falls into confusion.
> Let Sangine with her hot hand Choler hold,
> To take her moist my moisture will be bold:
> My cold, cold melancholy hand shall clasp;
> Her dry, dry Cholers other hand shall grasp.
> Two hot, two moist, two cold, two dry here be,
> A golden Ring, the Posey UNITY.
> (*Works*, 145–46)

This "Posey *Unity*," not an all-powerful or wrathful God, is the basis of
order in Bradstreet's universe.

Puritanism is part of the Western tradition that for the last two thousand years has regarded the earth as dark and dangerous and in need of
taming or reform. The colonial settlers brought the standards of European civilization with them to the New World but left behind the cultivated fields and the stone houses of the English countryside, the comforts
of the aristocratic manor of Lincolnshire, and the cobbled streets and
shops of London and Amsterdam. Instead, they found the primeval forest. In an effort to approximate the living standards of England and Europe, they cut down the trees, cleared large land areas, and built stone or
wood houses. This vigorous effort to re-create the communities left behind was partly motivated by custom and a longing to inhabit a familiar
world, but as Peter Carroll and Annette Kolodny point out, the Puritans
perceived nature as unregenerate—as a wild and threatening force that

needed to be subdued and tamed.[4] Before the seventeenth-century settlers arrived, the Indians of New England lived in symbiotic coexistence with nature revering the forests that the Puritans feared as the devil's hiding place. But in their zeal to reform the satanic wilderness, the settlers destroyed the delicate ecological balance that had evolved over thousands of years.[5]

Unlike the Puritan fathers, Bradstreet does not seem to have felt the need to impose sacred order on the landscape. Instead of trying to reform nature, she appreciates its cyclicity and diversity. Perhaps the tradition of feminine receptivity and nurturance freed her from the need to rigorously control her environment. In contrast to her male counterparts, Bradstreet repeatedly expresses her commitment to natural processes rather than abstract order. For her, an attachment to earthly existence is vain only because *it does not last*. "O Time the fatal wrack of mortal things" is Bradstreet's lament (*Works*, 381). Bradstreet's emphasis is on life—life on earth, to be followed by life in heaven. The difference between Anne Bradstreet's love of her world and the Puritan imperative to impose divine order on the landscape is rooted in the ancient schism between the gynecocratic values of pre-Hellenic culture and the Apollonian and Judeo-Christian traditions. Similarly, Bradstreet's responsiveness to the quotidian provides a dramatic contrast to the patriarchal transcendence that rejects mutability. As Bradstreet's poetry indicates, the sublime style is an expression of the traditional masculine effort to achieve supremacy over mundane existence, which is categorized as female. Because men dominated Bradstreet's literary world, she frequently feigned helplessness and inferiority to gain acceptance and to win their approval; however, her praise of men as superior beings was usually ironic, and most of her poetry presents a vision of life that values her experience as a woman. For example, "The Four Seasons," the fourth poem of Bradstreet's epic series, continues to stress process, the cooperative resolution of conflict, and the plenitude of nature, although it is somewhat more programmatic and more closely follows the style of Du Bartas. Using the conventions of pastoral poetry to describe the abundant diversity of life on earth as well as the intricate interrelationship between the zodiac and seasonal change, Bradstreet again differs from her models by concentrating on the earth's fertility rather than the order of God's creation, which was the subject of much seventeenth-century writing:

> The Sun in *Taurus* keeps his residence,
> And with his warmer beams glanceth from thence
> This is the month whose fruitful showrs produces
> All set and sown for all delights and uses:

The Pear, the Plum, and Apple-tree now flourish
The grass grows long the hungry beast to nourish.
The Primrose pale, and azure violet
Among the virduous grass hath nature set,
That when the Sun on's Love (the earth) doth shine
These might as lace set out her garment fine.

(*Works*, 170)

Fecundity, not sacredness, is expressed by the sexual metaphor of the potent sun courting the earth adorned with garments of lacy primrose, azure violet, and abundant grasses: generativity, not God's plan, is the focus of this poem.

Unlike Bradstreet's cyclical depiction of nature, the Puritans' New World garden was not a place of fertile abundance and growth, but a carefully ordered space that represented divine economy.[6] It was not a garden of fruits, grains, and vegetables to sustain the body and to celebrate life, but a tamed wilderness that soothed the soul. In the Puritan paradigm, human beings were set apart from nature and not subject to the decay and dissolution of lower forms of life. In contrast to the Puritan belief in the ultimate transcendence of nature, the earliest gardens are depicted in ancient religions as places where all life forms coexist. Ancient rites such as those celebrating the Eleusinian mysteries honored seasonal cyclicity, the phases of the moon, and the sun's varying path across the sky, associating the female power to give birth with the fruitful earth.

With the shift from the ancient religions to Hellenic and then to Judeo-Christian religions, the mantic force in all living creatures became embodied in individual heroes or male rulers. The Homeric sagas, for example, narrate the triumphs of the hero while the fertility rituals enacted a communal reality. As Jane Harrison observes, the eclipse of Gaia by Apollo marks the triumph of the sky, light, and reason over the earth, darkness, and mystery; mutability and mortality as represented by the changing seasons were overshadowed by a shift of interest to the more predictable movements of the stars and the concept of mortality.[7] According to Harrison, the religions of the goddesses implicitly accepted and acknowledged the terror of inevitable death through ritual sacrifices of animal and even human life, but for the Apollonian cultures that followed, the promise of eternal life muted existential fears. For the Puritans, like the Yawists and other biblical sects that gave rise to Protestantism, nature held no mantic power but was an expression of God's plan.[8]

Although Bradstreet used the Puritan belief that the history of the world was a divinely ordained progression culminating in the New World mission as a framework for "The Four Monarchies," the final poem in her epic series, her deepest energies were not engaged in the project. Not only is it less accomplished than the preceding poems, she never completed it. Written in the style of Du Bartas, it closely follows the text of Raleigh's *History of the World* as well as contemporary translations of Plutarch, Livy, Pliny, Xenophon, Hesiod, Homer, Ovid, and Thucydides.[9] Like Raleigh, Bradstreet narrates the rise and fall of the Assyrian, Persian, Grecian, and Roman empires in an effort to demonstrate the pattern of God's order in history. But "The Four Monarchies" ends with "An Apology" in which Bradstreet admits that she grew weary of the project "I hours not few did spend, / And weary lines (though lanke) I many pen'd" (*Works*, 329). In contrast to the lyrical and graceful composition of her later poetry, which appears in the second edition of *The Tenth Muse*, the doggedly written and mechanically rhymed lines of "The Four Monarchies" indicate that she was not actively interested in writing about traditional male subjects. But instead of admitting her boredom, she explains that she found the subject too elevated in the closing lines of this unfinished poem:

> My tyred brain leavs to some better pen,
> This task befits not women like to men:
> For what is past, I blush, excuse to make,
> But humbly stand, some grave reproof to take;
> Pardon to crave for errours, is but vain,
> The subject was too high, beyond my strain
> (*Works*, 321)

Although she feels—or protests—that she has failed because her attention was not engaged by the elevated subject matter that interested acclaimed male poets and historians, her best poetry in this volume is grounded in personal conviction and experience.

The last two poems of the first edition are concerned with traditional religious subjects. "David's Lamentation for Saul and Jonathan" is a paraphrase in rhymed couplets of 2 Sam. 1 : 19–27 of the Geneva Bible. The final poem, "Of the Vanity of all Worldly Creatures," is written in iambic couplets and restates the themes of renunciation of the world of Ecclesiastes as well as Revelation's promise of a heavenly paradise. Like "The Four Monarchies," these poems are programmatic and lack the depth and tension of the other poems in the volume. In spite of its flaws, however, the first edition of *The Tenth Muse* established Anne Bradstreet as the first woman poet in the New World and demonstrated that she was knowledgeable and accomplished in her craft.

THREE

"Be still, thou unregenerate part"

If physical suffering was a measure of piety, the numerous illnesses described in Anne Bradstreet's letters, occasional poems, and poetic aphorisms are proof of her struggling spirit: "I had a sore fitt of fainting, which lasted 2 or 3 dayes," she writes on July 8, 1656 (*Works*, 17). On September 30, she records, "It pleased God to visit me with my old Distemper," adding, "I can no more live without correction then without food" (*Works*, 23). Describing her sicknesses and afflictions as evidence of God's "abundant Love," Bradstreet tried to accept her infirmities and in accordance with the tenets of preparationism, which emphasized the importance of the broken spirit, she interpreted her illness as a sign of the intimate bond between herself and God, whom she acknowledged as a stern but not sadistic father:

> . . . God doth not afflict willingly, nor take delight in grieving the children of men: he hath no benefitt by my adversity, nor is he the better for my prosperity; but he doth it for my Advantage, and that I may bee a Gainer by it. And if he knowes that weaknes and a frail body is the best to make me a vessell fitt for his use, why should I not bare it, not only willingly but joyfully? (*Works*, 20)

As a young woman, Anne Bradstreet often doubted the existence of God and the promise of eternal life. So intense was her responsiveness to her immediate surroundings, her family and friends, that salvation frequently seemed ephemeral to her. Begging God to dispel her doubts by revealing himself to her in visible form, Bradstreet wrote on August 28, 1656, "O let me ever see Thee that Art invisible, and I shall not bee unwilling to come" (*Works*, 20). Of course, this plea for sensory evidence was antithetical to the demands of faith that require surrender of individual control or to use the Puritan's phrase, "the prideful monster of independence."

As one of the most strenuous forms of Christianity, Puritanism stresses the central paradox that the death of the body brings the possibility of eternal life of the spirit in union with God. The body pulls the Christian toward earth; "carnality" is Satan's lure. Satan tempts the beleaguered pilgrim with physical pleasure, while God calls on the faithful to accept the afflictions of the body as tests of belief in the far greater pleasures of the spirit. The mind and the body, then, become an arena for the battle between Satan and God. Much of Edward Taylor's poetry depicts an extreme form of the Puritan disgust with the filth and putrefaction of the body:

> A Sty of Filth, a Trough of Washing-Swill
> A Dunghill Pit, a Puddle of mere Slime.
> A Nest of Vipers, Hive of Hornets; Stings.
> A Bag of Poyson, Civit-Box of Sins [1]

In contrast to Taylor, for whom the body was a "dunghill," Anne Bradstreet did not loathe the flesh, but she did observe that it was easier for her to be pious when she was sick. She conveys the intensity of this struggle in her poem, "The Flesh and the Spirit," a dialogue between two sisters about physical desires and pleasures and the aspirations of the soul:

> Sister, quoth Flesh, what liv'st thou on
> Nothing but Meditation?
> Doth Contemplation feed thee so
> Regardlessly to let earth goe?
> (*Works*, 381–82)

Then Flesh adroitly proceeds to catalog the pleasures of this world—honor, fame, accolades, riches: "Earth hath more silver, pearls, and gold, / Then eyes can see or hands can hold." Spirit retorts:

> Be still, thou unregenerate part,
> Disturb no more my settled heart,
> For I have vow'd (and so will doe)
> Thee as a foe, still to pursue.
> And combate with thee will and must,
> Untill I see thee laid in th' dust.
> (*Works*, 382–83)

Discipline and resolute resistance are pitted against the tangible rewards and pleasures of earthly existence. The lines of battle drawn, Spirit berates Flesh for distracting her from God's glory with the "bait" of worldly treasures. Scorning secular achievement, Spirit announces, "My greatest honor it shall be / When I am victor over thee" (*Works*, 383). Bradstreet's poem expresses the tension, even enmity, of the body and the soul in the Christian ethos that is resolved only with the destruction of the body, "the unregenerate part," which liberates the spirit from the body's cage so that it can wear royal robes, "More glorious than the glistr'ing sun" in a place where disease and death—the infirmities of the flesh—do not exist. In heaven, mortality is subdued, conquered, and finally transcended; in the meantime, the battle between body and soul rages as it has since Adam and Eve's fall from grace.

In writing about the theme of enmity between the body and the soul, Bradstreet addressed the subject central to much Christian poetry. The dialogue between flesh and spirit was especially popular in medieval literature as well as in Elizabethan and metaphysical poetry. The Cavalier poets promulgated the materialist position that the mind cannot exist without the body and advised their readers to seize the day. Other poets such as Sir John Davies insisted that the spirit was separate from the flesh in such poems as "Of the Soule of Man, and the Immortalitie thereof":

> And though this Spirit be to the Bodie knit
> As an apt meane, her powers to exercise,
> Which are *life, motion, sense,* and *will* and *wit,*
> Yet she *survives,* although the Bodie *dies.*[2]

Andrew Marvell's poems embrace both sides of this dualism—eternity is portrayed as a vast desert devoid of youthful beauty and pleasure in "To His Coy Mistress," and in "A Dialogue between the Soul and Body" the spirit is depicted as being imprisoned in the flesh:

> A Soul hung up, as 'twere, in Chains
> Of Nerves, and Arteries, and Veins,
> Tortur'd, besides each other part,
> In a vain Head, and double Heart.[3]

Marvell takes an even more complex view of the mind/body problem in "A Dialogue between the Resolved Soul and Created Pleasure," which parallels Bradstreet's poem, "The Flesh and the Spirit." In both works, the soul battles the body and ultimately triumphs over the senses by force of will demonstrating, as Marvell writes, that "Nature wants an Art / To conquer one resolved Heart."[4] And the chorus in Marvell's poem exultantly declaims:

Earth cannot shew so brave a Sight
As when a single Soul does fence
The Batteries of alluring Sense,
And Heaven views it with delight,
  Then persevere: for still new Charges sound:
  And if thou overcom'st thou shalt be crown'd.[5]

Although the speakers of both poems are almost beguiled by lures of the flesh, faith enables them to resist the temptations of love, wealth, glory, and knowledge. However, there are significant differences between the attitudes of Bradstreet and the male poets in their search for heaven. Marvell emphasizes the moral trial and ultimate victory of the resolute spirit, while Bradstreet stresses the *pleasures* of eternity:

The stately Walls both high and strong,
Are made of pretious *Jasper* stone;
The Gates of Pearl, both rich and clear,
And Angels are for Porters there;
The Streets thereof transparent gold,
Such as no Eye did e're behold,
A Chrystal River there doth run,
Which doth proceed from the Lambs Throne
                    (*Works*, 384)

Using images drawn from Rev. 21:10–27 and 22:1–5, she describes heaven as far more luxurious and comfortable than earth. Even in heaven Bradstreet is more concerned with the senses than with spirituality. It is significant that male poets frequently use the metaphor of military campaigns and conquests to give form to the relationship between the mind and the body while Bradstreet describes herself as *bearing* the temptations of the flesh. The moral triumph in Marvell's poem is the result of assertive combat with sin while Bradstreet writes of passively enduring Satan's trials. This difference in consciousness is clearly influenced by gender roles because there is nothing in Puritan theology that explicitly differentiates the spiritual identity of men and women.

According to Puritan doctrine, the covenant of grace by which God "elected some to everlasting life" reversed the inevitable damnation of all people as a result of original sin. Through this covenant, salvation and redemption were granted to "the elect" who were chosen on the basis of divine grace not human merit. With the exclusion of some from the ranks of the saints, a division between the regenerate and unregenerate was established; a hierarchy of the saved and the damned—those with and without hope of eternal life—was created. Uncertainty about spiritual destiny caused extraordinary anxiety among many of the New World pilgrims. For example, Winthrop recorded in his journal in 1637 that "a woman of the Boston congregation having been in much trouble of mind about her spiritual estate, at length grew into utter desperation, and could not endure to her of any comfort, etc., so one day she took her little infant and threw it into a well, and then came into the house, and said, now she was sure she should be damned, for she had drowned her child." [6]

The preparationists such as Thomas Hooker and Thomas Shepard argued that because redemption was a gift from God whose infinite grace and mercy were extended to the elect, continual self-scrutiny and introspection were required in order to have a "heart prepared" to be called by God "to embrace Jesus Christ." [7] Urging their parishioners to scrutinize their lives for signs of salvation, for visible evidence of an invisible state of grace, Hooker and Shepard asserted that the prepared heart required constant testing, and therefore affliction and misfortune were to be welcomed as divine chastisement. Thomas Shepard explains the purpose of these moral trials in his journal: "if I had profited by former afflictions of this nature I should not have had the scourge." [8] Because each setback or crisis was seen as a necessary correction demonstrating God's love, paradoxically suffering was a form of joy as Anne Bradstreet explains in her spiritual autobiography:

> Among all my experiences of God's gratious Dealings with me I have constantly observed this, that he hath never suffered me long to sitt loose from him, but by one affliction or other hath made me look home, and search what was amisse—so usually thus it hath been with me that I have no sooner felt my heart out of order, but I have expected correction for it, which most commonly hath been upon my own person, in sicknesse, weaknes, paines, sometimes on my soul, in Doubts and feares of God's displeasure, and my sincerity toward him. (*Works*, 5–6)

The belief in God's regenerative power enabled the saints to endure their individual and collective tribulations and strengthened their commitment to their redemptive mission; so strong was their faith in God's plan for them that food shortages, Indian attacks, disease, and death were perceived as divine chastisement rather than disaster. As Perry Miller and Sacvan Bercovitch have demonstrated, these experiences were seen as emblematic of the Israelites' trials in their search for the promised land. [9] The Puritan tribe believed that ultimately history would vindicate them by revealing God's providential plan for his followers. Spiritual autobiographies, sermons, and jeremiads exhorted the holy army to redouble its efforts to build God's commonwealth in the face of formidable challenges of the New World.

In her later years, Anne Bradstreet accepted her illnesses as divine correction and as a chastening reminder of her moral frailty: "The Lord knowes I dare not desire that health that sometimes I have had, least my heart should bee drawn from him, and sett upon the world" (*Works*, 20). Elizabeth Wade White speculates that Anne Bradstreet suffered recurrent illnesses because of a rheumatic heart,[10] but it is significant that Bradstreet often became sick when she was unable to sustain the almost unbearable tension between spirit and flesh, faith and doubt, and renunciation and temptation that is the core of Puritanism.

Anne Bradstreet was not always able to sustain her faith during periods of severe testing; her doubt was, at times, overwhelming: "[S]ometimes I have said, Is there any faith upon the earth? And I have not known what to think" (*Works*, 9–10). Her despair even prevented her from sleeping:

> By night when others soundly slept,
> And had at once both ease and Rest,
> My waking eyes were open kept,
> And so to lye I found it best.
> (*Works*, 11)

The ambiguity created by "lye" in the last line underscores Bradstreet's misgivings about the promise of salvation and eternal life. Her wavering belief resulted in more than one dark night of the soul: "I have often been perplexed that I have not found that constant Joy in my Pilgrimage and refreshing which I supposed most servants of God have. . . . Yet have I have many Times sinkings and droopings, and not enjoyed that felicity that sometimes I have done" (*Works*, 7).

Although the preparationists stressed the difficulty of the journey, cautioning of obstacles intended to test faith that required continual renewal—each moment necessitated reaffirmation of commitment to God's will—there were dramatic differences in the spiritual experiences of the individual members of the New England congregations. The diaries of her male counterparts reveal a certainty of God's love that Bradstreet did not experience. Even though suffering was seen as proof of divine testing, it did not guarantee salvation. Nevertheless, the men tended to count themselves among the elect. In contrast to Bradstreet's agonizing uncertainty, John Winthrop's diary indicates that he emerged from his spiritual trial more assured of regeneration than she did. After undergoing a process of humiliation and preparation, Winthrop reports that he received confirmation of his faith: "The good spirit of the Lord breathed upon my soule, and said that I should live."[11] Winthrop experienced the emotional turmoil of the preparatory stages of conversion—conviction and repentance—prior to receiving sanctification, a sign of God's love. Unlike Bradstreet, however, he seems not to have felt abandoned by his Savior: "Hee left mee not till hee had overcome my heart to give up it selfe to him, and to bid farewell to all the world, and untill my heart could answer, Lord, what wilt thou have mee to doe?"[12] Although, as Edmund Morgan has observed, the soul's testing never ceased, permitting no rest for the Puritan conscience,[13] Winthrop seems to have felt comforted and sustained by God in his moments of doubt and adversity; he is more certain of redemption than Bradstreet, and he is more assured that the denial of the body brings forth spiritual life: "And the more I grew thus acquainted with the spirit of God, the more were my corruptions mortifyed, and the new man quickened."[14] Here Winthrop emphasizes regeneration and freedom from the body's bondage, and although the reshaping of his consciousness is arduous, he is convinced that he is ultimately transformed by God.

Thomas Shepard also believed that conversion did not happen in an instant of illumination but was a gradual process involving much moral backsliding; he too sees his unworthiness as a sign of his redemption: "I found the Lord helping me to see my unworthyness of any mercy, and that I was worthy to be cast out of his sight, and to leave myself with him to do with me what he would; and then, and never until then, I found rest, and so my heart was humbled."[15]

Fifty years later Cotton Mather's account of his soul's testing demonstrates that he also shared Winthrop's confidence in God's love. In his diary, Mather recorded an occasion full of doubt when he lay prostrate lamenting his "Loathesomeness" until he was overwhelmed "by a Flood of Tears, that ran down upon the floor. . . . This Conversation with Heaven, left a sweet, a calm, a considerate, a sanctifying, an Heavenly Impression upon my Soul."[16] Interpreting his self-loathing as a sign of ultimate worthiness, Mather assumes that he has received God's grace. Mather was so sure of God's concern for him that he even prayed for three days for the death of his son-in-law and was gratified, but not surprised, when the healthy man died suddenly.[17] In contrast to Winthrop, Shepard, and Mather who emerged reassured from their spiritual turmoils, Bradstreet's faith in God's grace was the result of *willed resolution*: "But when I have been in darkes and seen no light, yet have I desired to stay myself upon the Lord" (*Works*, 7). Her determination to submit to the authority of the church and to resist temptation enabled her to accept spiritual and physical affliction as God's "tender mercies."

Perhaps Anne Bradstreet's doubts about her worthiness were intensified by the fact that she did not actively shape her world; instead, she lived according to the rules established by the men in her life. Both her father and husband were intensely involved in the governing of the church during frequent disputes about covenant theology and the fine points of church membership. Dudley was a magistrate with Winthrop; as we have seen, he held the offices of governor of Massachusetts Bay, deputy governor, and justice of the peace; Simon Bradstreet also served as governor of the colony. As pillars of the community, these men were called upon to make decisions in both civil and ecclesiastical matters that gave them a sense of moral purpose and certainty. As New England patriarchs, their status was recognized and reinforced by the community, and their social prominence and concrete responsibilities tended to create the assumption that they were among the elect. This relationship between control and confidence is confirmed by the increasing belief of American women in the possibility of transforming their lives as they achieve recognition in the public sphere.

Unlike her father and husband, Anne Bradstreet participated very little in the public arena. As the mother of eight children—four boys and four girls—she had an elaborate household to administer; however, her life was very much directed by the decisions of Thomas Dudley and Simon Bradstreet, and her duty was to be an obedient daughter and a responsible wife. Not only did she leave England to come with them to the New World, she followed them to increasingly smaller and more distant settlements so they could improve their worldly estates—from Salem to Charlestown to Boston to Cambridge to Ipswich, and, finally, to Andover. But unlike the messianic pilgrimage of the men to build a city on a hill, Bradstreet's calling was domestic. Her mission was to create a home for her family in the savage outposts of the New World.

In addition to diffusing tensions about the spiritual destiny of the pilgrims, preparationism tended to enhance the authority of the church elders whose role it was to guide the congregation along the path to heaven. By insisting on the necessity of a broken spirit as the culmination of repeated trials and tests, the preparationists anticipated a certain amount of backsliding that would require counseling by the elders. Since no two souls were treated equally by God—"the Lord deals kindly and gently with one soul, and roughly with another"—members of the congregation often found it necessary to seek help from the ministers in an effort to interpret their moral turmoil.[18] The process of admitting new church members often involved an investigation of the conversion experience, and prospective members were constrained to offer some sign of belonging to the covenant of grace. This evidence was easier to obtain when a parishioner had been in the habit of confiding in a minister.[19]

By counseling sinners to make ready to receive the Lord's grace, preparationism offered hope to the unregenerate. Comforted in their despairing moments, sinners were assured that redemption was a gradual process that occurred through discipline and self-denial. According to Sacvan Bercovitch, this emphasis on the process of breaking down the resistance of the prideful self to God's saving mercy absorbed the rebellious impulses of the New England pilgrims that might otherwise have been directed toward social change. Emphasis on the "morphology of conversion," Bercovitch observes, is an effective method for domesticating the spirit or directing potentially radical energies toward acceptable social ends. By keeping the individual always on the alert for sin to be overcome, preparationism harnessed the potentially revolutionary energies of the soul.[20] Certainly, Anne Bradstreet's rebellious inclinations were restrained by this emphasis on a soul continually in the process of refinement and regeneration.

Preparationism was a more successful spiritual strategy for those men who believed in the efficacy of their efforts and who perceived themselves as capable of triumphing over sin. Salvation, then, was partly a matter of confidence, self-esteem, and spiritual expectation. As we have seen, it was extraordinarily difficult for Anne Bradstreet to imagine herself as triumphant over Satan who, after all, was a demonic male force whose assaults she had to endure. While Donne, Marvell, Shepard, and Winthrop welcomed the breaking of their spirits as a sign of their ultimate worthiness, Anne Bradstreet was never certain that she would survive her heart's battering. Instead of doing battle with Satan, Bradstreet was embattled.

FOUR

"The Rising Self"

Although the Puritans accepted Luther's proclamation that God could be served in a variety of ways—that all callings were equal—domestic piety was less impressive than public service. Confinement to private life narrows the arena in which faith can be exercised and tested. The exhortation of Peter to "declare the wonderful deeds of him that called you out of the darkness into his marvelous light" (1 Pet. 2:9–10) is difficult to execute in the kitchen or nursery; it is more easily done from the pulpit or podium. The field of service available to Anne Bradstreet was her home, her family, and her poetry. But even this internal, private landscape was treacherous.

Women who stepped beyond their domestic confines by means of literature, whether by reading or by writing, risked being branded as dangerous to themselves and to society. John Winthrop's journal entry for April 13, 1645, denouncing Anne Hopkins reflects the Puritan bias against intellectual women: "[Anne Hopkins] was fallen into a sad infirmity, the loss of her understanding and reason, which had been growing upon her divers years, by occasion of her giving herself wholly to reading and writing, and had written many books."[1] Winthrop goes on to observe that her husband, having been "loving and tender of her," failed in his duty to discipline her to stay in her place: "[H]e saw his errour, when it was too late. For if she had attended her household affairs, and such things as belong to women, and not gone out of her way and calling to meddle in such things as are proper for men, whose minds are stronger, . . . she had kept her wits, and might have improved them usefully and honorably in the place god had set her."[2] According to Winthrop, Anne Hopkins was punished for her excessive thinking by the loss of her reason.

Many other Puritans expressed considerable scorn for women who wrote or published. In 1650, Thomas Parker wrote a public letter condemning his sister for publishing a book in London: "Your printing of a Book beyond the Custom of your Sex, doth rankly smell."[3] This contemptuous attitude toward women writers was especially hard for Anne Bradstreet to accept because her childhood training had prepared her to think of herself as an intelligent and articulate person. Nevertheless, she was acutely aware of the risks of speaking openly in public because her younger sister, Sarah, was excommunicated from the church in 1646 and ostracized from the community for preaching. While accompanying her husband, Major Benjamin Keayne, on a business trip to London, Sarah talked so freely of her religious convictions that her brother-in-law, Stephen Winthrop, commented, "My she Cosin Keane is growne a great preacher."[4] After her return to Massachusetts, the Boston Church admonished her for "hir Irregular Prophesying in mixt Assemblies and for Refusing Ordinarily to heare in ye Churches of Christ,"[5] and her husband declared that he would "never againe to live with her as a Husband" because she had "ronne so faste from that highth of error in judgment, to that extremitie of error in practisse."[6] Divorce occurred rarely in the colonies, and Thomas Dudley was so angered by his daughter's conduct that he disinherited her.

The expulsion of Anne Hutchinson from Massachusetts Bay also demonstrated the very real dangers of stepping beyond the boundaries of prescribed behavior. Her trial warned against the dangers of listening to an inner voice that might be Satan's and not God's at all. The parallels in Hutchinson's and Bradstreet's lives are striking: both had fathers who were prominent public figures, and both of their mothers were women of advantaged backgrounds. Hutchinson's father was Thomas Marbury, a Puritan minister from Lincolnshire, England; her mother was related to the poet John Dryden. Both the Dudleys and the Hutchinsons had been members of John Cotton's congregation in England and were his strong supporters in the New World. As daughters of educated women and of men who were powerful in the Puritan community, Anne Bradstreet and Anne Hutchinson grew up in an environment in which they were exposed to intellectual discussion and independent thought. As women, they were in a double bind because their powerful intelligence was not permitted public expression even though the mission of the Puritans was to follow the admonition in Matt. 28:19 "to go forth and make disciples of all nations." Both women found private solutions—Bradstreet in her poetry, Hutchinson in her meetings at home that stressed the inner light, that is, the indwelling spirit of God's grace signaling redemption. Religious politics, however, proved to be more perilous than poetry writing, which was acceptable insofar as it praised God.

Anne Hutchinson was an extraordinarily effective public speaker, as Edward Johnson's report in *Wonder-Working Providence of Sions Saviour in New-England* (1654) reveals:

Come along with me. . . . I'le bring you to a Woman that preaches better Gospell than any of your black-coates that have been at the Ninneversity, a Woman of another kinde of Spirit, who hath had many Revelations of things to come, and for my part, . . . I had rather hear such a one that speakes from the meere motion of the Spirit without any study at all, than any of your learned Scollers.[7]

At first Hutchinson's meetings were tolerated because it was thought that they provided the older women of the community with an opportunity to instruct the younger women in religious and social virtues. This kind of teaching was praised in Titus 2 : 3 – 5 and could be considered beneficial to the community because "[aged women] may teach the young women to be sober, to love their husbands, to love their children, *to be* discreet, chaste, keepers at home, good, obedient to their own husbands, that the word of God be not blasphemed."[8]

But as the meetings became more popular and began to be attended by men as well as women, the ministers, fearing the erosion of their power, grew increasingly hostile. Hutchinson's brother-in-law, John Wheelwright, responded to their criticism by preaching militant sermons in her defense: "When enymies to truth oppose the way of God, we must lay loade upon them, we must kille them with the worde of the Lorde."[9] These fighting phrases further incensed the church authorities who then reviled Hutchinson as "the American Jezibel" and prohibited her "seditious" meetings. John Wilson, the pastor of the Boston Church, accused Hutchinson of the "*slighting of God's faithful Ministers and condemning and crying down them as Noboddies.*"[10]

Rejecting the preparationist emphasis on civil and spiritual discipline and on good works as a sign of regeneration, Hutchinson believed that conversion occurred in a moment of insight that was experienced as a transforming illumination and that salvation was a matter of emotional conviction or grace. As a midwife, she was active in the community and was very influential, too influential according to many of the ministers who felt she was undermining their authority. According to Winthrop, "it began to be as common here to distinguish between men, by being under a covenant of grace or a covenant of works, as in other countries between Protestants and papists."[11]

The underlying issue behind the Hutchinson controversy was that of control of the churches. By establishing her discussion groups, Hutchinson asserted the congregational principle of the gathered church—the right of the congregation to convene under the covenant of grace and to select a minister on the basis of shared needs and convictions. The elders of the established churches traditionally resisted this selection process based on popular support, insisting that approval of the magistrates and ministers was necessary before any new congregation could be formed.

By asserting that many of the New England ministers were functioning under the covenant of works, Hutchinson polarized two modes of religious thought—spiritism and legalism—which had coexisted in an uneasy alliance since the arrival of Bradford's expedition in the New World. The spiritists believed that God's promise of redemption was revealed to the elect who would join their savior in the millennium. These believers in the indwelling spirit were chiliastic and stressed the importance of prophecy and grace; they tended to be congregational, insisting on popular support of the minister by the parish. For them, the gathered church represented a consensus of the shepherd and his flock.[12] The legalists or preparationists stressed the importance of civil and spiritual discipline, which involved responsibility and duty; they emphasized the importance of self-scrutiny and right thinking as an aid to salvation. The spiritists accepted a diversity of experience and conviction while the legalists championed ecumenical principles and were hostile to the laissez-faire approach that they felt promoted enthusiasm; popular zeal was heretical and dangerous. The hostilities between these two groups had existed long before Anne Hutchinson catalyzed their differences.

In his *History*, Governor Winthrop, who pronounced Hutchinson "a woman of ready wit and bold spirit," charged her with two dangerous errors. She was accused of teaching that the "Holy Ghost dwells in a justified person" and that there is no "other sanctification but the Holy Ghost himself."[13] Because she believed that God's word could be understood through individual revelation, which was, for her, more genuine than the rules and rituals that upheld the authority of the church elders, she was accused and convicted of antinomianism—that is, of believing she was above Old Testament moral law. Hutchinson was charged with heresy by the General Court of Massachusetts and at a trial attended by hundreds, the enraged elders accused her of thirty errors—the Synod of Cambridge later increased the number of heresies to eighty-two. She was then excommunicated from the church and exiled from the community.[14] Her supporters were fined and disenfranchised; some, including Wheelwright, were banished from Massachusetts Bay.

In ejecting her from the church, John Wilson raged against her: "In the name of our Lord Jesus Christ and in the name of the Church . . . I *doe cast yow out . . . I doe deliver yow up to Sathan . . .* I doe account yow from this time forth to be Heathen and a Publican. . . . *I command yow* in the name of christ Jesus and of this Church *as a Leper to Withdraw your selfe*."[15] Reviling "this wretched woman," Thomas Hooker announced that Hutchinson was "to be cast out as unsavory salt, that she may not continue to be a pest in the place, that will be forever marvellous in the eyes of the saints." [16] Blaming her for all of the religious dissension in the community, Hooker warned the churches to "hear and fear." John Cotton, who had been one of the most articulate ministers in support of the congregational ideal and the transforming power of grace, reversed his position about church membership—apparently, the other ministers convinced him that inner-light theology was potentially damaging to the stability of the church and the ministry. [17] As Cotton's devoted disciple, Hutchinson based her statements on his argument that church membership was open to all those who had experienced the indwelling spirit, but during her trial Cotton defended the ministers' sacerdotal authority to determine who would be admitted to the Lord's Supper. This theological shift seems a bitter reversal, if not betrayal, of Anne Hutchinson.

Hutchinson's congregational zeal was shared by most members of the Boston Church and by Henry Vane who had been elected to replace Winthrop as governor in 1636. But John Wilson and most ministers of the New England churches along with John Winthrop opposed the spiritists whose informal approach to salvation threatened to erode the power of the pulpit. After Hutchinson's trial, Winthrop resumed the governorship and Vane returned to England. In the following September, Winthrop convened a synod that banished Anne Hutchinson from the colony. John Cotton tried to persuade Hutchinson's sons to join in the public condemnation and humiliation of their mother and warned the "sisters of the church to take heed" not to become similarly hardened to sin. Hutchinson, then, was blamed for the tensions within the church.

Spiritism made it easier for those Puritans outside the power structure of their society to consider themselves worthy of eternal life. In contrast, preparationism was derived from the male paradigm of combat with Satan and emphasized the necessity of a continual battle, a battle that was waged more effectively by those with sufficient aggressive energy and confidence that it could be won. Because most women, including Anne Bradstreet, were traditionally raised to be accepting rather than assertive, they found it almost impossible to perceive themselves as triumphant over Satan, a powerful demonic male. For those Puritans who were socially marginal—unable to shape or control the circumstances of their lives—grace offered an alternative to proving oneself in the moral arena by replacing the miseries of combat with the nurturing love of an all-wise parent.

By insisting that all believers were "one in Christ," Hutchinson not only made salvation accessible to a larger number of people but she also implied an equality of the sexes. The soul, not gender or social standing, was saved or damned. Winthrop was especially angered by Hutchinson's refusal to accept the limitations of traditional womanhood:

> In the assemblies which were held by the followers of Mrs. Hutchinson, there was nourished and trained a keen, contentious spirit, and an unbridled licence of tongue, of which the influence was speedily felt in the serious disturbance, first of domestic happiness, and then of public peace. The matrons of Boston were transformed into a synod of slanderous praters, whose inquisitional deliberations and audacious decrees, instilled their venom into the innermost recesses of society; and the spirits of a great majority of the citizens being in that combustible state in which a feeble spark will suffice to kindle a formidable conflagration, the whole Colony was inflamed and distracted by the incontinence of female spleen and presumption.[18]

According to Winthrop, religious enthusiasm, and the accompanying social disruption, was the result of unchecked female energy.

Winthrop described Hutchinson's exile as "a happy day to the churches of Christ here, and to many poor souls, who had been seduced by her."[19] The magistrates were so disturbed by Hutchinson's challenge to their authority over spiritual matters that they continued to publicly condemn her even after she was expelled from the community. In Boston, a lengthy lecture described in elaborate detail the malformations of the fetus that Hutchinson miscarried during her imprisonment on the Isle of Aquiday in Narragansett Bay. John Cotton, who had failed to defend Hutchinson at her trial in spite of the fact that she had been loyal to him when his preaching was the focus of controversy, moralized that the malformed fetus embodied her spiritual errors and that her miscarriage was caused by God to punish her for her sins.

Governor Winthrop interrogated the physician who attended Hutchinson for details of the miscarriage. After lengthy questioning, Dr. Clarke embellished his initial report that the fetus was a formless mass of lumps: "The lumps were twenty-six or twenty-seven distinct and not joined together; there came no secundine after them; six of them were as great as his fist, and one as great as two fists, the rest each less than the other, and the smallest about the bigness of the top of his thumb."[20] Then, not content with this description, Winthrop also questioned Mary Dyer, who was a close friend of Anne Hutchinson's and, like her, a midwife. Because she was afraid of banishment, Dyer permitted herself to be badgered into describing the fetus as the work of the devil:

It was a woman child . . . of ordinary bigness; it had a face, but no head, and the ears stood upon the shoulders and were like an ape's; it had no forehead, but over the eyes four horns, hard and sharp; two of them were above one inch long, the other two shorter; the eyes standing out, and the mouth also; the nose hooked upward; all over the breast and back full of sharp pricks and scales, like a thornback; the navel and all the belly, with the distinction of the sex, were where the back should be, and the back and the hips before, where the belly should have been; behind, between the shoulders, it had two mouths, and in each of them a piece of red flesh sticking out; it had arms and legs as other children; but instead of toes, it had on each foot three claws, like a young fowl, with sharp talons.[21]

Like Cotton, Winthrop lost no time in making the connection between the miscarriage and Hutchinson's spiritual errors: "And see how the wisdome of God fitted this judgment to her sinne every way, for look as she had vented mishapen opinions, so she must bring forth deformed monsters."[22]

No doubt Anne Bradstreet was familiar with the details of Hutchinson's trial and banishment. Her father and husband were among Hutchinson's main prosecutors, and both were on the board of public magistrates that convicted her. Thomas Dudley was especially hostile to Hutchinson, accusing her of being a troublemaker from the moment she landed at Massachusetts Bay and blaming her for endangering the foundation of the church. In addition to condemning her for questioning the ministers' abilities to interpret the New Testament and to act as God's agents on earth, he led the magistrates in accusing her of enthusiasm. During the trial, Dudley baited Hutchinson with the subtlest distinctions in points of theology, attempting to trick her at every turn with legalistic definitions of the difference between the covenants of works and grace to get her to perjure herself. Surely the lesson of Anne Hutchinson was not lost on Anne Bradstreet.

In view of the extraordinary anger toward her sister and Anne Hutchinson, Bradstreet must have been anxious at times about writing poetry in an environment that was hostile to independent women. Although more circumspect than Hutchinson in expressing her intellectual autonomy, Bradstreet sometimes came perilously close to challenging the authority of the Puritan divines in *The Tenth Muse*. When Bradstreet was besieged by doubt about eternal life and was tempted to accept her bond with the earth and hence the inevitability of decay and death, she worried that it was her imagination that was causing her to stray. In general, the

Puritans distrusted the imagination. As Richard Sibbes warned, "amongst all the *faculties* of the soul, most of the disquiet and unnecessary *trouble* of our lives arises from *vanity*, all ill government of that power of the soul, which we call the imagination."[23] Feared as "a faculty boundless, and impatient to any imposed limits, save those which it self maketh," the uncontrolled imagination was a subversive force used by Satan to undermine the faculties of reason and will.[24]

The unbounded imagination produced chaos and undermined psychic stability—its disruptive influence was one of the countless misfortunes of the Fall. The prelapsarian mind was balanced, but its beautiful harmony was shattered by the loss of God's grace. One of the punishments of Adam and Eve's exile from the garden of Eden was that they could no longer trust their perceptions. Again and again, Satan threatened to seduce them from God with alluring phantasms.

The concept of a self apart from God was responsible for the Fall: "Man's fall was his turning from God to himself; and his regeneration consisteth in the turning of him from himself to God. . . . [T]he very names of Self and Own, should sound in the watchful Christian's ears as very terrible, wakening words, that are next to the names of Sin and Satan."[25] Although the problems of inner-light theology—antinomianism—continued to plague the Puritan theocracy, and the issue of conversion on the basis of personal conviction persisted, continued efforts to rid the community of the perils of individualism were made. Kai Erikson argues that as cohesiveness in the Puritan commonwealth began to erode, crises were generated in order to unify the community by creating a common enemy. The crisis surrounding Hutchinson's exile, the witchcraft trials, and the controversy about the Half-Way Covenant are cited as rituals of cohesion, or rites of intensification, by Erikson.[26] Eventually compromises were made when it became clear that the church was losing membership; Solomon Stoddard sponsored the Half-Way Covenant as a means of admitting the unregenerate to communion; with Stoddard's compromise, church membership was a preparation for grace rather than a sign of having achieved it. Ironically, the effect of the Half-Way Covenant was to create even greater uncertainty about conversion and to intensify doubt and confusion about salvation. As Sacvan Bercovitch and Emory Elliott point out, after 1650 there was increasing anxiety about the basis for church membership.[27]

The Puritan social order was achieved by subordinating the individual to the community and emphasizing the necessity for traditional definitions of masculinity and femininity. The family was the basic unit of the Puritan commonwealth, and single people were not permitted to live alone—"to live for oneself." Cotton Mather asserted that "*well-ordered* families naturally produce Good Order in other *Societies*. When Families are under an *Ill Dicipline*, [they] will feel the error in the *First Concoction*." [28] In order to reinforce traditional patterns of authority, the relationship of husband and wife was clearly delineated: the wife's duty was to "keep at home, educating her children, keeping and improving what is got by the industry of the man," and she was to "guid the house and not guid the husband." [29] A wife was to remain in the domestic sphere and not venture beyond it even to the extent of advising or counseling her husband about his life outside their home. Male leadership and judgment ensured social stability, and those husbands who failed to maintain a dominant position were censured, as John Winthrop's excoriation of Anne Hutchinson's husband demonstrates: "A man of very mild temper and weak parts, and wholly guided by his wife." [30]

Citing biblical precedent, the Puritan elders used carefully defined sex roles as models for social stability. Their prescriptions for the proper behavior for men and women were intended to produce an ordered society that could be more easily guided or controlled in addition to reflecting God's plan, which subordinated women to men. Anne Hutchinson resisted this traditional view of society by insisting that men and women were equal in the eyes of God—that the soul transcends sexuality. In doing so, she was doubly culpable in the eyes of the magistrates: as a "mere woman," she dared to challenge the church elders' hegemony in matters of biblical interpretation and salvation, and she asserted that women and men were equally capable of comprehending God's grace.

Unlike her sister, Sarah Keayne, and Anne Hutchinson, Anne Bradstreet was able to combine public expression and domesticity and still remain within the framework of calling and vocation. For her, poetry became a way of preparing her heart for redemption. Although poetry provided her with a means of expressing her religious skepticism, it also enabled her to serve God through her daily meditations. Because poetry was her vocation, she could praise God and at the same time express her conflicts as a first-generation Puritan woman. Initially, her poetry documents her desire to be accepted as an accomplished artist; later, it celebrates her deep human attachments and records her trials and doubts. Finally, it helps her to subdue her worldly affections and to focus her attention more completely on life after death.

FIVE

"Were earthly comforts permanent"

When Thomas Dudley died in 1653, Anne Bradstreet was forty-one. With his death she experienced a transition from the rigorous public codes of the old divines to a more relaxed and private approach to faith. Although the compromises regarding church membership intensified anxiety by creating further ambiguity about salvation, at least the inner life was less subject to the scrutiny of the church elders. Perhaps the growing liberalism of the church following her father's death permitted Bradstreet greater freedom to express her deepest personal feelings in her work. During these years, she wrote primarily about her domestic life and her spiritual experiences. Ann Stanford observes that these later meditative poems are less ornate than her earlier work; the tortured heroic couplets, elaborate conceits, and extended metaphors of "The Four Ages of Man" and "The Four Monarchies" are replaced by supple lines more varied in length and more inventive in rhyme.[1]

The second edition of *The Tenth Muse*, which was not published until 1678, six years after Anne Bradstreet's death, contains her corrections of the first edition of the volume as well as several lyric poems that are deeply personal. Although she again apologizes for the "ill-formed off-spring of the feeble brain" (*Works*, 389), Bradstreet does publicly acknowledge her work. Using the metaphor of mother and child in the preface, "The Author to her Book," Bradstreet tells her readers that her child dressed in "homespun" is fatherless. On the surface it would appear that by describing her work as poor and illegitimate she was continuing her strategy of self-deprecation; however, it is important to note that the poems added to this volume no longer cite male writers as authorities or imitate their work. No longer does she cast herself in the role of awed apprentice, she now views her daily experience as a valid subject for her art.

Poetry writing enabled Bradstreet to endure the conflicts of her middle years when her affections were not sufficiently weaned from her family to permit her to put the demands of God first. Her craft also made it easier to accept the periods of isolation during her husband's frequent and sometimes long absences while he was on business for the church. Her poems to Simon Bradstreet, to whom she was married at sixteen, make it clear that she loved him deeply, as illustrated by the well-known lines from "To My Dear and Loving Husband":

> If ever two were one, then surely we.
> If ever man were lov'd by wife, then thee;
> If ever wife was happy in a man,
> Compare with me ye women if you can.
> (*Works*, 394)

In another poem, titled "A Letter to Her Husband, Absent Upon Public Employment," she asks, "How stayest thou there, whilst I at Ipswich lye?" (*Works*, 394). In still another, she laments:

> Commend me to the man more lov'd then life,
> Shew him the sorrows of his widdowed wife;
> My dumpish thoughts, my groans, my brakish tears
> My sobs, my longing hopes, my doubting fears,
> And if he love, how can he there abide?
> (*Works*, 396)

Since Puritans believed that spousal devotion was proof of piety, Anne Bradstreet's love for Simon was in harmony with God's plan for his creatures. But she must love him "in Christ" and not selfishly or carnally; to allow her emotional or physical desire for Simon to eclipse her greater commitment to God would be idolatry—a heresy committed by the familists, a sect that practiced free love in its zeal to be one in Christ. According to John Calvin, "conjugal union itself is appointed as a remedy for our necessity, that we may not break into unrestrained licentiousness."[2] Although Bradstreet experienced conflict between her passion for Simon and her duty to care for him selflessly, her love poems focus on her desire and longing rather than on duty or deference. In addition, there is no indication that she considers her social or domestic role subordinate to his:

> Together at one Tree, oh let us brouze,
> And like two turtles roost within one house,

And like the Mullets in one River glide,
Let's still remain but one, till death divide.
                    (*Works*, 398)

As governor, Simon Bradstreet's duties to his constituents were time-consuming, and his wife could not in good conscience claim more of his energy—to make further demands on him would mean that she was interfering with his calling by placing herself between her husband and God. Puritan custom carefully limited Anne Bradstreet's role as wife and mother by defining marriage as a partnership for producing young Christians in which the male had final authority.[3]

Although they accepted the necessity of marriage, Puritans worried that conjugal love would tempt the married couple to lose sight of God. John Cotton warned against such idolatrous unions: "[W]hen we exceedingly delight ourselves in Husbands or Wives, or Children, [it] much benumbs and dims the light of the Spirit."[4] Marriage, according to Cotton, should make husband and wife "better fitted for God's service, and bring them nearer to God."[5] This temporal union should not eclipse devotion to God: "Let this caution be minded, that they don't love inordinately, because death will soon part them."[6] Similarly, it was important not to love one's children excessively; in order to offset this peril, it was common to send adolescent children to board with other families. Anne Bradstreet's late poems reveal that she struggled with the conflict between her love for her husband and children and her devotion to God; repeatedly, she reminds herself of her duty as wife and mother and later grandmother to assist her family in the service of God. To love them for their own sake would indicate a dangerous attachment to this world.

Bradstreet's elegy to her grandchild, Elizabeth Bradstreet, who died in August 1665 at the age of a year and a half, expresses Bradstreet's effort to contain the opposing forces of familial love and religious duty:

Farewel dear babe, my hearts too much content,
Farewel sweet babe, the pleasure of mine eye,
Farewel fair flower that for a space was lent,
Then ta'en away unto Eternity.
                    (*Works*, 404)

Although Bradstreet's sorrow threatens to overwhelm her, the second stanza expresses resigned acceptance of Providence:

By nature Trees do rot when they are grown.
And Plumbs and Apples throughly ripe do fall,

> And corn and grass are in their season mown,
> And time brings down what is both strong and tall.
> But plants new set to be eradicate,
> And buds new blown, to have so short a date,
> Is by his hand alone that guides nature and fate.
>
> > (*Works*, 404)

The intricate rhyme scheme ababccc of six pentameter lines and the trip-let or alexandrine that conclude each stanza reflect the effort to master her grief. Rosemary Laughlin suggests that the slight irregularity in the meter creates a "somewhat tortured hesitation" indicating her reluctance to accept God's decree. Similarly, Ann Stanford emphasizes that the im-plied criticism of God in the first stanza is not entirely resolved by the pragmatic acceptance of his will in the second stanza.[7]

In another poem written four years later in 1669 in memory of another grandchild, Anne Bradstreet reveals an even deeper grief that borders on despair:

> With troubled heart & trembling hand I write,
> The Heavens have chang'd to sorrow my delight.
> How oft with disappointment have I met,
> When I on fading things my hopes have set?
> . . . .
> I knew she was but as a withering flour,
> That's here to day, perhaps gone in an hour;
> Like as a bubble, or the brittle glass,
> Or like a shadow turning as it was.
> More fool than I to look on what was lent,
> As if mine own, when thus impermanent.
>
> > (*Works*, 405–6)

Again, Bradstreet uses poetic form to help contain her loss, control her sadness, and sustain her faith in spite of her bereavement. Her poems la-menting the deaths of her grandchildren resemble Elizabethan elegies such as Ben Jonson's "On My First Son":

> Farewell, thou child of my right hand, and joy,
> My sin was too much hope of thee, loved boy;
> Seven years th' wert *lent* to me, and I thee pay,
> Exacted by thy fate, on the just day.
> O, I could lose all father now. For why
> Will man lament the state he should envy?

To have so soon 'scaped world's and flesh's rage,
And, if no other misery, yet age?
Rest in soft peace, and, asked, say here doth lie
Ben Jonson his best piece of poetry;
For whose sake, henceforth, all his vows be such
As what he loves may never like too much.[8]

By attributing their agony to excessive attachment, both Bradstreet and Jonson attempt to blunt the pain of their loss, but while Jonson chastises himself for the emotional indulgence of loving his child too much, Bradstreet feels cheated by the child's death.

Two additional elegies in the second edition of *The Tenth Muse* further demonstrate Bradstreet's profound tension between her familial attachments and her religious duty. Her elegies for her grandchild Simon and her daughter-in-law Mercy, both of whom died in the autumn of 1669, again reflect Bradstreet's resolution to sustain her faith in God's Providence in the face of bitter loss:

Chear up, (dear Son) thy fainting bleeding heart,
In him alone, that caused all this smart;
What though thy strokes full sad & grievous be,
He knows it is the best for thee and me.
(*Works*, 408)

In both poems, Anne Bradstreet's grief is controlled by her willed belief in a just and merciful God in spite of her experience that appears to contradict her faith. Although her resignation does not always eliminate her rage, she manages to subdue her incredulity in the name of obedience.

In 1867, John Harvard Ellis edited the first complete edition of Anne Bradstreet's works. In addition to the poems in both editions of *The Tenth Muse*, he included previously unpublished material—Bradstreet's spiritual autobiography, occasional poems, poems of gratitude for having survived a period of illness, prayers for the safety of her loved ones, and poems acknowledging the presence of God in her life as well as "Meditations Divine and Moral," dedicated to her son Simon on March 20, 1664. Although Bradstreet probably did not intend that this work be published because it is so personal, it is actually more technically accomplished and emotionally profound than much of the poetry of *The Tenth Muse*.

Like her poems of physical and spiritual affliction, Bradstreet's meditations began as religious exercises—as part of the process of preparation for conversion—but ultimately they provided her with comforting assurance of eternal life. Reiterating her desire to learn from her experience, Bradstreet writes: "I desire not only willingly, but thankfully, to submitt to him, for I trust it is out of his abundant Love to my straying Soul which in prosperity is too much in love with the world" (*Works*, 23). In her meditations, Bradstreet expresses the hope that she can help to instruct her children in their pilgrimage through life and to teach them the pattern of salvation: "Thus (dear children) have yee seen the many sicknesses and weaknesses that I have passed thro: to the end that, if you meet with the like, you may have recourse to the same God who hath heard and delivered me, and will do the like for you if you trust in him" (*Works*, 23–24). In these aphoristic observations, based on the *Bay Psalm Book* and intended to provide a virtuous model for her children, her daily domestic experience is correlated with spiritual truths:

(VI)   The finest bread hath the least bran; the purest hony, the least wax; and the sincerest christian, the least self love.

(X)   Diverse children have their different natures; some are like flesh which nothing but salt will keep from putrefaction; some again like tender fruits that are best preserved with sugar: those parents are wise that can fit their nurture according to their Nature.

(XVI)   That house which is not often swept, makes the cleanly inhabitant soone loath it, and that heart which is not continually purifieing it self, is no fit temple for the spirit of god to dwell in.

(*Works*, 49, 50, 51)

In terse form, they are spiritual exercises that document a pilgrim's progress:

(XXI)   He that walks among briars and thorns will be very carefull where he sets his foot. And he that passes through the wildernes of this world, had need ponder all his steps.

(*Works*, 52)

The spareness of language, the careful metaphors based on daily life prefigure the work of American poets such as Emily Dickinson and Robert Frost. As a Puritan, Bradstreet assumed that there were correspondences between the events of earth and heaven; this habit of finding spiritual meaning in the events of daily life has persisted as a dimension of American poetry.

Perhaps the poem that best expresses Bradstreet's love of life, temporal and eternal, is "Contemplations." This lyrical and carefully crafted poem has great force; it is so accomplished that some critics have speculated that it was read by the Romantic poets.[9] This poem follows the Puritan paradigm that viewed nature as a source of moral lessons and examples. Not only did God imbue nature with divine significance, but he expected his flock to enjoy earthly beauty as a harbinger of heavenly glory as the following passage from Calvin's *Institutes* indicates:

> Let us not be ashamed to take pious delight in the works of God open and manifest in this most beautiful theatre. . . . There is no doubt that the Lord would have us uninterruptedly occupied in this holy meditation; that while we contemplate his wisdom, justice, goodness, and power, we should not merely run over them cursorily, and so to speak, with a fleeting glance; but we should ponder them at length.[10]

In "Contemplations" Bradstreet again acknowledges the vanity of life on earth; nevertheless, she immerses herself in sensory experience and celebrates the plenitude of nature and the generative power of the elements. Paradoxically, the more the poet feels drawn by nature's power, the more she longs to transcend the world. Her metaphor drawn from the Nineteenth Psalm, which speaks of the sun as the earth's husband, is suffused with eroticism:

> Thou as a Bridegroom from my Chamber rushes,
> And as a strong man, joyes to run a race,
> The morn doth usher thee, with smiles & blushes,
> The Earth reflects her glances in thy face.
> Birds, insects, Animals with Vegative,
> Thy heart from death and dulness doth revive:
> And in the darksome womb of fruitful nature dive.
> (*Works*, 371)

Interestingly, in contrast to Bradstreet's secular poems, the life-giving power in this poem is associated primarily with the sun—the male principle. Earth is depicted as bearing fruit just as a woman bears children. Two centuries later, Emily Dickinson depicts the sun as the scorching man of noon who harms the flowers; for Dickinson, then, their attraction is fatal.

"Contemplations" interweaves the celebration of nature with a desire for eternal life. The opposition between earth's pull and heaven's promise is resolved when the poet accepts sensory pleasure as emblematic of eternal joy. Although the poem of thirty-three stanzas concludes with an acceptance of mutability and death, Bradstreet's ultimate decision to reject earthly pleasures is achieved by immersing herself in them. In the opening stanza, Bradstreet admits that she is enthralled with autumn's beauty: "Rapt were my senses at this delectable view" (*Works*, 370). She tells us that she would be tempted to capitulate to earthly delight if such pleasure were not finite. Her senses tell her that the sun is powerful, but faith is needed to believe in God's omniscience:

> Thy Swift Annual, and diurnal Course,
> Thy daily streight, and yearly oblique path,
> Thy pleasing fervor, and thy scorching force,
> All mortals here the feeling knowledg hath.
> Thy presence makes it day, thy absence night,
> Quarternal Seasons caused by thy might:
> Hail Creature, full of sweetness, beauty & delight.
>
> (*Works*, 372)

Interestingly, unlike Dickinson, Bradstreet sees the "scorching force" of the sun as a positive characteristic. But she reminds herself that if the sun is glorious, "How full of glory then must thy Creator be?" (*Works*, 372). Since death is inevitable, for "Man grows old, lies down, remains where once / he's laid," security can be found only in the permanence of eternal life: "Only above is found all with security" (*Works*, 376, 380).

Bradstreet is able to restrain her love of the temporal world not only by accepting its transitory nature but also by weaning her affections from it. The beauty of the world is emblematic of the promised glory of heaven. Personal delight in this world prefigures heavenly joy.[11] The Puritans, following Rom. 1:20, believed that the world was a source of figures and types that reflected divine truth; therefore, they were admonished to seek God's invisible wonders in his visible creation. Confronted with mutability, Bradstreet sought permanence in heaven. Because she lived in a culture that provided a religious scaffolding that enabled her to make the leap from known but finite earthly pleasures to the promised permanence of heaven, Bradstreet tried to subordinate her worldly desires to anticipated spiritual joy.

One of Anne Bradstreet's most effective poems in the second edition, certainly her most frequently anthologized, is "Verses Upon the Burning of Our House, July 10th, 1666." Like "Contemplations," this poem's power is the result of the very poignant tension between her worldly concerns, as represented by her household furnishings, and her spiritual aspirations:

> Here stood that Trunk, and there that chest;
> There lay that store I counted best:

My pleasant things in ashes lye,
And them behold no more shall I.
Under thy roof no guest shall sitt,
Nor at thy Table eat a bitt.
                    (*Works*, 41)

The poem leaves the reader with the painful impression of a woman in her mid-fifties, who having lost her domestic comforts is left to struggle with despair. Although her loss is mitigated by the promise of the greater rewards of heaven, the experience is deeply tragic: "Farewell my Pelf, farewell my Store. / The world no longer let me Love, / My hope and Treasure lyes Above" (*Works*, 42). But once again, the promise of a permanent house in heaven soothes her grief:

Thou hast a house on high erect,
Fram'd by that mighty Architect,
With glory richly furnished,
Stands permanent tho: this bee fled.
                    (*Works*, 41–42)

A poem written three years later on August 31, 1669, "Longing for Heaven," reveals a profound world-weariness; the clash between earth and heaven, temporal and eternal concerns, is muted; instead, there is longing for release from physical frailty and hope for immortality. Physical pain and old age have diminished her pleasure in life, and Bradstreet longs for freedom from her deteriorating body:

A pilgrim I, on earth, perplext
    wth sinns wth cares and sorrows vext
By age and paines brought to decay
    and my Clay house mouldring away
Oh how I long to be at rest
    and soare on high among the blest.
This body shall in silence sleep
    Mine eyes no more shall ever weep
No fainting fits shall me assaile
    nor grinding paines my body fraile
                    (*Works*, 43)

Josephine Piercy describes this poem as Bradstreet's "farewell to the world."[12]

Anne Bradstreet died on September 16, 1672; she was sixty years old. In the last months of her life Bradstreet was very sick; her son Simon wrote in his diary that she was "wasted to skin & bone. . . much troubled with rheum," and he noted that she had a badly ulcerated arm.[13] For much of her life, she tried to be the dutiful and loving wife of Simon Bradstreet, the devoted mother of eight children, and the resolute child of God. At the same time, her work reflects the tensions and conflicts of a person struggling for artistic expression in a culture outraged by individual autonomy and certain that the best poetry was written to praise God.

Although troubled by religious doubts throughout her life, Anne Bradstreet managed to subdue her love for her family, her domestic pleasures, and her love of nature's beauty. Her willed faith in the promise of heaven sustained her in times of spiritual confusion, but ultimately it was the beauty of *this* life that enabled her to believe in the next:

> Many times hath Satan troubled me concerning the verity of scriptures, many times by Atheisme how I could know whether there was a God; I never saw any miracles to confirm me, and those which I read of how did I know but they were feigned. That there was a God my Reason would soon tell me by the wondrous workes that I see, the vast frame of the Heaven and the Earth, the order of all things, night and day, Summer and Winter, Spring and Autumne, the dayly providing for this great household upon the Earth, the preserving and directing of All to its proper end. The consideration of these things would with amazement certainly resolve me that there is an Eternall Being. (*Works*, 8)

Although divine teleology supersedes Bradstreet's gynecocratic vision, it is her reverent identification with "the great household upon the Earth" that causes her to seek a designer. Her reluctance to believe that earthly life has its own agency and inner rhythm is consonant with her own experience of being subject to male control. Drawing a parallel between her own dependence on her husband and father for guidance and protection and earth's need for a divine father for the "preserving and directing of All to its proper end," Anne Bradstreet finally managed to believe in God. However, just as in bolder moments she hoped that her work could stand on its own so she sometimes surmised that earth exists for its own sake. Ultimately, Bradstreet's need for assurance triumphed over her desire for autonomy, but her faith was based on a profound desire to remain connected to life, whether in this world or the next. Repeatedly, she observes that if it were not for death and decay, earth would be heaven. Two hundred years later, Emily Dickinson decided that "heaven was superfluous" and found paradise on earth instead of looking for earth in heaven as Anne Bradstreet had done.

PART TWO
Emily Dickinson

"A Woman—white—to be"

A solemn thing—it was—I said—
A woman—white—to be—
And wear—if God should count me fit—
Her blameless mystery—

A hallowed thing—to drop a life
Into the purple well—
Too plummetless—that it return—
Eternity—until—

I pondered how the bliss would look—
And would it feel as big—
When I could take it in my hand—
As hovering—seen—through fog—

And then—the size of this "small" life—
The Sages—call it small—
Swelled—like Horizons—in my breast—
And I sneered—softly—"small"!

The Poems of Emily Dickinson,
1 : 193, no. 271

Introduction

Unlike Anne Bradstreet, Emily Dickinson (1830–86) did not depend on traditional religious beliefs to mediate her experiences and emotions; however, this does not mean that self-reliance came easily to her. There were many times when she felt extreme anxiety, helplessness, and anger, but no matter how confused or despairing she became, Dickinson did not subdue her existential fears and frustrations with the soothing assurances of salvation, filial piety, marriage, or a dutiful poetic apprenticeship. Even as a young woman, she rejected these comforting traditions, resisted male authority, and wrestled alone with her complex and often contrary emotions. Finally, she rejected all masters—God, father, potential husband, literary preceptor—to devote her life's energy to her poetry.

Although Emily Dickinson's poetry contains the kernel of the modern sensibility, with its awareness of mortality and the attendant anxiety, it also recapitulates the Puritan mission to build the city on a hill. Using the phrases, narratives, and images of the Bible, especially Matthew and Revelation, as well as the meters and stanzas of hymns, she forged a vision uniquely hers of earth as paradise in which nature and friendship were sacred. Embracing the ambiguity of experience from moment to moment, Dickinson's introspective poetry parallels Bradstreet's meditations on the testing of her spirit and the meaning of God's universe. By scrutinizing her emotions in all their contrariness, Dickinson created a cosmology in which consciousness replaces the soul, ecstasy parallels grace, human love replaces God's sanctification, and friends form the community of saints; nature is paradise, home is heaven, language is sacramental, and experience crystallized in art creates the possibility of eternal life.

To fully appreciate Emily Dickinson's life and work, it is necessary to understand her not only as a woman subject to the customs and constraints of Victorian society but also to see her in the context of American literary and cultural traditions. Like the rebels in American history and literature from Anne Hutchinson to Huck Finn, Emily Dickinson trusted her antinomian impulses, but her proving ground was not the community forum or the wide expanse of the Mississippi River and its surrounding woods but the mysterious labyrinth of her psyche—"within is so wild a place." Unlike those traditional women who provided solace and moral stability for their world-weary husbands compromised by the complex demands of an expanding marketplace, Emily Dickinson remained at home to pursue her own interests and priorities. At twenty-one, she wrote "I'm afraid I'm growing *Selfish* in my dear home, but I do love it so."[1] The underscoring of the pun on the word "selfish" indicates that her unusual life was a measure of her autonomy and determination rather than renunciation or denial: hers was a private rebellion in the service of her poetry, not an exercise in self-effacement. By remaining single and living in her father's house for her entire life, Dickinson created a haven in which she wrote nearly two thousand poems. Although she has been described as an eccentric spinster—the literary critic Thomas Wentworth Higginson called her life "abnormal" after meeting her—the emphasis should be placed on Emily Dickinson's courage. In a historical period that required women, even women writers, to conform to standards of piety and purity that were inimical to the creation of enduring poetry, she created the conditions necessary for her art.

Although Sandra Gilbert's provocative and illuminating study portrays Dickinson as the literal representation of the madwoman in Victorian literature—"a helpless agoraphobic trapped in a room in her father's house"—it is more accurate to view Dickinson's isolation as self-imposed, a measure of her freedom rather than her fear.[2] In *Emily Dickinson: When a Writer Is a Daughter*, Barbara Mossberg suggests that Emily Dickinson used the facade of filial obedience as a mode of rebellion, a strategy that enabled her to be outwardly deferential even though she was "seething with rage" about her second-class citizenship as a woman. This perceptive analysis is especially helpful in understanding Dickinson's conflicting needs for achievement and dependence especially as a young woman, but the emphasis must be placed on Dickinson's hard-won autonomy.[3] Ultimately, as Adrienne Rich observes, "Dickinson's life was deliberately organized on her own terms," and her domestic routines were designed to sustain her creative energy.[4] Not only did she have the best room in the house but she succeeded in gaining the support of her family, especially Lavinia, in her effort to write. Respecting her sister's artistic gifts, Lavinia took responsibility for directing the Dickinson household.

In the tradition of protest and reform that is a basic dimension of American culture, Emily Dickinson refused to be diminished by the constraints of feminine virtue and propriety that paralyzed so many Victorian women. Although she never lectured in the Lyceum on such issues as women's rights, immigration, and unions, as did her contemporary, Anna Dickinson (who was not a relative), Emily Dickinson was a pioneer who chose the domestic as her frontier because it provided the space and freedom to write. In doing so, she subverted the tradition of true womanhood to serve her poetic mission. Paradoxically, Emily Dickinson avoided the damaging effects of passive femininity by remaining in what she described as "the Infinite Power of Home" (1883). By creating and safeguarding her privacy, she made extraordinary discoveries unusual for anyone in the nineteenth century. Not only did she pierce the mystifications of evangelical Christianity as well as the mystique of redemptive femininity, but she also achieved a resolution of the mind/body dualism that prefigures twentieth-century scientific findings. Most important, she evolved a complicated understanding of emotional dynamics that is startlingly modern.

By struggling with her conflicting feelings of self-doubt and her desire "to be great," Dickinson experienced the extremes of despondency and exultation. Overwhelmed by fear and panic, she repeatedly fell into a psychic abyss, but she learned from these encounters with the depths of herself to discern a pattern of relationships in what threatened to be unbounded despair. Her initial forays enabled her to map points of consciousness, specific emotions, or states of mind, and after years of experience and careful observation, she recognized interconnections. That is what she meant by "circumference"—determining the periphery of experience, not just the center.

David Porter asserts Dickinson's poetry is impoverished by a lack of "controlling architecture" or system of beliefs that would enable her to reconcile the contradictory extremes of her experiences, and he concludes that she failed to resolve the conflict of love and death, or mutability and eternity, giving her work a "hard-edged fatalism."[5] But her poetry, and especially her letters, demonstrate that she deliberately avoided a system of categories that would prestructure or limit her perceptions. Dickinson's disjunctive states of awareness were the necessary concomitant to psychological and artistic autonomy. She was a pioneer precisely because she refused to dilute the intensity of her emotions by adopting a plan or a system of beliefs. Because she was committed to the process of living through her experience with all of its complicated ambivalences toward her family, toward nature, and even toward language itself, she sometimes experienced extraordinary discontinuities of consciousness that she accepted as part of her life.

In her poetry Dickinson eschews an epistemological system based on absolutes, preferring confusion, even chaos if necessary, in order to evolve a framework that corresponds to her actual experience. Joanne Feit Diehl suggests that the discontinuities in Dickinson's poetry express her determination to break free of the male literary tradition, and Margaret Homans observes that Dickinson's disparate states of consciousness challenge the hierarchy in language that is at the heart of male supremacy.[6] Much of Dickinson's innovative linguistic experimentation and her frequent and unusual oxymorons and metonyms embody her central concern with relationship and interconnection. Rejecting the assumption that each experience, idea, or event must always be subordinate to another, she explored the resonance and ambiguity of opposites instead of polarity and stratified differentiation. Noting that "the oxymoron served as the main structure for Dickinson's sense of the indecipherable ambiguity of existence," Karl Keller catalogs scores of these constructions: "Heavenly Hurt," "A Dome of Abyss," "Stolid Bliss," "Confident Despair," "Infinities of Nought," "the Scant Salvation," "Sumptuous Solitude," "a piercing Comfort," "numb Alarm," "sordid excellence," "abstemious ecstasy," and "a Hoary Boy" are but a few he has cited.[7]

Dickinson's women friends—her sister Lavinia, her cousins Louise and Frances Norcross, her closest friend Elizabeth Holland—sustained her as an artist. Although practically no attention has been given to these friendships, they were the lifeline that permitted her to descend into her emotional depths and to explore the discontinuities and contradictions that undercut androcentric categories. In the literally hundreds of letters that she wrote to her Norcross cousins and to Elizabeth Holland, she elaborated her belief that organic unfolding—what Thoreau described as "the bloom of the moment"—replaced categories of abstract principles. In a letter to her "kindred sister," Elizabeth Holland, she observed, "Had we the first intimation of the Definition of Life, the calmest of us would be Lunatics!" (*L*, 2:576, no. 492).

Implicit in Dickinson's letters, as in many of her poems, is a criticism of the narrowing of consciousness, not to mention conscience, in a society dominated by excessive competition and the profit motive. During the period of rapid economic expansion in which she lived, there was extraordinary social dislocation because of the population shift to the cities. In contrast to the jangling, stressful rhythms of Boston where she spent several months with her cousins in order to see an eye specialist, she preferred the pastoral simplicity of Amherst. Like Thoreau, she repeatedly observed that family, friends, and flowers were more important than productivity, profit, and power. For Dickinson, being "At Home," the wonderfully ambiguous phrase that her brother Austin used on her death certificate to designate occupation, meant not having to dissociate herself from her authentic responses in order to earn a living. Like many British and American romantic writers, Dickinson believed that the powers of the imagination superseded economic reality, but unlike her male counterparts, she managed to avoid what literary critics call the "egotistical sublime," which feminist critics observe was based on social privilege and a lack of concern for women. Like Wordsworth and Shelley whose work she admired, she cultivated the innocence of childhood, that is, a receptive consciousness that was not encrusted with tradition, but she remained grounded in the quotidian and did not share their desire for release, transcendence, or escape from the mundane world.

The young rebellious girl who dared to pick "Satan's flowers" became a woman who felt that the blossoms of her carefully tended garden and greenhouse were emblematic of the sacredness of life on earth. Dickinson was neither a proto-hippie nor a zealous proponent of matriarchal holism, but she did believe in the importance of nurturing people and plants, and her protest against an increasingly utilitarian society foreshadows important literary and political concerns of the twentieth century. For Dickinson, the joyous pleasures of this life supplanted the terrors of hell and promises of heaven. Her habit of presenting day lilies to her visitors and of sending baskets of geraniums, daphnes, violets or heliotrope, sprays of wisteria or cape jessamine, bouquets of hyacinths, primrose, or cassia carnations to her friends expressed her tenaciously held belief that she was "At Home—in Paradise" (P, 3:923, no. 1335). Her journey from the polarities of salvation and damnation to the cyclicity of the seasons was arduous and required unusual vision, and her reward was not the revelation of the saints but the revelation of the moment.

SIX

"The Soul selects her own Society"

As a young woman, Emily Dickinson experienced a series of struggles from which she emerged more fully in control of her energy and power. The first was an adolescent religious crisis; the second was a conflict with her father who finally acknowledged her need for time to write; the third focused on the choice between marriage or a life dedicated to poetry; and her last battle was waged with her preceptor Thomas Wentworth Higginson over the value of her poetry. In each contest, the adversary is a male figure—Christ, her father, a potential husband, and a poetic mentor. When overburdened by self-doubt, Dickinson was often tempted to relinquish her emotional and artistic priorities to gain protection and security from a male authority, but she learned from these crises that no one else could save her, that she must save herself. Dickinson's recognition of the need to create her own cosmology, to respect her intelligence and creativity, and to develop her poetic craft demonstrates unusual wisdom and independence, and it is this extraordinary individuality that characterizes her work and career. Finally secure in her power as a woman and as a poet, she could choose, as Adrienne Rich has written in her poem about Emily Dickinson, "to have it out at last / on [her] own premises." [1]

Strong social pressure was put on Dickinson during her adolescence to join the church. Amherst had been in the grip of Calvinist congregationalism for eight generations, and her resistance to religious conversion alienated her from the community in which Jonathan Edwards and Solomon Stoddard had set the moral tone decades earlier. Dickinson's refusal to commit her soul to Christ meant that she had spurned a tradition honored by her family for several generations. The Dickinson ancestors had come from England to Massachusetts with the first settlers, and Emily, Austin, and Lavinia were the fifth generation of Dickinsons in Amherst. [2] Even her father, who initially refused to be converted, relented and finally joined the church. In his civic speeches, the newly sanctified Edward Dickinson hailed Amherst as a model of moral purity and piety, and praised its Puritan tradition: "And first of all, we should render devout thanks to Almighty God, for our ancestry; that the kingdoms of the Old World were sifted to procure the seed to plant this continent; that the purest of that seed was sown in this beautiful valley; that the blood of the Puritans flows in our veins."[3]

Clearly Dickinson was defying the deeply embedded social and religious values of her family as well as of the larger community when she declared to her friend Jane Humphrey on April 30, 1850, "I am standing alone in rebellion."[4] Several of her friends and neighbors who had been converted during the Amherst revivals repeatedly urged her "to accept Christ as her Saviour," and these pressures increased at Mount Holyoke Seminary, where she was sent to school after completing her studies at Amherst Academy. At Holyoke Dickinson attended numerous meetings in which Mary Lyon preached about sin and the evil of hardheartedness toward God. Using Jonathan Edwards's sermon "Sinners in the Hands of an Angry God" as a model, she convinced her students that their efforts to resist God were not only foolish but dangerous: "How vain to resist God. Did you ever see the insect fall into the flame, see it struggle and strive to escape? How vain—just so you are in the hands of an *angry* God! . . . oh! how vain! How much better to submit."[5] When Edwards delivered his famous sermon, people wept, shrieked, and fainted and were converted by the hundreds, and Lyon's skillful application of Edwards's rhetoric was sufficiently powerful to convert the majority of Holyoke students. In addition to the sermons, each student had to present an assessment of the state of her soul to the assembled group. For meeting after meeting, Dickinson remained "without hope," and, on one occasion, she was the only student who remained impenitent.[6] The conflict between accepting Christ as her master or remaining true to her personal convictions was intense, as her letter to her close friend Abiah Root discloses:

> Abiah, you may be surprised to hear me speak as I do, knowing that I express no interest in the all-important subject, but I am not happy, and I regret that last term, when that golden opportunity was mine, that I did not give up and become a Christian. It is not now too late, so my friends tell me, so my offended conscience whispers, but it is hard for me to give up the world. (*L*, 1 : 67, no. 23)

On one hand, she fears she has become hopelessly hardened in sin, but, on the other, she sees salvation as giving up—as the capitulation and sacrifice of her individual being. Whereas Anne Bradstreet continued to struggle against her own impulses and inclinations, Emily Dickinson honors her feelings and does not permit her personal responses to be extinguished by external authority.

That Dickinson was not simply being arbitrary in her resistance to conversion is evident in another letter she wrote to Abiah Root on January 31, 1846: "I am far from being thoughtless on the subject of religion. I continually hear Christ saying to me, Daughter give me thine heart. . . . I am continually putting off becoming a christian. Evil voices lisp in my ear—There is yet time enough" (L, 1:27, no. 10). Nine months later, she confided to Abiah, "I know not why, I feel that the world holds a predominant place in my affections. I do not feel I could give up all for Christ, were I called to die" (L, 1:38, no. 13). At the point where Anne Bradstreet tried to subdue her senses as an act of faith, Dickinson chose to honor her own inclination and experience. This demonstrates remarkable independence for a young girl who very much wanted to be accepted by her friends.

Even though Emily Dickinson thought that her spiritual recalcitrance had alienated her friend—Abiah Root stopped writing to her at this time—she nevertheless continued to place greater value on friendship than on salvation: "Six long months have tried hard to make us strangers, but I love you better than ever not withstanding the link which bound us in that golden chain is sadly dimmed, I feel more reluctant to lose you from that bright circle, whom I've called *my friends*" (L, 1:71, no. 26). For Dickinson, intimacy, not conversion, was the sacred tie; friendship superseded salvation, and the pleasures of companionship were more important to her than the promise of eternal life. Dickinson's version of sanctification was the privilege to choose her own friends, as her well-known poem written two years later reveals:

> The Soul selects her own Society—
> Then—shuts the Door—
> To her divine Majority—
> Present no more—
> (P, 1:225, no. 303)[7]

When read in the context of her religious struggle and fierce resolution to remain committed to this life instead of the next, the imperial—and imperious—metaphor of the queenly soul to describe her own consciousness takes on greater resonance. Not even her sister Lavinia's conversion swayed Emily Dickinson's resolute independence. Writing to another friend, Jane Humphrey, on April 30, 1850, she observed ruefully: "Christ is calling everyone here, all my companions have answered, even my darling Vinne believes she loves, and trusts him, and I am standing alone in rebellion, and growing very careless. . . . How strange is this sanctification . . . that brings Christ down, and shews him, and lets him select his friends!" (*L*, 1:94, no. 35). Admitting that she was affected by the new-found serenity and intense certainty of her friends who were saved, she added, "They seem so very tranquil, and their voices are kind and gentle, and the tears fill their eyes so often, I really think I envy them."[8]

While scrutinizing the meaning of her life in order to forge a personal cosmology, Dickinson was hounded by fears of worthlessness: "*I* am one of the lingering *bad* ones, and so do *I* slink away, and pause, and ponder, and ponder, and pause, and do work without knowing why—not surely for *this* brief world, and more sure it is not for Heaven" (*L*, 1:98, no. 36). In spite of the risk of damnation, she accepted the responsibility for her own life with all of its uncertainties instead of committing herself to God's care: "the shore is safer, Abiah," she wrote on December 31, 1850, "but I love to buffet the sea" (*L*, 1:104, no. 39). Dickinson's humorous remarks about religion underscore her determination to separate herself from narrow sectarianism. Echoing Emerson's assertion in "Self Reliance," "If I am the Devil's child, then I will live from the devil," to buttress her newfound independence, she wryly commented to Jane Humphrey on January 23, 1850, "My hardheartedness gets me many prayers" (*L*, 1:84, no. 30). Nine years after her religious turmoil, her satiric barbs indicate that she continued to reject conventional piety: "I wish the 'faith of the fathers' did'nt wear brogans and carry blue umbrellas" (*L*, 2:359, no. 213).

The second crisis in Emily Dickinson's adolescence was precipitated by her father's directive that she was not to return to Holyoke (*L*, 1:66, no. 23). Like many Victorian fathers, Edward Dickinson decided that school was harmful to his daughter's health and that ambition in a daughter was debilitating as well as unseemly. His unilateral directive was bitterly disappointing to his daughter who loved her academic studies and was an exceptional student. At seventeen, she received excellent grades in chemistry, physiology, algebra, astronomy, and rhetoric (*L*, 1:57, 59, 67, no. 19, no. 20, no. 23). When her brother Austin "arrived in full sail, with orders from head-quarters to bring [her] home at all events," she begged, pleaded, and cried to stay, but "Austin was victorious, and poor, defeated [Emily] was led off in triumph" (*L*, 1:65, no. 23).

After their arrival in Amherst, Edward Dickinson took the reins from his son: "Father is quite a hand to give medicine, especially if it is not desirable to the patient, and I was dosed for about a month after my return home, without any mercy." Not subdued, she added, "I went on with my studies at home, and kept up with my class" (*L*, 1:66, no. 23). With a strong instinct for survival, Dickinson resisted her father's effort to deny her intellectual autonomy and pursued her academic interests within the confines of the home. While successfully playing the role of dutiful daughter, she did not relinquish her aspirations. To Abiah Root she wrote, "I am now working a pair of slippers to adorn my father's feet. . . . We'll finish an education sometime, won't we? You may then be Plato, and I will be Socrates, provided you won't be wiser than I am" (*L*, 1:10, no. 5). The painful contradiction of achieving philosophic heights while plying her needle represents the cognitive dissonance experienced by many genteel women of the nineteenth century. No matter how gifted or intelligent their daughters, most Victorian fathers felt that their female children could not survive in the male world of doctors, lawyers, businessmen, and college professors.

Although a trustee of Amherst College, Edward Dickinson was more conservative about the issue of women's education than other members of the board who permitted girls to attend lectures. After a visit to Amherst, Harriet Martineau observed that "no evil had been found to result from it. It was a gladdening sight."[9] Edward Dickinson was clearly ambivalent about Emily Dickinson as a thinking woman, as her letter to Higginson reveals: "Father . . . buys me many Books—but begs me not to read them—because he fears they joggle the Mind" (*L*, 2:404, no. 261). This anxiety about psychological agitation caused by reading reflected a traditional belief that women should not be intellectually active because mental exertion was considered detrimental to female health. Reading and cerebral activity were felt to drain energy from the womb resulting in impairment of the reproductive function, and a woman who asserted her intelligence was often thought to be a monstrous aberration of nature.[10]

In spite of Edward Dickinson's fears about female education, the Dickinson family library contained abundant materials for his daughter's self-education. She had access to the Bible, Bunyan, Shakespeare, Milton, Sir Thomas Browne, Ruskin, Carlyle, and Jean-Paul Richter. In addition, there were scores of novels by Dickens, the Brontës, George Eliot, and Hawthorne as well as extensive volumes of poetry by Keats, the Brownings, Byron, Shelley, Tennyson, Longfellow, Bryant, Emerson, and Goethe, and essays by Emerson and Thoreau.[11] Several conduct books filled with sentimental platitudes about the angelic, self-sacrificing role of women, such as *The Frugal Housewife* (1830) by Lydia Maria Child and *The Mother at Home; or, The Principles of Maternal Duty* by John Abbott (1833) were also in the Dickinson library. But the books that Emily Dickinson loved best were those written by George Eliot and Emily and Charlotte Brontë. She described *Daniel Deronda* as a "wise and tender Book" (*L*, 3:865, no. 974); her admiration for Eliot was unbounded—Eliot was "the Lane to the Indes, Columbus was looking for" (*L*, 2:551, no. 456). These British writers sustained Dickinson throughout her life. In many respects, she was more fortunate than the novelists she admired. Unlike Eliot and the Brontës, Dickinson did not have to work at unrewarding or humiliating jobs to support herself, nor did she have to marry for pragmatic reasons. Although her freedom was severely curtailed, she did not experience the grinding burden of poverty that threatened to crush the will of her British counterparts.

Although Dickinson clashed frequently with her father about her domestic responsibilities and her social life, her letters indicate that she stood her ground. She wrote to Austin, who was attending school in Boston: "[I]t is pretty much all sobriety, and we do not have much poetry, father having made up his mind that its pretty much all *real life*. Father's real life and *mine* sometimes come into collision, but as yet, escape unhurt!" (*L*, 1:161, no. 65). But sometimes their conflicts alarmed her: "[A]fter tea I went to see Sue—had a nice little visit with her—then went to see Emily Fowler, and arrived home at 9—found Father in great agitation at my protracted stay—and mother and Vinnie in tears, for fear that he would kill me" (*L*, 1:111, no. 42). These fierce battles indicate that Emily Dickinson was strong-willed and did not capitulate gracefully. Also, implicit in her detailed reports to her brother is resentment that as a son he is allowed freedom that she is denied.

That Edward Dickinson was a stern man is evident by the fact that his children alternately feared and were fascinated by him. Emily Dickinson often refers to him as "my master," a habit common to Victorian women, and Austin and Lavinia were always careful to defer to him. During his years as a legislator in Boston, he was away from home for weeks, sometimes months, at a time. His wife's letters to him during his absence have much the same longing and loneliness for her husband as do the letters of Anne Bradstreet for Simon Bradstreet. In response, Edward Dickinson's letters to his wife were full of admonitions: "Don't get worn out with company. Take care of the little boy—& not let him get bad habits—Pay all debts you contract, if you can. . . . Women must keep clear of debt," he wrote on June 7, 1829.[12] Throughout their marriage, he issued instructions about caring for the children's health as well as Mrs. Dickinson's safety: "[The children] must be very careful about taking cold, in this pleasant weather—Lavinia, particularly, is exposed to croup, & must be closely watched. . . . be careful about fire . . . *You must not go into the yard, yourself*, on any account—there is no necessity for it, and *you must not do it*—."[13] There are repeated warnings about taking appropriate precautions against unspecified dangers: "Keep your doors all safely locked at nights," [14] and "Do not overdo—nor exert yourself too much—don't go out, evenings, on any account—nor too much, in the afternoon." [15]

Mr. Dickinson's moral imperatives represented the male sphere of law and duty, and Mrs. Dickinson's obedience to his rule embodied feminine propriety. The Dickinson family was organized according to the Victorian precept that men were stern, logical, and committed to reason while women were loving and sympathetic but in need of direction. As a child Emily Dickinson received emotional support from her mother and dispassionate guidance from her father. Their common letter to her during her visit to her aunt Lavinia's reveals their separate concerns: "We are lonely without you, but we hope you are enjoying yourself," Mrs. Dickinson wrote. Mr. Dickinson cautioned: "You must be a good girl—not make any more trouble than you can help—be careful about wetting your feet or taking cold—and not get lost." [16] Throughout her life, Emily Dickinson associated compassion with women and duty with men. In October 1851, when Austin was teaching in Boston, she lamented the rigors of masculinity and begged him to return to the family circle: "Duty is black and brown—home is bright and shining" (L, 1 : 146, no. 57). Even though Austin had considerably more mobility than his sisters, Emily considered herself fortunate to have freedom from pragmatic and utilitarian concerns. As a woman from a professional family, she had leisure and privacy to pursue her interests while Austin was expected to follow his father's example and prepare for life as a husband and provider. In many respects, the Victorian restrictions on female activities worked in Emily Dickinson's favor as Austin himself implies in his complaints about being obliged to live in Boston—a city he disliked—in order to prepare for a profession.

Both Edward and Austin Dickinson were very much affected by the cultural emphasis on hard work and success. Although they were relatively isolated from the commercial centers for most of their lives, they played a part in the economic expansion of Amherst in the nineteenth century. As a young man, Edward Dickinson wanted to make a lot of money; on September 7, 1835, he wrote to his wife:

> Tell your father I wish he would speculate a little for me in "Maine land." . . . I must make some money in some way . . . when the next fever attacks me—nothing human shall stop me from making one desperate attempt to make my fortune—To be shut up forever "under a bushel" while hundreds of mere Jacanapes are getting their tens of thousands and hundreds of thousands, is rather too

much for my spirit—I must spread myself over more ground—half a house, and a rod square for a garden, won't answer my terms.[17]

The Dickinson men had always occupied positions of legislative and financial prominence in Amherst. Edward Dickinson became a successful lawyer and a man of considerable property. His house was "A large country lawyer's house, brown brick, with great trees & a garden" (L, 2:473, no. 342a). Like his forebears he was prominent in state politics and promoted the economic growth of Amherst; he spearheaded the effort to have the railroad line extended from Boston and made speeches in favor of business in which men and women play dramatically different roles: "Then may our 'daughters become corner-stones and our sons become pillars' in the great temple of industry, which, by its beauty and splendor, will attract universal admiration, and around which all true Americans may rally, as the Citadel of our country's security and prosperity."[18] Edward Dickinson's vision is a transmutation of the Puritan dream of the city on a hill to the nineteenth-century American dream of the temple of commerce.

A stern, deliberate man, Edward Dickinson would not allow himself the luxury of complaining about his sometimes burdensome financial responsibilities. Even at home, he did not relax. "Father steps like Cromwell when he gets the kindlings," Emily observed (L, 2:470, no. 339). Unlike his resolute father, Austin grudgingly devoted his life to business, and he frequently complained about his responsibilities. Declining an invitation to dinner, he grumbled: "I am not a man of leisure, and haven't the control of my time. Don't think I am careless or indifferent—and add this to the burden of my self-sacrifice. . . . A man with an expensive family relying on his daily labor for the delights of life isn't reliable for a good time."[19]

Although Emily Dickinson was often angered by her father's conservative and austere habits, she was also fearful of exciting his wrath. Her unresolved conflicts caused her to take an "approach/avoidance" stance toward him. Because he was harsh, emotional intimacy seemed dangerous; nevertheless, she longed for his love. Emily Dickinson was not subdued by her father and ultimately she triumphed. Over the years Edward Dickinson made many concessions to his strong-willed daughter, the most important of which was permitting her to keep her own hours to write and giving her the best bedroom in the house—a spacious, sunny room that overlooked the main street of Amherst. Initially, Emily Dickinson remained at home to please her father, but in her middle years she made a virtue of what had been a necessity. For example, she wrote to the well-known literary figure T. W. Higginson that she could not accept an invitation to visit because her father might miss her or need something; she was especially proud of the fact that he would eat only the bread she baked (*L*, 2:474, no. 343a).[20] This is an ironic shift in view of the fact that twenty years earlier, on May 17, 1850, she had written Abiah Root that "Father and Austin still clamor for food, and I, like a martyr am feeding them" (*L*, 1:99, no. 36). But in her middle years Emily Dickinson was not self-sacrificing. In fact, her culinary efforts consisted of making breads and puddings and the rest was left to Lavinia and to Maggie, the cook. When she was not writing poetry, she engaged in the decorative activities of proper Victorian women—sewing, playing the piano, reading widely from Shakespeare to sentimental novels, and tending her greenhouse and garden.

Edward Dickinson was parsimonious with his affection and rarely showed his love for any of his children; his emotional inaccessibility created a longing for acceptance that Emily Dickinson later transferred to other unresponsive men such as Samuel Bowles and T. W. Higginson. Like her father, these men were professionally prominent and somewhat distant. Perhaps Emily Dickinson subconsciously chose these two men as confidants and friends because they were aloof. Out of her desperate need for approval from her father, she chose the very men who were most likely to neglect her. Both Bowles and Higginson were married and very much preoccupied with their work; Bowles was the editor of the *Springfield Republican* and Higginson was a much respected poet and editor. Even though both men rejected her as a poet, she tried to win them over. Paradoxically, their inability or refusal to accept her as a poet or as a woman gave Emily Dickinson her freedom, but it was a painful liberation because initially she felt cast out and abandoned. Before achieving autonomy, Dickinson alternated between the extremes of abject helplessness and scornful superiority. In many poems she adopts the persona of the orphan, the waif, or the beggar as an expression of her feelings of utter dependency; in others, she adopts the compensatory stance of the all-powerful queen. In an oversimple bifurcation of her experience, she perceived herself either as a forlorn, neglected child or as an indomitable empress.

As we have seen, Anne Bradstreet also alternated between portraying herself as insignificant and vulnerable (to ward off attacks by hostile reviewers and readers) and reveling in female power as embodied by Elizabeth I. Dickinson's literary use of ethical and emotional opposites was the nineteenth-century version of the Puritan view of life, which envisaged an eternal struggle between God and Satan and divided the world into realms of saints and sinners, spirit and flesh. The polarization of experience is a psychological counterpart of the Ramistic dualism of virtue or vice, salvation or damnation on which Puritanism was based, and it is an emotional habit that persisted into the nineteenth century and persists today. Melville's preoccupation with innocence and experience, good and evil, Hawthorne's recurrent themes of virtue and vice, the fair maiden and dark temptress are the fictional parallels to Dickinson's persona of the waif or the queen.

Emily Dickinson's mother, Emily Norcross, was a submissive and sickly woman who was unable to provide strong female guidance for her gifted daughter. Resentful of her mother's weakness, Dickinson once said to T. W. Higginson: "I never had a mother" (L, 2:475, no. 342b), and on another occasion she disparaged her mother's intellectual deficiencies, commenting scornfully: "My Mother does not care for thought" (L, 2:404, no. 261). She also referred to her mother's chronic invalidism in scathing tones: "On the lounge asleep, lies my sick mother, suffering intensely from Acute Neuralgia" (L, 1:97, no. 36). Clearly, it did not occur to Dickinson that her mother's perpetual invalidism was a physical enactment of the insignificant and insubstantial position she held in her husband's world, a world that literally rendered her invalid.[21] It was not until her mother was permanently bedridden that Dickinson could express genuine concern for her. Even then, an undercurrent of anger remained, as her letter to her cousins Louise and Frances Norcross in September 1880 reveals: "Mother's dear little wants so engross the time,—to read to her, to fan her, to tell her health will come tomorrow. . . . I hardly have said 'Good-morning, mother,' when I hear myself saying 'Mother, good-night'" (L, 3:675, no. 666). Emily Norcross Dickinson's illness was diagnosed as neuralgia, or "nerves," a widespread complaint of Victorian women; the frailty of the health of the confined housewife in the United States in the nineteenth century was a common phenomenon.[22] It was generally believed that the female constitution was inherently weak, and many doctors believed that menstruation, pregnancy, and menopause were intrinsically pathological and the cause of illness.[23] Bed rest, social isolation, and intellectual inactivity—a treatment known as the "rest cure"—were frequently prescribed for women with nervous disorders, but as Elaine Showalter points out, "the rest cure was a sinister parody of idealized Victorian femininity: inertia, privatization, narcissism, dependency."[24] It is significant that many women whose experience was trivialized and whose preferences were considered inconsequential became permanently bedridden, literally acting out their culturally enforced passivity.

As a young woman, Mrs. Dickinson had resisted her husband's harsh rule. Lafayette Stebbins, a housepainter in the community, recalled that when Mr. Dickinson forbade his wife to have her bedroom painted, she secretly contacted the painter and arranged for him to do the job while Emily was being born.[25] But over the years her will was worn down by her husband's domination, and instead of continuing to defy him, however indirectly, she retreated into invalidism. Emily Dickinson learned from her mother that physical maladies could bring freedom from onerous domestic duties as well as from incessant conflicts with Mr. Dickinson, and her own withdrawal from domestic and social obligations was a version of her mother's strategy.

As an adolescent, Dickinson railed against the heavy burdens imposed on her by her mother's illness. She complained to Abiah Root on May 17, 1850: "When I am not at work in the kitchen, I sit by the side of mother, provide for her little wants—and try to cheer, and encourage her. I ought to be glad, and grateful that I *can* do anything now, but I do feel so very lonely, and so anxious to have to her cured" (*L*, 1:97, no. 36). Angered by her parents' insistence that her domestic responsibilities should take precedence over her writing, she mocked their moralistic demands in a letter to her friend Jane Humphrey on January 23, 1850: "[M]y hands but *two*—not four, or five as they ought to be—and so *many* wants—and me so *very* handy—and my time of so *little* account—and my writing so *very* needless . . . mind the house—and the food—*sweep* if the spirits were low—nothing like exercise to strengthen—and invigorate—and help away such foolishness" (*L*, 1:82, no. 30). As she continues her complaint, it becomes clear that her parents consider her poetry writing useless, perhaps even sinful; nevertheless, the twenty-year-old Emily Dickinson confided that she preferred to pick Satan's flowers:

> "[W]ork makes one strong, and cheerful. . . . Somehow or other I incline to other things—and Satan covers them up with flowers, and I reach out to pick them. The path of duty looks very ugly indeed—and the place where I want to go more amiable—a great deal—it is so much easier to do wrong than right—so much pleasanter to be evil than good, I dont wonder that the good angels weep—and bad ones sing songs. (*L*, 1:82, no. 30)

In the same letter she parodied the Victorian edict that women should suffer and be still: "We . . . *will* try to be still—tho' we really had rather complain."[26]

As we have seen, Dickinson managed to gain more and more control over her time by staying up late at night to write and sleeping in the morning, a major victory in her struggle for autonomy. One of her poems, written in 1858, was prefaced with a note thanking her father for her exemption from the household schedule: "To my father—to whose untiring efforts in my behalf, I am indebted for my *morning-hours*—viz—3.AM. to 12.PM." These grateful lines are inscribed by his "aff Daughter" (*L*, 2:344, no. 198). This hard-won recognition of her need to keep her own hours meant that, unlike Anne Bradstreet, Dickinson did not have to sacrifice sleep in order to write poetry.

Not only did Dickinson have to obtain permission from her father for time of her own but she had to get Lavinia Dickinson's cooperation as well: her identity as a poet would not have been possible without her sister's willingness to assume the role of domestic caretaker. In the skirmish for territory and identity that occurs in all families, Emily Dickinson won the right "to think." As Lavinia Dickinson observed years later when the family patterns were firmly established, Emily "had to think—she was the only one of us who had that to do. Father believed; and Mother loved; and Austin had Amherst; and I had the family to keep track of."[27]

Since Austin and Lavinia Dickinson also wrote poetry, the psychological maneuvers necessary for Emily Dickinson to win the role of poet must have been quite complicated.[28] Composing occasional verse was a common recreation in the Dickinson household, but when she was twenty-two Emily served notice that she was the serious writer in the family:

> And Austin is a Poet, Austin writes a psalm. Out of the way, Pegasus, Olympus enough "to him," and just say to those "nine muses" that we have done with them!
>
> Raised a living muse ourselves, worth the whole nine of them. Up, off, tramp!
>
> Now Brother Pegasus, I'll tell you what it is—I've been in the habit *myself* of writing some few things, and it rather appears to me that you're getting away my patent, so you'd better be somewhat careful, or I'll call the police! (*L*, 1:235, no. 110)

Unlike Anne Bradstreet who depicted herself as being chased from Olympus by the muses, Dickinson calls her brother an interloper and accuses him of encroaching on her territory. Like Bradstreet, she has given birth to a muse of her own—a tenth muse—and as this letter asserts, she did not define her creativity according to male convention. Rejecting passive inspiration, she announces to Austin that as a woman she has direct access to her creative energy and does not need external assistance: she herself has "raised a living muse." Relegating Austin to the instrumental role of Pegasus, the winged horse ridden by the Muses, Emily Dickinson assumes a proprietary stance insisting that she will protect her interest in any way necessary.

Austin Dickinson was clearly the most important child, and his needs were given priority, especially by Edward Dickinson.[29] As the eldest child and only son, Austin attended college and received his degree from Harvard Law School; it is likely that he understood that he was to pursue his father's profession and therefore did not contest his sister's claim to poetry. When Austin left home to attend Harvard, both Emily and Vinnie missed him very much, but perhaps they were depressed because he was more significant to their father than they were. On March 18, 1853, Emily wrote to Austin that their father "takes great delight in your remarks to him—puts on his spectacles and reads them o'er and o'er as if it were a blessing to have an only son" (*L*, 1 : 231, no. 108). However, the cosmopolitan pleasures of Boston were not appealing to Austin; he wrote to Susan Gilbert, his future wife, that he was homesick for Amherst, where he was honored as a leading citizen, and as soon as he graduated from law school, he returned home to become a leader of the community in the tradition of his father.

The skirmish with Lavinia for the role of poet was probably more complicated for Emily. Vinnie emerged as the "angel in the house," content to be the caretaker, the good daughter, while Emily was considered willful, independent, even rebellious. Interestingly, once Lavinia assumed responsibility for the household, Emily became quite dependent on her: "Vinnie you know is away—and that I am very lonely is too plain for me to tell you—I am *alone—all* alone," she wrote to Jane Humphrey on January 23, 1850 (*L*, 1 : 83, no. 30). As the years passed, Emily Dickinson began to feel that she could not survive without Lavinia's tender care: "Vinnie has been all, so long, I feel the oddest fright at parting with her for an hour, lest a storm arise, and I go unsheltered," she wrote to her friend Mary Emerson Haven nine years later (*L*, 2 : 346, no. 200). The relationship between the two sisters became so intensely symbiotic that Emily Dickinson was, at times, unable to differentiate between her feelings and her sister's: "Vinnie is sick to-night, which gives the world a russet tinge, usually so red. . . . When she is well, time leaps. When she is ill, he lags, or, stops entirely," she wrote to Dr. and Mrs. Holland in September 1859 (*L*, 2 : 353, no. 201). And Vinnie seemed pleased to be her sister's protectress: after Emily's death in 1886 Lavinia cried, "How can I ever live without her? Ever since we were little girls we have been wonderfully dear to each other—and many times when desirable offers of marriage have been made to Emily she has said—I have never seen anyone that I cared for as much as you Vinnie."[30] Mabel Todd, a family friend, remarked: "Those two sisters were everything to each other, & how Vinnie will ever survive it I cannot see."[31]

This symbiotic division of psychological identities is quite common, especially in large families.[32] The March family in Louisa May Alcott's *Lit-*

tle Women is the fictional counterpart of the Dickinsons. The differentiation of roles and talents as well as responsibilities diffuses their sibling rivalry by establishing agreed-upon territories much as the division of spheres does for men and women. Like the March girls, the Dickinson children were sufficiently able to avoid competition to feel great fondness for one another. There was a sense of community in these families based on shared experiences, loyalty, and love that Emily Dickinson then extended to her women friends.

Emily Dickinson was forty-three years old when her father died, and his death was the beginning of an unbroken cycle of loss and grief until her own death twelve years later of Bright's disease, a kidney disorder. Mr. Dickinson had collapsed while giving a speech before the legislature in Boston and died of a reaction to the morphine administered by his doctor.[33] Although the funeral was held on the front lawn of the Dickinson house, Emily would not leave her room to attend it and refused to see anyone but Samuel Bowles. The funeral was a major event in Amherst; the entire town was present, and the village stores were closed in Edward Dickinson's honor. Austin was said to have kissed his father in the open casket, lamenting, "There father, I never dared do that while you were living."[34] Describing her father's stern morality, Emily Dickinson wrote shortly after his death that "His Heart was pure and terrible and I think no other like it exists" (*L*, 2:528, no. 418).

Edward Dickinson's death was a major emotional and spiritual crisis for Emily Dickinson. A letter, written a little more than two years after his funeral, indicates that she was reexperiencing an acute conflict between her desire to believe in a Christian afterlife and her conviction that life ends when the body dies: "I dream about father every night, always a different dream, and forget what I am doing daytimes, wondering where he is. Without any body, I keep thinking. What kind can that be?" (*L*, 2:559, no. 471). In contrast to Anne Bradstreet, Dickinson did not feel that an incorporeal existence could compensate for the loss of bodily life. After her father's death, she depended on Reverend Charles Wadsworth, a minister from Philadelphia, for guidance during this crisis, frequently enclosing notes for him in her letters to her friend Mrs. Holland. In mid-December 1877, Wadsworth wrote a letter to Dickinson that many scholars have interpreted as an indication of a romantic liaison between them. However, his letter is clearly not an expression of passion but of consolation. Extending his "sympathy," he tells her he is "distressed" by her grief and offers his "constant, earnest prayers." He then concludes his letter by urging her to write him of her "trial," although he says, "I have no right to intrude upon your sorrow."[35] It is difficult to imagine how Wadsworth's concern could be construed as an expression of romantic love, especially since he misspells her name![36] Emily Dickinson turned to Wadsworth for spiritual counsel and was so grateful for his help that she considered him "her closest friend," as she told Higginson. After her father died, Emily Dickinson sought paternal guidance from men like Wadsworth, Bowles, and Higginson.

SEVEN

"Your Wayward Scholar"

Apart from her father and brother, Emily Dickinson probably loved Samuel Bowles more than any other man in her life.[1] With his dark beard and flashing eyes, the handsome editor of the *Springfield Republican* was admired for his wit and intelligence. Described as a "vital, fructifying personality" by his biographer George Merriam, Bowles was a bit of a ladies' man, and his attraction for intellectual women such as Maria Whitney, Kate Scot Anthon, and Sue Dickinson was acknowledged by his friends and, not entirely without distress, by his wife.[2] Bowles was a close friend of Austin and Sue Dickinson, and Emily saw him and his wife frequently at lively gatherings at "The Evergreens," the home of the junior Dickinsons. Emily Dickinson said of these evenings: "I think Jerusalem must be like Sue's Drawing Room, when we are talking and laughing there, and you and Mrs. Bowles are by" (*L*, 2:334, no. 189). Dickinson's early letters to Bowles reveal a playful, affectionate relationship between the two in which Emily generally mentions his wife—"love to Mary," "we never forget Mary." Initially, then, Bowles was essentially a favorite "uncle" and very much associated with the Dickinson family as a group, but her feelings deepened and Austin is reported to have said that Emily loved the dashing editor "beyond sentimentality."[3]

In 1860, about the year she seems to have dedicated her life to writing, Dickinson shifts the tone of her correspondence by sending the following poem, prefaced by the line, "I can't explain it, Mr. Bowles" (*L*, 2:363, no. 219):

> Two swimmers wrestled on the spar—
> Until the morning sun—
> When One—turned smiling to the land—
> Oh God! the Other One!
>
> The stray ships—passing—
> Spied a face—

> Upon the waters borne—
> With eyes in death—still begging raised—
> And hands—beseeching—thrown!
>
> (P, 1:143, no. 201)

In addition to revealing the ambivalence Dickinson felt toward Bowles and the other men who were important to her, this poem expresses the conflict she was experiencing between two aspects of herself—the romantic and the creative. The romantic self is not only filled with desire and passionate yearning, but it is even willing to capitulate to a master, to accept its weakness and dependence on another's strength and will. The other swimmer, the creative self, wants to survive and prevail as an autonomous being—or, at least, to be sustained by art. Signaling a resolution to Dickinson's struggle between autonomy and dependence, this poem affirms her creative identity.

During this phase of her correspondence with Bowles, Emily Dickinson also wrote the "Master" letters, which have puzzled and intrigued Dickinson scholars. It has generally been thought that Reverend Wadsworth was the "Master." However, recently Ruth Miller, David Higgins, and Richard Sewall have suggested that the "Master" letters were written to Bowles. Certainly much of the language and style of Emily Dickinson's letters and poems sent to Bowles during the years 1860 to 1862 echoes the "Master" letters. Although it is impossible to identify with certainty the recipient of these letters, Samuel Bowles was the man most likely to have received them *if* they were ever sent.

These letters contain the same dichotomy of purpose—the same conflicting desires to be autonomous and to be dominated. These three letters (L, 2:333, no. 187; L, 2:373–74, no. 233; L, 2:391–92, no. 248) express "Daisy's" intense, even worshiping love for "Master," who neither acknowledges nor returns her passion. Full of longing, grief, despair, and hope, these letters were written from the point of view of a little girl who is pleading for acceptance:

> Master—open your life wide, and take me in forever, I will never be tired—I will never be noisy when you want to be still. I will be . . . your best little girl—nobody else will see me, but you—but that is enough—I shall not want any more—and all that Heaven only will disappoint me—will be because it's not so dear (L, 2: 392, no. 248).

The first letter (no. 187), dated by Thomas Johnson "about 1858,"[4] is the most optimistic and conveys her love for "Master" in sensuous language: "I wish that I were great, like Mr. Michael Angelo, and could paint for you. You ask me what my flowers said—then they were disobedient—I gave them messages. They said what the lips in the West, say, when the sun goes down, and so says the Dawn" (*L*, 2:333, no. 187). The second letter (no. 233), written approximately three years later according to the Johnson dating, makes it clear that "Daisy," as she identifies herself, is suffering acutely from unreciprocated love. Pain and confusion pervade the letter as she likens herself to a bird who has been shot and tells him of the "gash that stains your Daisy's bosom." Like Anne Bradstreet, Emily Dickinson uses the traditional metaphor of the daisy or "day's eye" that follows the sun's path across the sky to describe the romantic relationship between a dependent woman and a powerful man. Again she depicts herself as unassuming and without guile, explaining that she cannot control her tumultuous emotions: "[God] built the heart in me—Bye and bye it outgrew me—and like the little mother—with the big child—I got tired holding him" (*L*, 2:373–74, no. 233). Then, revealing the extremes of her feelings, she rapidly vacillated between the image of the ineffectual frail child she felt that she was and the queen she longed to be: "[I]f I wish with a might I cannot repress—that mine were the Queen's place—the love of the Plantagenet is my only apology—." In this letter she says that he has "altered" her and that she will wait for him "till my hazel hair is dappled—and you carry the cane—."

This third letter is flooded with humiliation. The little girl is alone with "A love so big it scares her, rushing among her small heart—pushing aside the blood and leaving her faint [all] and white in the gust's arm —." Berating herself for offending her beloved, "perhaps her odd—Backwoodsman [life] ways [troubled] teased his finer nature (sense)," she begs him to "teach her majesty—Slow (Dull) at patrician things—" (*L*, 2:391–92, no. 248). These letters are startlingly similar to the letters written a few years earlier by Charlotte Brontë to Constantin Heger, the headmaster of the school she attended in Brussels:

> All I know is, that I cannot, that I will not, resign myself to lose wholly the friendship of my master. I would rather suffer the greatest physical pain than always have my heart lacerated by smarting regrets. If my master withdraws his friendship from me entirely I shall be altogether without hope; if he gives me a little—just a little—I shall be satisfied—happy; I shall have reason for going on, for working.[5]

The torment and suffering that Dickinson and Brontë experience is an externalization of their feelings of inadequacy, inferiority, and insignificance as intelligent creative women in a society that ignores their talents. The yearning for a connection to a strong man expresses a desire to re-

102 · Emily Dickinson

claim a dimension of the self denied to them by their culture. Although it is very disturbing to read these letters of abject humiliation—Helene Moglen describes the Byronic mode as "sadomasochistic"—it is also important to understand that they represent an effort to achieve psychological wholeness.[6]

As we have seen, the Puritans considered suffering and self-abnegation a sign of testing by God and the capacity to sustain this suffering a sign of moral strength, even triumph. Certainly, Emily Dickinson's emotional patterns reflect this heritage; an exultant dimension to the torment of her "Master" letters and her turmoil paradoxically leads to spiritual serenity. This triumphant suffering is described by Sandra Gilbert and Susan Gubar as "Strength in Agony" and, according to this formula, women prove their strength by bearing extraordinary emotional burdens without complaint.[7] Paralleling Bradstreet's abject entreaties to God, Dickinson's despairing "Master" letters reflect the transition from Puritanism to Romanticism, in which the relationship of an all-powerful God to helpless sinners was transferred to the willful and autocratic Byronic hero and his abject guilt-ridden female supplicant. After rejecting the dichotomies of Edwardsean Calvinism, Dickinson was able to modulate her alternating self-hatred and moral triumph and to evolve her mature identity by confronting the conflicts and contradictions of her life. As her perspective deepened, she saw herself as an "Empress of Calvary" who reigned over her suffering. By fusing two aspects of the same psychological state, abnegation and invincibility, she became stronger by acknowledging her pain and living through it rather than denying or repressing it.

It is likely that Dickinson's "Master" letters were written to Bowles but never actually sent to him. In them, Emily Dickinson experienced feelings that were charged and dangerous. While exploring her impulse for self-abnegation and renunciation, she permitted herself to shrink almost to nothingness. But she held on and did not extinguish herself. She is numbed by her fear, but she survives and actually emerges stronger from the conflict. In doing so, she successfully resists the Romantic tradition that casts women in subordinate roles—her sense of self survives and even triumphs over an extraordinarily powerful cultural paradigm that threatens to destroy her. Dickinson's "Master" poems and letters are efforts to resolve her conflicts with a rejecting man. Struggling with her feelings of grief and rage, she is finally able to accept these emotions. Eventually she is able to reclaim the energy and power that she had assigned to the significant men in her life, whether God, her father, Bowles, or Higginson. This is a choice that Anne Bradstreet was not able to make.

In addition to its being a common reference to God or any respected male authority, Adrienne Rich and Joanne Feit Diehl speculate that Dickinson's use of "Master" might also have referred to her active, creative self—her own inner agency, which she feared would desert or destroy her.[8] Her British counterparts commonly assumed male or at least neuter pseudonyms—Mary Ann Evans became George Eliot, Charlotte and Emily Brontë chose Currer and Ellis Bell—and it is possible that Dickinson also referred to her creative self as male.

An early letter to Abiah Root reveals that Dickinson was in the habit of personifying aspects of herself as male. Entertaining her absent friend with a fantasy of appearing suddenly out of nowhere, she casts herself in the role of a famous man: "[I shall] loom up from Hindoostan, or drop from an Appenine, or peer at you suddenly from the hollow of a tree calling myself King Charles, Sancho Panza, or Herod, King of the Jews" (L, 1 : 228–29, no. 107). Two years later, she writes a poem about her alter ego or imaginative faculty as a boy named Tim. Whether "Master" refers to a man, to a series of men, or to her imagination, the important point is that during this period of her life, Emily Dickinson was undergoing an acute conflict between her active and passive and creative and conventional selves. Even more important, she emerged from the struggle in command of her energy and fully committed to writing.

Poem no. 508, "I'm ceded—I've stopped being Their's—" (P, 2 : 389–90) written during the period of the "Master" letters, signals Dickinson's commitment to poetry. The poem concludes, "With Will to choose, or to reject, / And I choose, just a Crown—." In addition to being the sign of royalty, "Crown" refers to the ancient laurel wreath awarded to poets; "ceded" refers to Dickinson herself—she is the territory that others must relinquish; self-centered, she now claims the right to devote her energy to her own work. Another poem written in the same period also expresses Emily Dickinson's increasing autonomy:

> Title divine—is mine!
> The Wife—without the Sign!
> Acute Degree—conferred on me—
> Empress of Calvary!
> Royal—all but the Crown!
> Betrothed—without the swoon
> God sends us Women—
> When you—hold—Garnet to Garnet—
> Gold—to Gold—
> Born—Bridalled—Shrouded—
> In a Day—

> "My Husband"—women say—
> Stroking the Melody—
> Is *this*—the way?
> > (*P*, 2:758, no. 1072)

Ironically reversing the image of herself as the helpless waif, Dickinson presents herself as "Royal," an "Empress of Calvary." Having sustained and learned from her suffering, she has mastered it. This is a love poem, but it is also an announcement of her power—her capacity to experience intense emotions and to survive their annihilating potential. Although her love has been unrequited, she has not been defeated by her suffering. She is not ruled by a master—she reigns over herself. As we have seen, the compensatory image of the queen in command of her energy appears repeatedly in Dickinson's poetry as an antidote to the destructive impact of romantic imagery on women. This poem also takes an ironic view of conventional marriage, revealing Dickinson's scorn for the loss of self women experience when they wed; there is a pun on "bridalled" and bridled, as the wife's expectations about her new life—"Born"—are contrasted with the reality of her now constricted world—"Shrouded." For Emily Dickinson, the wife's expectations of security in marriage are as illusory as the converted sinner's hopes of heaven.

These issues of autonomy and relationship were also explored by other nineteenth-century women. For example, in *Woman in the Nineteenth Century* (1845) Margaret Fuller writes: "Woman, self-centered, would never be absorbed by any relation; it would be only an experience as to a man. It is a vulgar error that love, *a* love, to woman is her whole existence; she is also born for Truth and Love in their universal energy."[9] Margaret Fuller drowned along with her husband and baby in the famous shipwreck off Fire Island in 1850 when Dickinson was nineteen; it is possible that Dickinson was familiar with this treatise in which Fuller concluded that in a highly polarized society men cannot understand women's needs for self-development. Because men programmatically perceive women as "the other," they cannot be trustworthy guides, and Fuller advises women to seek their own counsel:

> But men do *not* look at both sides, and women must leave off asking them and being influenced by them, but retire within themselves, and explore the ground-work of life till they find their peculiar secret. Then, when they come forth again, renovated and baptized, they will know how to turn all dross to gold, and will be rich and free though they live in a hut, tranquil if in a crowd. Then their sweet singing shall not be from passionate impulse, but the lyrical

overflow of a divine rapture, and a new music shall be evolved from this many chorded world.[10]

Whether or not Dickinson knew this work, she followed Fuller's advice and used similar images to describe the perspective of the autonomous woman.

Soon after Samuel Bowles sailed to Europe on *The China* on April 15, 1862, Emily Dickinson wrote to the literary critic T. W. Higginson in another attempt to receive external validation from a recognized authority. Higginson had just published an essay of advice to young writers in the April 1862 *Atlantic Monthly* and was greatly admired by the literary community, which ranked him with Hawthorne as one of America's foremost men of letters.[11] Although her correspondence with Bowles continued, the intensity of her concern regarding her destiny as a poet shifted to Higginson. In her first letter written on April 15, 1862, Dickinson enclosed four poems: "I'll tell you how the Sun rose" (no. 318), "We play at Paste" (no. 320), "Safe in Their Alabaster Chambers" (no. 216), and "The Nearest Dream Recedes Unrealized" (no. 319).[12] The covering letter asks quite simply, "[Is] my Verse alive?" She tells him that "The Mind is so near itself—it cannot see, distinctly—and I have none to ask—" (*L*, 2:403, no. 260). Again, she has placed herself at the mercy of a powerful male; not only did she beg for guidance, but she made it clear that she would respect his judgment. Higginson lost no time in responding to her request and ten days later Emily Dickinson wrote him a second letter thanking him for editing her poems, which she described as "the surgery." Answering his questions regarding her reading, she cites Keats, the Brownings, Ruskin, Sir Thomas Browne, and Revelation. She also told him that her first teacher—Benjamin Newton—has died, and her second—Samuel Bowles—"was not contented I be his scholar—so he left the Land" (*L*, 2:404, no. 261). She asks if he will be her third teacher: "Could you tell me how to grow—or is it unconveyed—like Melody—or Witchcraft?" Confiding that two editors have asked her for her work, she admitted that she was not sure whether her poems merit the world's scrutiny: "I could not weigh myself—Myself— / My size felt small—to me" (*L*, 2:405, no. 261). Echoing Anne Bradstreet's self-effacing descriptions of herself, Emily Dickinson persists in presenting herself as insubstantial, even though she has successfully weathered her religious and romantic crises.

In her third letter, dated June 7, 1862, Emily Dickinson concealed what must have been disappointment at his advice that she "delay" publication of her work. Demurring that "[publication] was as foreign to my thought as Firmament to Fin," she preserved her dignity and protected herself from the charge of indelicate ambition. Wishing to safeguard her respectability, Dickinson disclaimed an interest in fame: "If fame belonged to me / I could not escape her—" (*L*, 2:408, no. 265). However, she expressed alarm that Higginson was dismissing her work as rough, crude, and unruly: "You think my gait 'spasmodic'—I am in danger—Sir— / You think me 'uncontrolled'—I have no Tribunal" (*L*, 2:409, no. 265). Like Anne Bradstreet, Emily Dickinson belittled herself in an effort to gain favor: "I have a little shape—it would not crowd your Desk—nor make much Racket as the Mouse, that dents your Galleries —." Although irony moderates her hopeful expectations, she nevertheless asks, "But, will you be my Preceptor, Mr. Higginson?" (*L*, 2:409, no. 265).

The next letter written in July 1862 sets the tone of their relationship for many years to come. "I am happy to be your scholar," she writes cordially, "and will deserve the kindness, I cannot repay" (*L*, 2:412, no. 268). It is noteworthy that Emily Dickinson had the strength to ask for criticism; she urged Higginson to be straightforward and unsparing in his advice: "Men do not call the surgeon, to commend—the Bone, but to set it" (*L*, 2:412, no. 268). But it is too bad that she lacked the judgment not to seek Higginson's advice in the first place. However, he was an important critic, and it would be unrealistic to expect her to ignore his opinions. In this letter she encloses four more poems, "Your Riches—taught me—Poverty" (*P*, 1:218, no. 299), "Success is counted sweetest" (*P*, 1:53, no. 67), "Some keep the Sabbath going to Church" (*P*, 1:254–55, no. 324), and "Of Tribulation, these are They" (*P*, 1:256, no. 325).

Continuing the self-deprecating pose, she apologizes for having no portrait of herself but describes herself in the following manner: "[I am] small, like the Wren, and my Hair is bold, like the Chestnut Bur—and my eyes, like the Sherry in the Glass, the Guest leaves—" (*L*, 2:411, no. 268). Again like Anne Bradstreet, Emily Dickinson assumes a diminutive pose to conceal her ambition and disarm a potential critic. In a subsequent letter written in August 1862, she makes an effort to curb her "Wayward" tendencies, dutifully signing her letter as "Your Scholar." This letter again expresses Dickinson's conflict between her need for external validation and her desire to trust her own experience. Echoing Blake's image of angels in the trees, she covertly questions external authority, including Higginson, with the following story: "When much in the Woods as a little Girl, I was told that the Snake would bite me . . . but I went along and met no one but Angels, who were far shyer of me, than I could be of them, so I hav'nt that confidence in fraud which many exercise" (*L*, 2:415, no. 271). It is tempting to infer from this story that she knew Higginson's advice was erroneous, for in the preceding paragraph she had observed: "You say 'Beyond your knowledge.' You would not jest with me, because I believe you—but Preceptor—you cannot mean it? All men say 'What' to me, but I thought it a fashion—" (*L*, 2:415, no. 271).

This was a critical juncture in their correspondence, because Dickinson had to decide between Higginson's judgment and her own. Rather than violate the code of feminine decorum, she appeared to respect his judgment about publication; however, the fact that she continued to send him poems for the next twenty-four years indicates that she had confidence in her work.[13] Unfortunately, when she first asked Higginson for his advice, she did not personally know any women writers who could instruct her in the practical matters of publication. Dickinson greatly admired George Eliot, the Brontës, and Elizabeth Barrett Browning, but they were distant ideals.

When her poem "A narrow Fellow in the Grass" (*P*, 2:711–12, no. 986) was published as "The Snake" in both the *Daily* and *Weekly Republican*, Dickinson wrote to Higginson obliquely expressing anger about the orthographic changes made by the editors: "Lest you meet my Snake and suppose I deceive it was robbed of me—defeated too of the third line by the punctuation. The third and fourth were one—I had told you I did not print—I feared you might think me ostensible" (*L*, 2:450, no. 316). Although she again assumes a self-effacing stance and apologizes for appearing to be presumptuous for having published her work, the real message here is that she would not tolerate editorial tampering with her work. For her, diction, rhythm, accent, and punctuation were eternal:

> A word is dead
> When it is said,
> Some say.
> I say it just
> Begins to live
> That day.
> (*P*, 3:845, no. 1212)

Although Higginson did not encourage Dickinson to publish, he did acknowledge her brilliance. Commenting on her solitary existence, he wrote on May 11, 1869, "Yet it isolates one anywhere to think beyond a certain point or have such luminous flashes as come to you—so perhaps the place does not make much difference" (*L*, 2:461, no. 330a). From this point on, Emily Dickinson knows she has a certain stature—she thanks him for saving her life—and she relies upon her growing strength and continues in her chosen direction (*L*, 2:460, no. 330). Repeatedly declining his invitations to come to Boston for literary parties and musical festivals, she invited him to visit Amherst as her guest at the inn. By this time, she was more confident of his basic esteem: "Your opinion gives me a serious feeling. I would like to be what you deem me" (*L*, 2:453, no. 319). She began to pepper her letters with ambiguous phrases such as "to escape enchantment, one must always flee." Higginson admitted that he felt the "strange power" of her letters and verse and that he feared to "miss that fine edge of thought" (*L*, 2:461, no. 330a).

When Higginson did visit Dickinson in Amherst, he was impressed by her genius and eccentricity. Years later in the *Atlantic Monthly*, he commented that she "was much too enigmatical a being for me to solve in an hour's interview, and [I had] an intuition that the slightest attempt at direct cross-examination would make her withdraw into her shell. I could only sit and watch, as one does in the wood." [14] Referring to her as his "half cracked poetess," Higginson carefully recorded Dickinson's comments that revealed her profound visceral response to art rather than cerebral judgment: "If I read a book [and] it makes my whole body so cold no fire ever can warm me I know *that* is poetry. If I feel physically as if the top of my head were taken off, I know *that* is poetry. These are the only way [*sic*] I know it. Is there any other way" (*L*, 2:473–74, no. 342a).

Dickinson's intense energy aroused considerable anxiety in Higginson, and he wrote to his wife: "I was never with anyone who drained my nerve power so much. . . . I am glad not to live near her" (*L*, 2:476, no. 342b). The correspondence with Higginson continued until Dickinson's death. Including Higginson in her circle of friends, she sent him flowers and notes to commemorate important occasions in his life. When his wife, Mary, died in September 1877, she shared her wisdom with him: "The Wilderness is new—to you. Master, let me lead you" (*L*, 2:590, no. 517). She knew her way through grief's maze: "Danger is not at first, for then we are unconscious, but in the after—slower—Days—" (*L*, 2:594, no. 522). These direct letters freely express her deep feelings, but Higginson rarely responded; in fact Dickinson received most of the news about his life from the social columns of the *Springfield Republican*.

In October 1876, Dickinson asked for Higginson's advice in regard to the popular poet Helen Hunt Jackson's request for a poem for the "No Name Series"—an anthology of poems to be published by Roberts Brothers of Boston and edited by Thomas Niles. Jackson had written, "Surely, in the shelter of *double* anonymousness as that will be, you need not shrink. I want to see some of your verses in print. Unless you forbid me, I will send some that I have. May I?" (*L*, 2:563–64, no. 476a). Apparently, Higginson misunderstood that Dickinson was asking him for his opinion about whether or not to send a poem to Jackson because he answered, "I should not have thought of advising you to write stories," and he tells her to do what she likes (*L*, 2 : 564, no. 476b). Dickinson reiterated her request for advice, delicately inquiring, "But may I tell her just the same that you dont prefer it? Thank you, if I may, for it seems almost sordid to refuse from myself again" (*L*, 2 : 566, no. 477). There is no letter on record to indicate that Higginson answered her. However, Dickinson's poem, "Success is counted sweetest" (*P*, 1 : 53, no. 67) appeared in the collection, *The Masque of Poets*; significantly, it was one of two poems singled out for praise by the reviewer of the *New York Times*.[15]

In November 1880, Dickinson again asked Higginson's advice about a few "hymns" that she "promised . . . to charity" (*L*, 3 : 681, no. 675). These poems are emphatically secular, but Dickinson's irony was lost on Higginson; again he failed to give her useful advice.[16] One wonders what might have happened to Dickinson's career if she had chosen a more supportive guide. In contrast to Higginson's lack of judgment, Helen Hunt Jackson valued Dickinson's poetry and wanted to make it available to the public. Apart from the British writers Elizabeth Barrett Browning, the Brontës, and Eliot, whom Dickinson, of course, had never met, Jackson was the only woman artist Dickinson knew.

Over a period of several years Emily Dickinson seems to have come to terms with the fact that Samuel Bowles loved Maria Whitney, a teacher of the modern languages at Smith College. The relationship between Bowles and Whitney has been largely ignored, but it is obvious that they were either lovers or at the very least devoted companions. A letter written by Bowles to Whitney while he was in Switzerland in 1862 reveals their intimacy: "What will you have—if you can get it? A pound of fresh grapes, a row on the lake with me, or a stroll among the vineyards and the grapes, and up the hill-sides? Come and you shall have your choice— all three if you are greedy."[17]

After traveling with Bowles and his children in Europe, Whitney actually lived in the Bowles household in 1868 as a tutor to his children while Mrs. Bowles was ill; Mrs. Bowles was bedridden much of her married life from the stress of complicated pregnancies and several stillbirths. When rumors began to circulate that Mrs. Bowles tolerated her husband's friendship "to avoid further separation" from him, Maria Whitney confided to her sister Lizzie: "I know such a friendship is open to objection, but I feel that there are reasons for this which do not often exist. . . . The friendship is as precious to me as to him, and he has not attempted at any time to persuade me to any thing my judgement and inclinations do not sanction."[18]

Maria Whitney left the household, but she and Bowles continued to work and travel together,[19] and apparently Emily Dickinson accepted their intimacy. When Bowles became seriously ill in 1878, Emily Dickinson wrote to Whitney, who was "allowed to see him" twice a week: "I fear we think too lightly of the gift of mortality, which, too gigantic to comprehend, certainly cannot be estimated" (L, 2:595, no. 524). After Bowles's death in the same year, Dickinson wrote frequently to Maria Whitney as a testimony to their common grief: "I have thought of you often since the darkness,—though we cannot assist another's night" (L, 2:602, no. 537). Dickinson did not attend Bowles's memorial service, at which J. G. Holland observed in his elegy: "The women whom he loved and who loved him were good women, of the highest intellectual grade."[20] If she had attended the service, Emily Dickinson would surely have counted herself in this circle.

Shortly after Bowles's death, Emily Dickinson's long-standing friendship with Judge Otis P. Lord, who was eighteen years her senior, became increasingly intimate, and she finally admitted that she loved him: "Oh, my too beloved, save me from the idolatry which would crush us both" (L, 2:616, no. 560).[21] Although she expressed some concern about the consequences of her love for him, Dickinson's life and work remained very much her own. A letter written after the first of Lord's many visits indicates that her growing security and confidence enabled her to take deep pleasure in his love for her:

> I do—do want you tenderly. The Air is soft as Italy, but when it touches me, I spurn it with a Sigh, because it is not you. . . . Our life together was long forgiveness on your part toward me. The trespass of my rustic Love upon your Realms of Ermine, only a Sovreign [sic] could forgive—I never knelt to other—The Spirit never twice alike, but every time another—that other more divine. Oh, had I found it sooner! Yet Tenderness has not a Date—it comes—and overwhelms. (L, 3:728, no. 750)

Again, feminine inadequacy is contrasted with masculine superiority, but this time the image is literary and this time Dickinson's affection is reciprocated. As she was about to post the letter, she received a message from Austin that the *Republican* had carried an announcement that Lord was critically ill—unconscious and delirious. While Lord was convalescing, her own mother, who had been bedridden since Edward Dickinson's death, died. Although Lavinia took most of the responsibility for Mrs. Dickinson's care, Emily confessed that her mother's invalidism activated her own anxiety about mortality: "Brave Vinnie is well—Mother does not yet stand alone and fears she never shall walk, but I tell her we all shall fly so soon, not to let it grieve her, and what indeed is Earth but a

Nest, from whose rim we are all falling?" (*L*, 2:648, no. 619). Indeed, Emily Dickinson was able to accept her mother's death as part of a natural process, observing that "she slipped from our fingers like a flake gathered by the wind, and is now part of the drift called 'the infinite'" (*L*, 3:750, no. 785).

Soon after Mrs. Dickinson's funeral, Emily Dickinson wrote to O. P. Lord: "Emily 'Jumbo'! Sweetest name, but I know a sweeter—Emily Jumbo Lord. Have I your approval?" (*L*, 3:747, no. 780). Her mother's death had intensified her love of her living friends, and perhaps Dickinson at last felt that she was free to express openly her feelings for Lord. Although he responded to her letter with an invitation to visit him, Dickinson did not alter her course—she remained at home. In spite of their separate lives, the relationship remained charged with emotion:

> The withdrawal of the Fuel of Rapture does not withdraw the Rapture itself.
> Like Powder in a Drawer, we pass it with a Prayer, it's Thunders only dormant. (*L*, 3:786, no. 842)

Such intense friendships were essential to Dickinson, and when Lord died on March 13, 1884, she grieved deeply:

> So give me back to Death—
> The Death I never feared
> Except that it deprived of thee—
> And now, by Life deprived,
> In my own Grave I breathe
> And estimate it's size—
> It's size is all that Hell can guess—
> And all that Heaven was—
> (*P*, 3:1119–20, no. 1632)

This lyrical and flowing poem expresses Emily Dickinson's intense sorrow and deepening awareness of her own mortality. There is no attempt to diminish the intensity of the pain with false promises of reunion in an afterlife. Again, her sorrow is more acute than was Anne Bradstreet's because she has no faith in a divine plan.

The final decade of Dickinson's life was marred by the death of many of her most beloved friends and family members: in addition to her parents, Bowles, and Lord, Wadsworth, Holland, and her favorite nephew, Gilbert, also died. Although each death severely taxed her emotional resources, Dickinson never relinquished her belief in the sanctity of this life. She observed that she was "constantly more astonished that the Body contains the Spirit—Except for overmastering work it could not be borne" (*L*, 3:661, no. 643). Bradstreet's sorrow was mitigated by resigned acceptance of God's will. Although she questioned God's wisdom in taking the lives of innocent children, she nevertheless depended on the concept of Providence to subdue her own emotions. Dickinson had no choice but to accept her painful losses as being irrevocably permanent. During these years of the illness and death of her relatives and closest friends, Dickinson's letters are punctuated by the recognition of death's inevitability, made even more striking by images drawn from her garden: "I trust your garden was willing to die—I do not think mine was—it perished with beautiful reluctance, like an evening star—" (*L*, 3:676, no. 668). Her joy in living became bittersweet: "Consciousness is the only home of which we *now* know. That sunny adverb had been enough, were it not foreclosed" (*L*, 2:634, no. 591). In spite of the sadness she felt about decay and dissolution, Dickinson was not lured by the comforts of theology:

> The Moon upon her fluent Route
> Defiant of a Road
> The Star's Etruscan Argument
> Substantiate a God—
> How archly the Heaven "to come"—
> If such perspective be—
> By superseding Destiny
> And dwelling there Today—
> (*P*, 3:1054, no. 1528)[22]

When Gilbert Dickinson died of typhoid fever on October 5, 1883, Dickinson's belief in the sanctity of earthly life was severely shaken. In order to be with her nephew, Emily Dickinson went to her brother's house for the first time in fifteen years. A friend wrote of her violent reaction to the visit: "[T]he odor of disinfectants used, sickened her so that she was obliged to go home about 3 AM—and vomited—went to bed and has been feeble ever since, with a terrible pain in the back of her head."[23] In spite of her own mourning, Emily Dickinson immediately tried to comfort her sister-in-law and lead her through grief's labyrinth: "The first section of Darkness is the densest, Dear—After that, Light trembles in—" (*L*, 3:803, no. 874). But by offering solace to Sue she did not escape her own dark night of mourning. In her grief, she recapitulates her own conflict regarding belief in an afterlife. Her letter to her friend

Elizabeth Holland echoes the question posed to Abiah Root decades earlier:

> "Open the Door, open the Door, they are waiting for me," was Gilbert's sweet command in delirium. *Who* were waiting for him, all we possess we would give to know—Anguish at last opened it, and he ran to the little Grave at his Grandparents' feet—All this and more, though *is* there more? More than Love and Death? Then tell me it's name! (*L*, 3:803, no. 873)

Interestingly, in a much later letter describing Gilbert's death, Dickinson revised his last words: "[O]pen the door, the boys are waiting for me," which has the effect of erasing any possible doubt that she had about Gilbert's fate. Although Gilbert's death was a major loss, Dickinson once again chose to concentrate on the present world, reiterating her belief that loved ones are kept alive through memory: "To 'know in whom' we 'have believed,' is Immortality" (*L*, 3:852, no. 953), and "Show me Eternity, and I will show you Memory—" (*L*, 3:830, no. 912). And acting on her philosophy, she immortalized her nephew in her poems.

Gilbert's death made Dickinson even more intensely aware of life's beauty and brevity. She wrote to Elizabeth Holland: "Sweet Sister. . . . [R]ecall that Earth's most graphic transaction is placed within a syllable, nay, even a gaze—" (*L*, 3:802, no. 873). In the final years of her life, Emily Dickinson respectfully acknowledged the complex and mysterious connection of life and death. She reiterated her belief that to accept the connection between life and death is to grow as a person; to deny it is to bury a part of oneself in repression and denial: "Tis a dangerous moment for any one when the meaning goes out of things and life stands straight— and punctual—and yet no . . . [signal] comes. Yet such moments are. If we survive them they expand us, but if we do not, but that is Death, whose if is everlasting." [24]

Throughout this period of intense mourning and acute awareness of life's tenuous character, Emily Dickinson retained her sense of humor, which was sometimes bantering, often salty or wry:

> Those—dying then,
> Knew where they went—
> They went to God's Right Hand—
> That Hand is amputated now
> and God cannot be found—
>
> The Abdication of Belief
> Makes the Behavior small—

> Better an ignis fatuus
> Than no illume at all—
>   (*P*, 3 : 1069, no. 1551)

Dickinson's comprehensive vision, her commitment to circumference, or the entire range as well as the outer edge of experience, permitted her to accept life in its many aspects—grief and joy, despair and hope, tears and laughter. She continued to take pleasure in flowers, in food, in friendship, and often sent humorous notes along with her gifts: "Maggie 'dragged' the garden for this bud for you. You have heard of the 'last rose of summer.' This is that rose's son" (*L*, 2 : 466, no. 337). The following note was sent with two roasting chickens: "Enclosed please find the birds which do not go South" (*L*, 3 : 879, no. 997).

From her girlhood, Emily Dickinson was known for her sardonic wit; her salty humor was in the tradition of John J. Hopper's *The Adventures of Simon Suggs* and Seba Smith's "Major Jack Downing Letters," which appeared in the *Springfield Republican*, and Mark Twain's sketches, "Old Times on the Mississippi," which were published in the *Atlantic*.[25] But there was a darker side to her comic remarks that may aptly be termed "gallows humor." One of her favorite stories concerned an old woman who asked for directions; Dickinson obliged the woman by directing her to the "cemetery to save the expense of moving," and she was known to laugh loudly at reports in the *Republican* of "those funny accidents, where railroads meet each other unexpectedly, and gentlemen in factories get their heads cut off quite informally" (*L*, 1 : 264, no. 133).

As she grew older, Dickinson's parodies of the Bible became increasingly sardonic: "[W]e read in a tremendous Book about 'an enemy,' and armed a confidential fort to scatter him away. The time has passed, and years have come, and not yet any 'Satan.' I think he must be making war upon some other nation" (*L*, 3 : 694, no. 693). Commenting ironically on Gal. 5 : 22, "But the fruit of the spirit is love," she wrote: "We have no Fruit this year, the Frost having barreled that in the Bud—except the 'Fruits of the Spirit,' but Vinnie prefers Baldwins—" (*L*, 3 : 839–40, no. 936). She even joked lightly about her own death in a letter to Frances and Louise Norcross in August 1884: "Eight Saturday noons ago, I was making a loaf of cake with Maggie, when I saw a great darkness coming and knew no more until late at night. I woke to find Austin and Vinnie and a strange physician bending over me, and supposed I was dying, or had died, all was so kind and hallowed" (*L*, 3 : 826–27, no. 907). But underneath the bantering, the sad memory of Gilbert remained: "The little boy we laid away never fluctuates, and his dim society is companion still. But it is growing damp and I must go in. Memory's fog is rising" (*L*, 3:827, no. 907).

Emily Dickinson never married, but her life was full of intense emotion and deep attachments to friends and family. Although her youthful romantic love for Bowles was not reciprocated, she ultimately received Otis Lord's rapturous attention. Through her painful struggle with Bowles and Higginson, she learned not to project her strength onto men and reclaimed her energy for her work. Remaining single in a society that placed enormous burdens on wives, Dickinson was able to concentrate on writing poetry.

EIGHT

"A Word made Flesh"

Emily Dickinson died of Bright's disease, a kidney disorder, on May 15, 1886; she was fifty-five years old. Shortly after her burial in the family plot, her sister Lavinia found a locked box of poems sewn in forty-four packets or "fascicles," as Lavinia called them; in addition, there were several poems written on loose sheets and scraps of paper. These poems, totaling 1,775, would probably never have been published if Lavinia Dickinson had not enlisted the aid of Mabel Loomis Todd, Austin's mistress and a family friend, to prepare them for publication.[1] There has been much critical speculation about Emily Dickinson's failure to publish the bulk of her poetry during her lifetime. With the exception of five poems published in the *Springfield Republican*, edited by her friend Samuel Bowles, and two others published in *The Round Table* and *A Masque of Poets*, her poems were read only by her closest friends.[2]

It has been difficult for readers and critics to comprehend the enigma of the sequestered Dickinson who persisted in writing her poems—some jotted down on scraps of paper, some carefully sewn together—over a period of twenty-eight years without public confirmation of her achievement. It is equally difficult to understand why she failed to give more specific instructions about the ordering and possible publication of her work after her death. Yet a closer look at the circumstances of her life in her letters as well as in the poems themselves reveals that Emily Dickinson dedicated her life to art—poetry was her "calling" and hence its own justification. Poetry writing was a process as sacred and necessary to her survival as the writing of diaries, chronicles, narratives, and histories was to the spiritual survival of the Puritans. Like the Puritan diarists, who continually scrutinized their lives in order to have a heart prepared for conversion, Emily Dickinson wrote to explore her consciousness and to chronicle her inner life. As Albert Gelpi has observed: "As an artist she made permanent the momentary acts of consciousness despite time's inexorable wheel."[3] In this respect, Emily Dickinson was a "heart's remembrancer"—poetry writing helped her to understand and give shape to her experience and enabled her to record the joys and sorrows of human fellowship as well as to celebrate the wonders of nature.

Words were sacred to Dickinson because, for her, language *was* life: "this loved philology" gave form and substance to experience. Words made perceptions palpable; language made emotion and thought possible:

> A Word made Flesh is seldom
> And tremblingly partook
> Nor then perhaps reported
> But have I not mistook
> Each one of us has tasted
> With ecstasies of stealth
> The very food debated
> To our specific strength—
>
> A Word that breathes distinctly
> Has not the power to die
> Cohesive as the Spirit
> It may expire if He—
> "Made Flesh and dwelt among us"
> Could condescension be
> Like this consent of Language
> This loved Philology.
>   (*P*, 3 : 1129, no. 1651)

Punning on "condescension," Dickinson playfully replaces the religious concept of Christ's salvation of true believers with the redemptive power of poetry. The clue to Dickinson's cosmology can be found in the contrast between condescension and consent; the former is a descent from a superior position and implies disdain while the latter indicates a harmony and accord that springs from union.

Dickinson's excavations of the psyche disclose emotional patterns as complex as Puritan conversion with its requisite phases of sanctification, justification, and grace. The war between God and Satan is transmuted into opposing forces of life and death, eros and agape. In Dickinson's poetic scenario, the prepared heart is modulated into intense existential awareness:

> This Consciousness that is aware
> Of Neighbors and the Sun
> Will be the one aware of Death
> And that itself alone

Is traversing the interval
Experience between
And most profound experiment
Appointed unto Men—

How adequate unto itself
It's properties shall be
Itself unto itself and none
Shall make discovery.

Adventure most unto itself
The Soul condemned to be—
Attended by a single Hound
It's own identity.
                    (*P*, 2:622–23, no. 822)

In this poem, consciousness replaces Christ and self-awareness supersedes salvation. Critics have traditionally focused on Dickinson as a religious poet and have failed to see that, for her, temporal life is not extended after death but becomes an "experiment" or "adventure."[4] No longer framed by a divine plan, the drama of the poet focuses on what happens between birth and death, not on the ultimate destiny of heaven or hell.

Anticipating the modernists like Wallace Stevens, Marianne Moore, William Carlos Williams, and Theodore Roethke, Dickinson believed that death gives meaning to life: "Sweet is it as Life, with it's enhancing Shadow of Death." For her, generativity in all its forms took precedence over the theological quest for salvation. The primacy of the bee, the flower, the child supplanted the distant ideal of the city on a hill—"Redemption leaves nothing for the Earth to add," she observed. To strive to be counted among the elect at the expense of responding to this life was a perversion of its purpose: "O Matchless Earth," she wrote in December 1870, "We underrate the chance to dwell in thee" (*L*, 2:478, no. 347). Unlike Anne Bradstreet who felt constrained to discount her earthly existence, Emily Dickinson celebrated the pleasures of daily life.

Clara Newman Turner witnessed Dickinson's profound attachment to nature: "Her events were the coming of the first bird;—the bursting of a young chrysalis;—the detection of the first fascinating spring fuzz of green in the air—the wonderful opening of the new world of every little flower; an unusual sunset; the autumn changes—and the inexhaustible life."[5] Echoing Emerson's observations of nature, the following poem illustrates Dickinson's conviction that "Nature is Heaven":

"Nature" is what we see—
The Hill—the Afternoon—

Squirrel—Eclipse—the Bumble bee—
Nay—Nature is Heaven—
Nature is what we hear—
The Bobolink—the Sea—
Thunder—the Cricket—
Nay—Nature is Harmony—
Nature is what we know—
Yet have no art to say—
So impotent Our Wisdom is
To her Simplicity
                    (*P*, 2 : 5 1 5, no. 668)

Poem by poem, Dickinson reshaped the Puritan ideal of the city on a hill into a vision of *Earth as paradise*: "I find ecstasy in living—the mere sense of living is joy enough" (*L*, 2 : 474, no. 342).

As we have seen, Emily Dickinson experienced an acute conflict between accepting the received wisdom of religious tradition and following her personal inclination during her adolescence. Wrestling with the question of conversion during these formative years, she often felt that she was wicked to resist salvation: "[T]he world allured me and . . . I listened to her syren voice" (*L*, 1 : 30, no. 1 1). Because she inherited the legacy of the Puritan distrust of the imagination along with the fear of metaphor as irrational and wicked, the young Dickinson worried that her will was demonic, but as she grew older and began to trust her experience more fully, Dickinson committed herself to living in this world and to writing poetry as a chronicle of her experience: "I have dared to do strange things—bold things, and have asked no advice from any—I have heeded beautiful tempters, yet do not think I am wrong. . . . I hope human nature has truth in it. . . . Nobody *thinks* of the joy, nobody *guesses* . . . but there *now* is nothing old, things are budding, and springing, and you rather think you are in a green grove, and its branches that go, and come."[6] In spite of the threat of damnation, Dickinson chose a bower thick with life instead of divine prospects.

Dickinson's language captures the multivalent nature of her experience that not only was complicated but at times even risky:

I stepped from Plank to Plank
A slow and cautious way
The Stars about my Head I felt
About my Feet the Sea.

I knew not but the next
Would be my final inch—

> This gave me that precarious Gait
> Some call Experience.
>
> (P, 2:650, no. 875)

Unlike Shelley, Wordsworth, and Keats, she does not use images of flight and escape from earthly restraints but as this poem reveals she proceeds cautiously and is connected to her actual experience, however perilous it seems to be. Although the stars whirl around her head, and the sea swirls at her feet, she remains grounded, however tentatively, in the moment. In other poems her considerable suffering and pain in response to the uncertainty of her direction is evident:

> The Soul has Bandaged moments—
> When too appalled to stir—
> She feels some ghastly Fright come up
> And stop to look at her—
>
> (P, 2:393, no. 512)

Instead of describing fear as a personal response to an external event or set of circumstances, Dickinson personifies it as a predatory entity that can hound her. In this poem she depicts her soul as vulnerable to this negative force; the passive soul has no choice but to wait for fear to strike and to endure his attack. Here Emily Dickinson uses the traditional distinction between female powerlessness and male aggression to structure her poem. Interestingly, by externalizing terror, she gains psychological and artistic control over the turmoil and despair that threatens to engulf her. Just as Emily Dickinson derived poetic images from the Bible and other literary works, she used the nineteenth-century paradigm of separate masculine and feminine spheres as a source of metaphors. As we have seen, she depicted her own aggressive impulses as male whether in the form of Master, or a playmate called Tim. Sometimes she portrayed the negative force in nature as male—a marauding bee who assaults a flower's tranquillity, the rapining sun who seduces and then scorches nature's delicate vegetation, or death as the inevitable abductor. This aesthetic application of traditional gender roles resulted in metaphors of startling variety and vitality. Emily Dickinson depicted organic growth as female and accepted, somewhat ruefully, the male principle as the necessary concomitant to this growth. Ultimately, she evolved a cosmology based on cyclicity and honoring generativity in all of its forms. An early poem playfully expresses her creed:

In the name of the Bee—
And of the Butterfly—
And of the Breeze—Amen!
          (*P*, 1 : 21, no. 18)

Unlike Anne Bradstreet, who was unable to accept fully the validity of her experience as an American woman, Emily Dickinson writes poetry that is grounded on her own perceptions of the universe.

There are parallels between Emily Dickinson's cosmology and the transcendentalism of Emerson and Thoreau. Dickinson shared Thoreau's aversion to the "unmanly love of wealth" and the "commercial spirit" that desecrates nature, and she also agreed with Thoreau's conviction that the earth is more to be "admired and enjoyed than used."[7] And Dickinson understood that human beings in a commercial society rarely transcended "custom and gross sense."[8] Describing Emerson's *Representative Men* as "a little Granite Book you can lean upon" (*L*, 2 : 569, no. 481), she followed Emerson's advice to poets and abandoned herself to "the nature of things."[9] Although Emerson and Dickinson shared a sense of surprise and discovery in the world of process, their approach to experience was dramatically different. Unlike Dickinson, Emerson was impelled to develop his metaphors into metaphysics, resulting in a philosophical system that was the secular equivalent of Puritanism. For example, Emerson's definition of will functions as faith did for the saints; like faith, will penetrates the perceptual wilderness clearing spaces and shaping forms in the experiential thicket. Even though Emerson knows that these arbitrary forms ultimately will be broken, that life is essentially a succession of moments, that the self is a discontinuous collection of habits, he develops a concept of will to eliminate ambiguity and flux. For Emerson, and for his precursor Kant, consciousness is a burden. Although he dislikes the effort of having to maintain social structures on quicksand, he is not able to free himself of the conditioned masculine reflex to order his perceptions and to create form out of apparent chaos. Although the discontinuities of consciousness caused Dickinson considerable anxiety, her deliberately contrived environment freed her from the need to control her emotions. She often reacted with pain and fear to the ambiguities of her experience, but she did not repress the darker aspects of her vision in order to create the illusion of control.

In his essays, Emerson articulates alternative points of view, arguing first one side, then the other. His experience is circular, but it is quite unlike Dickinson's circumferential vision. Emerson returns where he began, contemplating the circuit between subject and object, but, unlike Dickinson, he does not experience himself as coexisting with the universe. In contrast to Dickinson's concern with simultaneous events and synchronic perceptions that are expressed as synaesthetic moments in her poems, Emerson's circular arguments attempt to join discrete thoughts like beads on a string. For Emerson, there is always a gap to be bridged, and he maintained that it is the responsibility of the poet and the philosopher to leap over the chasm of the unknown; for him, the universe is the bride, the consciousness is the groom, and the two are never congruent.[10] Emerson's philosophical system, then, repeats the traditional paradigm of male mind subduing female matter. In a discussion of Emerson's journals, Joel Porte discusses a dream that Emerson recorded in his journal in which he described himself as eating the earth as though it were an apple; this lofty and omnivorous perspective contrasts dramatically with Dickinson's depiction of the earth as a nest or garden.[11]

As we have seen, Dickinson perceives the universe in terms of patterned wholes, as resonating fullness rather than sequential opposites: there is no need for the dialectic of unity and variety, no need to hurtle herself through essentially disjunctive moments; no need to strive to "attain the universe," as Emerson writes in *Representative Men* and *Nature*. Dickinson is connected to the universe, just as it is connected to her. Emerson believes in limitless possibility; Dickinson is concerned with unfolding moments. While Emerson struggles to rise above nature, Dickinson remains grounded. Her perceptions remain centered in the present, and her lyric poems express the absorption in the moment. For Emerson, death is "the reality that will not dodge us," but for Dickinson it is the cessation of life: "That it will never come again / Is what makes life so sweet" (*P*, 3:1171, no. 1741).[12] Emerson and Dickinson represent two modes of consciousness, the linear and the holistic. This is not to suggest that Dickinson's comprehensive vision was easily achieved; her fear of death, her longing for love had to be resolved first. Her commitment to unfolding experience explains why her grief and despair threaten to overwhelm her at times; she had no assurance that these emotions would end. Learning the complex interrelationships of her feelings was a lifelong task.

The linear mode that is associated with the left side of the brain and the right side of the body is analytic, sequential, focused, specialized, concerned with cause and effect and logical argument. This thought pattern is characteristic of science and other logical disciplines such as law. The right brain is associated with the arts—music, literature, dance—and is characterized by recognition of a pattern or "gestalt." Because the linear and holistic modes are associated with the left and right sides of the brain, respectively, it has been conjectured that socialization patterns emphasize left-brain skills for men and right-brain skills for women or that men tend to be dominated by the left cerebral hemisphere and women by the right. In any event, the dichotomy between these two modes of thought associated with the left and right brain leads to opposition of simultaneous and sequential perception of time, the comprehensive and the specialized, the synchronic and the causal, experience and analysis, intuition and logic.[13] Buddhist and Jungian psychology and many other systems of thought differentiate between the analytic and mystical modes, associating the former with day, history, intellect or "mind," masculine or "yang" elements, and the latter with night, eternity, senses or "body," feminine or "yin." Other characteristics that have been associated with analytical versus mystical modes are bounded versus unbounded, agentic versus passive, mastery versus receptivity, conscious versus unconscious. Instead of the hierarchical order, logical causality, and abstraction characteristic of traditional masculinity, Dickinson concentrated on relationship, synchronicity, and textured details associated with feminine sensibility.

Dickinson regarded the unfolding present as infinite. This unbounded, nonlinear, timeless mode parallels the phenomenon of egolessness or being outside of oneself—literally, ecstasy—that Dickinson felt was the highest form of consciousness:

> Take all away from me, but leave me Ecstasy,
> And I am richer than all my Fellow Men—
> Ill it becometh me to dwell so wealthily
> When at my very Door are those possessing more,
> In abject poverty—
>
> (*P*, 3 : 1123, no. 1640)

In many respects this selflessness is an intensification of the conditioned egolessness of traditional womanhood. By carrying the Victorian dictate of feminine receptivity to its extreme, Dickinson discovered what mystics call the joy of cosmic fusion, or being one with the universe. Struggling with complex problems such as the artificial distinction between subject and object that characterizes patriarchal modes of perception, Dickinson remained focused on the actual and immediate rather than on the transcendent dimension of her experience:

> The Sun went down—no Man looked on—
> The Earth and I, alone,
> Were present at the Majesty—
> He triumphed, and went on—

The Sun went up—no Man looked on—
The Earth and I and One
A nameless Bird—a Stranger
Were Witness for the Crown—
(*P*, 2:763, no. 1079)

In this poem, Dickinson is not overwhelmed by the sunrise or sunset, nor does she trivialize or sentimentalize the experience. Instead, she, the earth, and a nameless bird are silent but responsive observers. The pun on witness—a word that refers to religious conversion—is significant because she delimits God's omnipresence as well as the sun's power with her observation and acknowledgment of nature's glory. Dickinson does not perceive herself to be separate or alienated from the experience; she, the bird, and the earth are equally present, coexisting with the sunset and the sunrise. The parallel stanzas with the repetitive phrase "no Man looked on" capture diurnal rhythms and differentiate the poet's responsiveness to nature from masculine agency. In her private world, Dickinson often suspended the boundaries between herself and the events she witnessed, observing life not in distinct categories but in an interconnected pattern:

Circumference thou Bride of Awe
Possessing thou shalt be
Possessed by every hallowed Knight
That dares to covet thee
(*P*, 3:1111, no. 1620)

With this poetic elaboration of Emerson's observation, "the Universe is the Bride of the Soul," Dickinson provides an alternative to Keats's "Ode on a Grecian Urn," in which the pursuer never achieves the pursued. Here Dickinson celebrates joyous fusion of self and other—seeking and finding are no longer eternal opposites. Circumference, from the Latin "to carry around," then, is the perception of the universe as an eternal and cyclic whole. It also refers to organic boundaries that, unlike those of a circle, are not geometrical. Dickinson's primary concern was to trace the encompassing periphery rather than focus on a central goal; her philosophical and poetic commitment was to rendering experience as continuous movement rather than categorical classification.[14]

Emerson wrote that it was the "poet who re-attaches things to nature and the Whole."[15] This imaginative leap is difficult if constrained by the burden of the socially constructed self. As Emerson understood, memory is, in part, a form of selective consciousness that enables the individual to maintain a coherent sense of self. But like the ego, memory, with its arbitrary divisions of past and present, falsifies experience by interfering with the perception of the moment. In "Self Reliance," Emerson asks, "Why drag about this corpse of your memory?," and he counsels his audience to "bring the past for judgment into the thousand-eyed present, and live ever in a new day." [16] Arbitrary categories of past, present, and future are mechanical divisions that serve the public presentation of self, schedules for the production of goods but not the truths of the psyche or nature.

While Emerson followed the lecture circuit and received wide public acclaim for his work, Emily Dickinson remained at home. Thoreau also lectured (*Walden* began as a lecture at the Concord Lyceum), and his seclusion in the woods was an interlude in an otherwise active life. Like Thoreau, Dickinson isolated herself, but Amherst was not Walden. Thoreau chose solitude while Dickinson made a virtue of necessity; as an unmarried woman from a traditional family, she was constrained by her father's decision that she should remain in his house. [17] Walden gave Thoreau a chance to confront life in order to determine whether or not it was essentially "mean," but he was not restricted by the sentimental tradition of domestic womanhood. In his search for the natural life, Thoreau followed his inclinations, eating, walking, and housekeeping whenever he chose. In spite of the psychological independence she achieved as a mature woman, Emily Dickinson was still bound by the routines and rituals of a patriarchal household: as a young woman she cooked, she sewed, she gardened, she entertained guests and, in later years, helped to care for her invalid mother. Like Anne Bradstreet who was constrained to serve God at home, Dickinson's activities were strongly limited by custom. Because neither could fully participate in a wider life, both women evolved poetic visions based on female priorities as alternatives to the Puritanism and transcendentalism that excluded them.

Like Thoreau, Dickinson avoided reflexive sociability. For Dickinson, privacy—being secluded from observation—became a privilege which enabled her to explore her experience; free of social scrutiny, she was able to nurture her poetic gifts. Dickinson's distaste for polite society was evident in her adolescence. When she was nineteen, she confided to her close friend Abiah Root: "I stayed at home all Saturday afternoon, and treated some disagreeable people who insisted upon calling here as tolerably as I could" (*L*, 1:87, no. 31). For her, the silent meditation of nature was far preferable to obligatory conversation:

My best Acquaintances are those
With Whom I spoke no Word—

The Stars that stated come to Town
Esteemed Me never rude
Although to their Celestial Call
I failed to make reply—
My constant—reverential Face
Sufficient Courtesy.

(*P*, 2:679, no. 932)

On the one hand, Dickinson's seclusion was a form of romantic individualism; on the other, it liberated her from the continual round of parties, picnics, concerts, lectures, fairs, sleighrides, receptions, levees, temperance dinners, church socials, weddings, baptisms, and funerals that composed the social life of a town like Amherst.

As in most small towns, gossip was the staple of social life, and much of the conversation was concerned with narrow, moralistic judgments, as this letter from George C. Shepard to his nephew Lucius M. Boltwood indicates: "At Amherst, where I lived for years, this fault-finding spirit *greatly prevails*. It seems a large part of the business of that village to tell of the *wicked doings* of men, or of committees."[18] Since the Dickinson home was located on one of the central streets of Amherst, even a short walk meant the likelihood of social encounters that she preferred to avoid. Near the Dickinson house and meadow lived Professor Richard Mather and family. The village church and parsonage were also nearby, as were the railroad intersection, the town hall, and the Grace Episcopal Church. Even to venture across the lawn to Austin and Sue Dickinson's home was risky because her sister-in-law was one of the most active hostesses in Amherst.[19]

Dickinson's seclusion helped her avoid the prefabricated perceptions of her social context, and as a mature woman, she safeguarded her freedom: "The Fence is the only Sanctuary," she wrote to Elizabeth Holland in January 1871 when she was nearly forty (*L*, 2:485, no. 359). John Cody has argued that Emily Dickinson's isolation was a neurotic response to the pressure of adult life, but as Thomas Johnson observes, "She organized her daily routines so that she could live and think and express her thoughts as she herself wished them lived and expressed."[20] Her room functioned much as a retreat does for the clergy, or as an ashram for the Buddhist monk; it was a protected place that enabled her to keep her perceptual powers "cleansed," to use Blake's word. Even more than the very real conflict between the demands of art and traditional womanhood, Dickinson experienced a tension between the demands of conventional sociability and psychological autonomy. In order to have a wider range of perceptions that, as Emerson suggested in "The Poet," would enrich her art, Dickinson deliberately removed herself from the social life of Amherst. She would have agreed with Virginia Woolf's observation that "All the being and the doing, expansive, glittering, vocal, evaporated; and one shrunk, with a sense of solemnity, to being oneself, a wedge-shaped core of darkness, something invisible to others . . . and this self having shed its attachments was free for the strangest adventures. When life sank down for a moment, the range of experiences seemed limitless."[21] In her diaries, Woolf expresses a recurrent conflict between her desire to concentrate on her writing and her need for intelligent conversation. Repeatedly, she complains that teas, dinner parties, and other social engagements throw her off her rhythm for days, sometimes weeks afterwards. By shunning conventional social life, Dickinson avoided the codified habits of perception that would have dulled her sensitivity and limited the range of her understanding. Paradoxically, by simplifying her world—by remaining single, by excluding random social encounters, by always wearing white—she remained receptive to the intricate patterns and complicated textures of her experience.

In order to protect herself from stultifying social obligations, Dickinson turned the code that confined nineteenth-century women to the private sphere into a privilege that permitted her time and space to write. Instead of passively enduring the limitations of true womanhood, Dickinson used the feminine ideals of piety and purity as a moral and aesthetic rationale for her art. Just as Anne Bradstreet used the Puritan imperatives to praise God and to have a "prepared heart" as justification for her writing, Emily Dickinson used the Victorian ideal of the leisured woman, cloistered in the sanctity of the home, to create time for her poetry. For her, privacy permitted the blurring of the boundaries that separated her from the world around her. In contrast to men who are traditionally trained to think "oppositionally," as Nancy Chodorow argues, to perceive themselves as separate from other people and forms of life, Emily Dickinson was free of the necessity of having to polarize subject and object.[22] Dickinson used her privacy to write poetry that was grounded in her experience as a nineteenth-century woman.

Although the concept of separate selfhood, and its corollary self-interest, facilitates life in a stratified, commercial society by stressing the specialized economic function of the individual, it restricts the multiplicity of experience. Dickinson's seclusion permitted her to develop an extraordinarily vivid awareness of the natural world, and her poetry demonstrates that she understood the extent to which everyday social circumstances would impoverish her receptivity to her surroundings:

A Light exists in Spring
Not present on the Year
At any other period—
When March is scarcely here

A Color stands abroad
On Solitary Fields
That Science cannot overtake
But Human Nature feels.

It waits upon the Lawn,
It shows the furthest Tree
Upon the furthest Slope you know
It almost speaks to you.

Then as Horizons step
Or Noons report away
Without the Formula of sound
It passes and we stay—

A quality of loss
Affecting our Content
As Trade had suddenly encroached
Upon a Sacrament.
                    (*P*, 2:613, no. 812)

To be sufficiently aware of the quality of early spring light requires concentration that could not be sustained in a law office where her brother and father worked, or a library where her cousin Frances Norcross spent her days, or especially at the tea parties that occupied Susan Gilbert's afternoons.

For Dickinson, the public self was a collection of reified, or objectified, habits that did not constitute the fundamental person. She believed in a deeper identity that she called the "soul":

The Outer—from the Inner
Derives its Magnitude—
'Tis Duke, or Dwarf, according
As is the Central Mood—

The fine—unvarying Axis
That regulates the Wheel—
Though Spokes—spin—more conspicuous
And fling a dust—the while.
                    (*P*, 1:348, no. 451)

Whereas the ritualized awareness of roles makes possible the smooth functioning of society, it does so at the expense of more complex perceptions. It is dangerous to eliminate the protective mask or to relinquish ego boundaries in a social system that is based on predatory individualism. Although the unshielded self—Dickinson's "Costumeless Consciousness" (*P*, 3 : 1007, no. 1454)—is vulnerable in a territorial world, the socialized self can survive. A person can be defined as a "have" or a "have not," a magistrate, shopkeeper, charwoman, but every role filters experience. In her room and garden, Dickinson gained some freedom from bounded, categorized existence, and she understood that a rigid persona restricts perceptions just as conventional religious treatments of mortality and salvation reduce sensitivity to the presence of eternity in our midst.

Like the heroine of her favorite poem, "Aurora Leigh," Dickinson wore white to emphasize that she had rejected marriage to dedicate herself to art.[23] Wearing white, secluding herself from the social life of Amherst, Dickinson became the high priestess of her poetry. Although her strange behavior intrigued the local gossips who referred to her as an eccentric spinster, Suzanne Juhasz, Allen Tate, and Inder Kher observe that by setting herself apart, Dickinson reinforced her identity as a poet.[24]

Like Anne Bradstreet, Emily Dickinson came from an economically advantaged family, and the circumstances of the lives of both women were similar. Bradstreet's father was a magistrate and her husband a church elder; Dickinson's father was a state legislator and her father and brother were lawyers and trustees of Amherst College. Both women lived in large houses where there were some servants; both were extremely attached to their immediate families and bound to their loved ones by elaborate ties of love and responsibility. But there were dramatic differences as well. Anne Bradstreet was the mother of eight children, and although she had some domestic help, her responsibilities were far more elaborate and time-consuming than Dickinson's. Since Dickinson remained unmarried, she could dispose of her time more freely. However, both women lived in a social universe that was highly polarized. The worlds of men and women were separate, and both Bradstreet and Dickinson defined their lives entirely within the spheres assigned to them by social custom.

As the domestic and commercial worlds became increasingly bifurcated in the nineteenth century, the traditional woman was counseled to concentrate on family responsibilities, but, as Nancy Cott and Nina Baym point out, most women did not protest their confinement to home. For them, the sewing circle, the nursery, and the kitchen were as important as the office and marketplace were to men.[25] However, many nineteenth-century women resisted the narrowing influence of the domestic ethos and perceived their homes as a place of captivity; political activists like Susan B. Anthony and Elizabeth Cady Stanton as well as writers like Charlotte Perkins Gilman, Elizabeth Stuart Phelps, and Margaret Fuller felt that women needed to participate in public life.[26]

Not until the twentieth century did a significant number of women attempt to combine marriage and a career or attempt to have both love and work.[27] During the decade of the 1920s, poets like Marianne Moore, Louise Bogan, and Edna St. Vincent Millay gained public recognition as artists, but in spite of the increasing autonomy of women, these poets were subjects of gossip and censure: Bogan had several nervous breakdowns, Millay's life was considered scandalous, and Moore denied that she had a personal life in order to escape public scrutiny. The role of the romantic artist—antisocial, rebellious, daring—was not an option for women, and these poets often felt embattled by the conflicting demands of convention and creativity.

From the time she was an adolescent, Dickinson parodied the standards of "female propriety & sedate deportment" (*L*, 1:62, no. 22); like Mark Twain, who wore white suits in ironic deference to the genteel tradition and the code of the cavalier gentleman, Emily Dickinson wore long white dresses in playful mockery of the Victorian ideal of angelic femininity. Furthermore, her white dresses announcing her "white election" were her secular version of the pristine robes of the saints of Revelation. Just as the faithful dedicated their lives to God, Dickinson consecrated herself to "the white heat of poetry." Because the Victorian code of domestic womanhood provided Dickinson with a rationale for using her time to write poetry, she was able to adapt creatively to a social system that imposed enormous limitations on women. Although the sentimental idealization of "true womanhood" was experienced as confining and destructive by many women, Dickinson protected herself by subverting the definition of woman as a private creature to serve her poetic mission.

NINE

"Earth is Heaven"

Whereas Anne Bradstreet scanned nature to discern God's message, Emily Dickinson observed the universe for its own sake. Bradstreet was taught that nature was a pale version of a glorious world to come, but Dickinson concluded that nature *was* paradise: "Earth is Heaven—/ Whether Heaven is Heaven or not" (*P*, 3 : 977, no. 1408). In contrast to the Puritans who were convinced that the will of God was revealed in the events of nature, Dickinson thought that all forms of life were interconnected and that human truths could be learned from the close observation of the animal, vegetable, and mineral worlds. Dickinson's Eden was not a lost paradise but could be found in her own garden: "if God had been here this summer and seen the things I have seen—I guess that He would think his Paradise superfluous," she wrote to Elizabeth Holland in 1856 (*L*, 2 : 329, no. 185). And in one of her poems she wrote: "Eden is that old-fashioned House / We dwell in every day" (*P*, 3 : 1131, no. 1657).

God was at the center of the Puritan world and gave significance to all events. Consciousness illuminated Dickinson's universe; instead of discerning God's will, she sought life's comprehensive pattern which she called "circumference." Unlike Bradstreet, she did not perceive the world as having a divine purpose but as an end in itself. Dickinson looked for connecting patterns instead of metaphysical explanations, and she was less concerned with what *should be* than with what *was*. For her, free will superseded faith, and life was not a foreordained event but an adventure in which exploration and discovery were most important. Emily Dickinson's poetic vision is essentially holistic, generative, and comprehensive rather than linear, compartmentalized, and categorical. The interconnection of sight and sound, word and object, form and feeling, poetic image and natural phenomena fascinated her and her poetry manifests her desire to resolve the dualisms of flesh and spirit, salvation and damnation, mortality and immortality. Instead of Anne Bradstreet's moral allegories or religious meditations that attempt to explain the ways of God to man, Dickinson used pun and paradox, enigmatic images and cryptic phrases to explore the conundrum of Puritan dichotomies.[1]

Most of Dickinson's poems are short—many are only four lines long—and although some readers find them diminutive and self-effacing, her terse verses tease the mind, piercing religious and cultural illusions with their wry observations and ironic wit: "Existence with a wall / Is better to consider / Than not exist at all—" (P, 3 : 1130, no. 1652). By disrupting conventional linguistic habits, her condensed phrases, inverted syntax, and frequent dashes bring words that might otherwise be ignored to our attention and her highly individualized poetic method and style forces us to examine our language and our lives. This re-vision of our habitual perceptions is what Pound meant when he urged poets to "make it new" and what William Carlos Williams wanted when he called for the "birth of a new language."[2] Like Walt Whitman, Emily Dickinson succeeded in creating an American idiom, but there are dramatic differences between Whitman's expansive, assertive lines and Dickinson's involuted, concise stanzas. Although both poets were influenced by Emerson and both were alienated from commercialism as well as traditional definitions of gender, the white-robed recluse and the peripatetic homosexual had very different views. Their contrasting styles and visions characterize the essential differences between patriarchal and gynecocentric modes of perception—differences that can easily be seen in two appositive sets of poems about spiders and about locomotives. The first set—Whitman's "A noiseless patient spider" and Dickinson's "The Spider holds a Silver Ball"—represents contrasting views of projective and interior consciousness:

A noiseless patient spider,
I mark'd where on a little promontory it stood isolated,
Mark'd how to explore the vacant vast surrounding,
It launch'd forth filament, filament, filament, out of itself,
Ever unreeling down, ever tirelessly speeding them.

And you O my soul where you stand,
Surrounded, detached, in measureless oceans of space,
Ceaselessly musing, venturing, throwing, seeking the spheres to
  connect them,
Till the bridge you will need be form'd, till the ductile anchor hold,
Till the gossamer thread you fling catch somewhere, O my soul.[3]

In the first stanza of Whitman's poem, the poet-observer portrays the spider as "isolated" on a phallic promontory "launching forth," or ejaculating, threads out of itself in order to build a bridge to the external world.

Significantly, only the spider's tireless efforts can connect the two realms of subject and object. This separation of the spider from the "vacant vast surrounding" is characteristic of the masculine oppositional mode. In the second stanza, the spider's activity is a metaphor for the poet's soul which is also differentiated from its surroundings—"detached, in measureless oceans of space." Like the spider seeking to anchor itself in the external world through its prodigious spinning, the soul must persevere in its effort to connect with the realms outside itself. Although the outer space is boundless, the poet is confident that industrious activity will enable the spider, and the soul, to impinge on its vastness. Whitman's confidence in projective effort mirrors the conviction of the nineteenth-century industrialists and their Puritan ancestors who, in the name of progress or God, saw themselves as bringing civilization to the wilderness or divine order to unregenerate chaos.

Dickinson's spider is observed for its own sake—its activities and territory are not subsumed by the poet's egocentric identification with it as in Whitman's poem. And in contrast to Whitman's filament-launching spider whose activities are directed toward an external goal, Dickinson's spider listens to its internal rhythm "dancing softly to Himself":

The Spider holds a Silver Ball
In unperceived Hands—
And dancing softly to Himself
His yarn of Pearl—unwinds—

He plies from Nought to Nought—
In unsubstantial Trade—
Supplants our Tapestries with His—
In half the period—

An Hour to rear supreme
His Continents of Light—
Then dangle from the Housewife's Broom—
His boundaries—forgot—
(P, 2:464, no. 605)

Dickinson's poem describes the actual process of creating a web while Whitman describes an imaginary activity—spiders do not randomly cast threads into the void but, in fact, follow a careful pattern attaching threads securely to objects whether they be ceiling beams or tree branches. In place of Whitman's bridge-building metaphor, Dickinson describes her spider as weaving evanescent webs. The emphasis is on the playful process of spinning rather than on the achievement of an external goal. In addition,

Dickinson writes from the spider's point of view and does not subsume its identity. In contrast to Whitman's spider whose activities produce lasting results, the intricate tapestries of Dickinson's spider are created in an hour, and these "Continents of Light" can be destroyed in an instant by the "Housewife's Broom." Impermanence rather than permanence is stressed as is the process of spinning rather than productive activity. Receptivity to internal rhythms rather than mastery or agency is Dickinson's concern. If Dickinson's spider is a metaphor for her soul, one can safely say that her view of herself as a poet is less assertive, more self-contained, less egocentric, and more aware of relative perspectives than is Whitman's.

Another pair of poems that illuminates these stylistic differences is Whitman's "To a Locomotive in Winter," and Dickinson's "I like to see it lap the Miles—" (P, 2:447–48, no. 585). Both poets choose the metaphor of the horse to convey the size and speed of the train, but Whitman's steed is wild and threatens to gallop out of control while Dickinson's ultimately submits to its reins. Invoking the majestic power of the engine, Whitman likens it to a mighty stallion whose awesome power is epic in scale: "Thy black cylindric body, golden brass and silvery steel / Thy ponderous side-bars, parallel and connecting rods, gyrating / Shuttling at thy sides."[4] Although Dickinson's locomotive is also larger than life—"I like to see it lap the miles— / And lick the Valleys Up"—its force is not overwhelming. Unlike Whitman's "Fierce-throated beauty" with its "lawless music," Dickinson's horse is controlled by its bridle—its Boanergeian neigh silenced at the will of its rider:

> Then—punctual as a Star
> Stop—docile and omnipotent
> At its own stable door—
> (P, 2:447–48, no. 585)

Dickinson views the locomotive with wry amusement; she does not mythologize the engine as the embodiment of freedom, "Law of thyself complete," as Whitman does. In contrast to Whitman's glorification of the machine as an embodiment of national power and collective energy, her irony does not let us forget for a minute that this powerful horse is a mechanical device that can be turned on and off. Whitman's locomotive has agency—it dominates the landscape subject to no external restraints—while Dickinson's prodigious train follows definite tracks, and though it consumes the space it traverses, it is inherently tame. A letter to Austin on February 6, 1852, reveals Dickinson's lack of enthusiasm for technology, which she sees as an expression of the masculine need to control the environment as well as to make money: "Since we have seen you, the grand Rail Road decision is made, and there is great rejoicing throughout the town. . . . Father is really *sober* from excessive satisfaction."[5] Like Thoreau, Dickinson resented the railroad's invasion of the pastoral life of the New England villages.

In general, these two sets of poems by Dickinson and Whitman reflect the differences in traditional masculine and feminine consciousness in the nineteenth century. Whitman's declarative style expresses confidence in male agency, aggression, and ultimate mastery. His poems are replete with assertive phrases—"I challenge," "I see," "I say," "I swear," "I teach," and "I think." As the following lines from "Song of Myself" demonstrate, Whitman stands in the center of the universe: "All the forces have been steadily employ'd to complete and delight me, / Now in this spot I stand with my robust soul."[6] In contrast to this cheerful egocentricity, Dickinson is primarily concerned with relationship, interconnection, and empathic representation. She is more sensitive to the subtle textures of her private world, whereas Whitman's catalogs of places and lists of names create sweeping panoramas of public life. Paradoxically, the sequestered Dickinson is much less self-absorbed than the freely roaming Whitman.

The renegade Whitman wandered the streets and cities of America and embraced the role of mythmaker for a growing nation, but the role of artist as creator initially frightened Dickinson, who, as we have seen, inherited the Puritan legacy of distrust of the unfettered imagination; like Hawthorne and Melville, she was sometimes paralyzed by artistic autonomy. Not only was the artist's ability to create a world apart from God an awesome responsibility but Dickinson's anxiety was intensified by nineteenth-century proscriptions against female assertion. As Sandra Gilbert and Susan Gubar observe, female literary achievement was enormously difficult in a world that expected women to be submissive.[7]

For Dickinson, the wilderness was not a primeval forest but the unknown landscape of her psyche. Her poems explore emotional mysteries—love, grief, joy, fury, exhilaration, tenderness—which are observed and charted. Sometimes she leaps into the void, or "infinity," in an effort to understand what follows death. As she voyaged into new psychic territory, she wrote to illuminate her path, and her poems exist as points of bright light in the sometimes dark expanse of her experience. Although much of Dickinson's life and work can be described as part of the Romantic tradition, especially insofar as she grants primacy to her imagination, she nevertheless remains grounded in the quotidian, and it is this commitment to mundane experience that constitutes the basis of the female literary countertradition. As we have seen, Anne Bradstreet was reluctant to relinquish her attachment to daily life in order to undergo the divine translation to heaven, and Emily Dickinson refuses to deny the centrality of her immediate experience, even if it is negative, in the name of imaginative transcendence.[8] Implicit in the female ethos is the conviction that the individual can neither tame nature nor control the external world and that the hierarchical ordering of the body as inferior to the mind and women as inferior to men is an expression of male dominance. Therefore Dickinson had no need to discount her physical experiences. On the contrary, she trusted her senses to teach her important truths. No flower's petal or bee's wing went unnoticed. Her ears were alert to bird-songs, thunder, the morning breeze. Unlike Bradstreet, who ultimately tried to subdue her physical self in an effort to liberate her soul, Dickinson did not reject her corporeal being. In her version of the dialogue between the mind and the body, she wrote:

> The Spirit lurks within the Flesh
> Like Tides within the Sea
> That make the Water live, estranged
> What would the Either be?
> (P, 3:1086, no. 1576)

Sensory experience, then, was a source of emotional or spiritual knowledge. Because Victorian society, like Puritan society, was based on the bifurcation of the flesh and the spirit, Emily Dickinson's belief in the interdependence of body and mind, like Anne Hutchinson's concept of the genderless soul, had startling social implications.

As a Victorian woman, Emily Dickinson was trained to think relationally and did not automatically divide her world into the opposing realms of self and other; therefore, the brooding alienation of much Romantic poetry is absent in her work. Instead of willful individualism and an effort to transcend the temporal world, Dickinson evolved a nurturing vision based on a cyclical flux of interconnected life forms. Paralleling Dickinson's understanding of the spiritual symbiosis of mind and body is her awareness that life and death are inextricably intertwined. Death was a painful certainty for Dickinson, yet life was more precious because it offered an opportunity, however brief, to be part of the immense and complicated earth. The acceptance of mortality sharpened her awareness and appreciation of life and gave depth and resonance to her work:

> To be alive—is Power—
> Existence—in itself—

Without a further function—
Omnipotence—Enough—

To be alive—and Will!
'Tis able as a God—
The Maker—of Ourselves—be what—
Such being Finitude!
(*P*, 2:523, no. 677)

This poem contains the kernel of Dickinson's cosmology: life as an end in itself is inherently powerful, while life dedicated to control can create the illusion of omnipotence but ultimately exposes the limitations of human will. As we have seen, Emily Dickinson tends to equate respect for life force with women and the desire to dominate existence with men.

In keeping with her description of herself as a poet of the "Barefoot Rank" (*L*, 2:408, no. 265), the recurrent themes of her poetry—the undeniable yet fearful fact of mortality, the power of the nurturing ethos, nature's plenitude, the joy of solitude, the pleasure of friendship—are common chords of human experience. The language of her poems is generally plain, unadorned, and not elaborately ornamental: "I watched her face to see which way / She took the awful news" (*P*, 3:1136, no. 1667). Her images are taken from ordinary, everyday experience, which is nevertheless highly personal. It is this radical subjectivity that makes her metaphors so startling and powerful: death is described as "the Supple Suitor" (*P*, 3:1001, no. 1445); nature as "the Gentlest Mother" (*P*, 1:596, no. 790); frost as "the blonde Assassin" (*P*, 3:1114, no. 1624); the hills as "My Strong Madonnas" (*P*, 2:553, no. 722); God as the "Frontier" (*P*, 2:769, no. 1090); sin as "a distinguished Precipice" (*P*, 3:1066, no. 1545). "Consciousness is—Noon" (*P*, 2:745, no. 1056); "Experience is the Angled Road" (*P*, 2:668, no. 910); the moon a "Chin of Gold" (*P*, 2:562, no. 737). Mixing visual and auditory images, she creates highly individual effects: "There's a certain Slant of light, / Winter Afternoons—That oppresses, like the Heft of Cathedral Tunes—" (*P*, 1:185, no. 258), or "The wind drew off / like hungry dogs" (*P*, 3:1149, no. 1694). Sometimes she describes the psyche in geographical metaphors: "The Heart is the Capital of the Mind—" (*P*, 3:935, no. 1354). Often her visual effects are as starkly dramatic as an abstract painting: "A Lane of Yellow led the eye / Unto a Purple Wood" (*P*, 3:1129, no. 1650). Other poems capture the precise texture of the subject with photographic exactness: "The Bat is dun, with wrinkled Wings—" (*P*, 3:1035, no. 1575).

Like Anne Bradstreet, Dickinson incorporates biblical phrases and images in her poetry, but Dickinson's attitude was playful, not pious. Ironic use of religious mythology characterizes much of her work:

> The Bible is an antique Volume—
> Written by faded Men
> At the suggestion of Holy Spectres—
> Subjects—Bethlehem—
> Eden—the ancient Homestead—
> Satan—the Brigadier—
> Judas—the Great Defaulter—
> David—the Troubadour—
> Sin—a distinguished Precipice
> Others must resist—
> Boys that "believe" are very lonesome—
> Other Boys are "lost"—
> Had but the Tale a warbling Teller—
> All Boys would come—
> Orpheus' Sermon captivated—
> It did not condemn—
> (P, 3 : 1065–66, no. 1545)

Not only does Dickinson relegate theology to the province of men and boys, but she criticizes the punitive orientation of the Judeo-Christian heritage with a reference to the myth of Orpheus whose music charmed the rulers of the underworld. In addition, she parodies the patterns of language and metrical forms of traditional hymns, especially those of the well-known hymnist Isaac Watts (1674–1748). The rigid 4–3–4–3 meters of Watts's hymns provide the ground bass against which she syncopates many of her poetic lines. Dickinson's version has the rhythmic complexity of jazz in contrast to the rigid regularity of Watts's heavily rhymed lines. Although she reacted against Watts's predictable meters, they did provide a springboard for her variations.

The following hymn by Watts illustrates his steady cadences and inexorable rhymes:

> God of the Seas, thy thundering Voice
> Makes all the roaring Waves rejoyce,
> And one soft Word of thy Command
> Can sink them silent in the Sand.
> If but a Moses wave thy Rod,
> The Sea divides and owns its God;

The stormy Floods their maker knew,
And let his chosen Armies thro!

The Scaly Flocks amidst the Sea
To thee their Lord a Tribute pay;
The meanest Fish that swims the Flood
Leaps up, and means a Praise to God.[9]

The slant rhymes, lively rhythms, and colloquial language of Dickinson's poem on the same theme provide a dramatic contrast with the pedestrian couplets and metrical regularity of Watts's hymn:

"Red Sea," indeed! Talk not to me
Of purple Pharaoh—
I have a Navy in the West
Would pierce his Column thro'
Guileless, yet of such Glory fine
That all along the Line
Is it, or is it not, Marine—
Is it, or not divine—
The Eye inquires with a sigh
That Earth should be so big—
What Exultation in the Woe—
What Wine in the fatigue!
            (P, 3:1124, no. 1642)

Here Dickinson satirizes the biblical narrative of the avenging God who commands the seas to part and undercuts the notion that all earthly life should pay obeisance to a master. The last stanza implies that God's faithful band takes immense pleasure in the strenuous opposition to deadly foes. Again, while undermining hierarchical religion and male mastery, Emily Dickinson associates diversity and vitality with the female earth and constricting domination with the male God and his heaven.

Similarly, Dickinson mocked the pious certainties of Watts's "Christ Jesus, the Lamb of God, worshiped by all the creation" from Rev. 5:11, 12, 13:

Let all that dwell above the sky,
      And Air, and Earth, and Seas
Conspire to lift thy Glory high,
      And speak thine endless Praise.

The whole Creation join in one,
    To bless the Sacred Name
Of him that sits upon the Throne,
    And to adore the Lamb.[10]

Dickinson's version playfully undercuts the swelling grandeur of Watts's lines, reiterating her conviction that earth is paradise:

Who has not found the Heaven—below—
Will fail of it above—
For Angels rent the House next our's,
Wherever we remove—
               (*P*, 3 : 1065, no. 1544)

Dickinson rebelled against Watts's metrics, just as she resisted Calvinist theology. Sometimes she satirized his strict scansion, which she found too confining; for her, poetry was defined by the phrase and not the meticulous convention of the foot. Instead of inexorable and deadening metrical stress, Dickinson used dashes to indicate pauses. Her innovative poetics had a profound influence on modern poets. William Carlos Williams, who called Emily Dickinson "his patron saint," acknowledged her influence on his poetry. His concept of the variable foot as a relative, not a fixed, stress, using the breath and inflection of American speech instead of rigid accent and measured syllables to determine phrase and line length, is based on Dickinson's flexible, organic metrics.[11] Similarly inspired by Dickinson's poetry are Robert Frost's "sentence sounds"— the rhythms of everyday speech loosely structured by standard poetic forms—and Ezra Pound's "functional," as opposed to "forced," metrics.

Often jagged and unpredictable, Dickinson's unusual poetic rhythms capture the surprise and wonder with which she approached life. Higginson complained that her meters were too "spasmodic," that her poetic rhythms were rough and untutored (*L*, 2:409, no. 265). Yet it is this highly individual verbal timing that makes Dickinson's poems so vivid and charged. Sometimes her rhymes zigzag across the line proceeding at strange angles. Sometimes there is a driving energy in the rhythm: "To pile like Thunder to it's close / Then crumble grand away" (*P*, 3:866, no. 1247). At other times the rhythms are syncopated:

Uncertain lease—developes lustre
On Time
Uncertain grasp, appreciation
of Sum—

The shorter Fate—is oftener the chiefest
Because
Inheritors upon a tenure
Prize—

(P, 2:642, no. 857)

The irregular or inverted syntax of Dickinson's poems sometimes confused her friends and continues to puzzle readers today, but Lois Cuddy
has demonstrated that many of Dickinson's idiosyncratic constructions
are actually derived from her adaptation of Latin models for her own
purposes.[12] As Cuddy points out, her strange inversions of language—
"Rekindled by some action quaint" (P, 3:1017, no. 1468); omission of
auxiliary verbs, "Before it [can] see the Sun!" (P, 3:870, no. 1255); use
of adjectives and verbs as nouns, "We talk in *careless*—and in *toss*—" (P,
2:510, no. 663); use of adverbs as nouns, "I lingered with Before—" (P,
2:467, no. 609); conclusion of sentences or clauses with verbs, "Nor
what consoled it, I could trace—" (P, 2:447, no. 584)—are actually
based on rules of grammar outlined in *A Grammar of the Latin Language: For the Use of Schools and Colleges* (Boston, 1843) that Dickinson used as a student.[13] Just as Dickinson used Watts's hymns as ground-
ing for her poetic variations, she used classical forms of grammar and
syntax—hyperbaton, anastrophe, hysteron proteron, hypallage, syn-
crisis, enallage, aphaeresis, parenthesis, and ellipsis—to create her own
highly individual meters and rhymes, which Higginson dismissed as "uncontrolled" but which, in fact, help to make her style essentially modern.

As we have seen, many of Dickinson's poems reflect the rhythms of nature—the rising and setting of the sun, a succession of the seasons; they
are concerned with the unfolding present and with cyclic rather than sequential time. Higginson recalled that Dickinson could not tell conventional clock time until she was an adolescent: "I never knew how to tell
time by the clock until I was fifteen. My father thought he had taught me,
but I did not understand and I was afraid to ask anyone lest he should
know."[14] Although nineteenth-century society was becoming increasingly
dependent on clocks, timetables, and schedules, Dickinson's world was
largely atemporal. As Thoreau observed in *Walden*, once the railroad
schedule becomes a social priority, the rhythms of nature are lost. The
preoccupation with hours and minutes—linear time—obscures broader
experiential patterns. Sharon Cameron suggests that Dickinson experienced considerable conflict between the opposing forces of time and eternity, but, in fact, Dickinson simply did not accept traditional definitions
of temporality or life everlasting.[15]

Dickinson's resistance to clock time paralleled her refusal to accept conventional notions of eternity. Throughout her life she questioned belief in heaven as it was depicted in the Bible and resented the traditional effort to measure and quantify time that for her was shaped by emotional intensity and experiential content:

Two Lengths has every Day—
It's absolute extent
And Area superior
By Hope or Horror lent—

Eternity will be
Velocity or Pause
At Fundamental Signals
From Fundamental Laws

To die is not to go—
On Doom's consummate Chart
No Territory new is staked—
Remain thou as thou art.
   (*P*, 3:898–99, no. 1295)

Just as time measured in hours, minutes, and seconds constricts awareness, so the traditional notion of an afterlife as a specific time and place following death impoverishes our experience of the present. In addition, dying is not a "divine translation" into a new being as the Puritans believed but a bequest of legacies to loved ones. Prefiguring such modern poets as Wallace Stevens who wrote "death is the mother of beauty," Dickinson makes it clear that accepting and constantly remembering the reality of death affects our experience of life:

The Admirations—and Contempts—of time—
Show justest—through an Open Tomb—
The Dying—as it were a Hight
Reorganizes Estimate
And what We saw not
We distinguish clear—
and mostly—see not
What We saw before—

'Tis Compound Vision—
Light—enabling Light—
The Finite—furnished
With the Infinite—
Convex—and Concave Witness—

> Back—toward Time—
> And forward—
> Toward the God of Him—
> (*P*, 2:666, no. 906)

This "Compound Vision" composed of what is and is not there, presence and absence, past and future, "Convex" and "Concave," enables us to distinguish and appreciate the texture of the moment that is thrown into relief by the reality of death. For Dickinson, eternity lends depth to the present; it is not a transcendent place or a numeric extension of days and nights into an endless future but a perspective of time, an additional dimension illuminating every moment:

> The Blunder is in estimate
> Eternity is there
> We say, as of a Station
> Meanwhile he is so near
> He joins me in my Ramble
> Divides abode with me
> No Friend have I that so persists
> As this Eternity
> (*P*, 3:1144–45, no. 1684)

In both poems the word "estimate" is characteristic of hierarchical thought—it represents an effort to determine, measure, define, or locate such phenomena as time and eternity that cannot by their nature be concretized or quantified. For Dickinson, eternity is the unfolding present, not a destination or location.

Dickinson's belief that "Forever—is composed of Nows—" (*P*, 2:480, no. 624) (which Adrienne Rich echoes in her poem "Not Somewhere Else, But Here") reinforced her commitment to process and her immersion in the present. Even her work habits express this orientation. In his introduction to the standard edition of her poetry, Thomas Johnson tells us that she often wrote on scraps of paper, on flaps or backs of envelopes, discarded letters, wrapping paper, edges of newspaper—in fact, on anything that lay conveniently at hand.[16] She continually revised her poems, and "more than once she turned a fair copy into a worksheet draft which she ultimately abandoned, thus leaving the poem in a particularly chaotic state."[17] Some of her poems were polished, some were still in the process of achieving final form when she died. Her writing technique was very much like patchwork quilting; each poem was composed of carefully worked lines and each group of poems made the larger pattern visible.[18]

Often she used phrases from her letters in her poems; sometimes she used the same expression several times in letters to her various friends; for example, she used the phrase "box of Phantoms" to refer to lost friendships in her letters to Susan Gilbert (L, 2:315, no. 177) and John Graves (L, 2:330, no. 186). This repeated use of the same phrase indicates Dickinson's striving for artistic effect. Although there has been considerable controversy about the ordering of Dickinson's poems, it seems clear that her use of fascicles was an attempt to create an organic mode for the presentation of her poems.[19] The word *fascicle*, which her sister Lavinia used to describe the packets of sewn poems, is also a botanical term referring to a flower pattern in which the petals spring irregularly from the top of a main stem like a peony. In binding her poems in fascicular packets, Emily Dickinson chose an appropriate form for the blossoming of her poems; each poem was a petal, each packet a flower.

Hers was an aristocratic existence. Like the Touchetts who are served tea while they sit in capacious wicker chairs on a carpet on the lawn of their Gardencourt estate outside of London in the opening paragraphs of Henry James's *Portrait of a Lady*, Emily Dickinson savored her comfortable life. Her leisure, provided by her father's wealth, enabled her to perceive life in terms of wholes; utilitarian necessity did not contract her world into automatic patterns of perception. In the protected space of home, she was able to experience intense emotions fully and to correlate the patterns of her inner life with those she found in nature. And she used her protected status to evolve an ethos that was based on feminine values; to coexist with nature, not to control it, was her purpose.

Dickinson's upper-middle-class background permitted her the leisure to pursue her philosophical and aesthetic priorities. Since Dickinson was not driven to publish for money, she could develop and express her imagination however she chose. In addition, Dickinson could worship the fertility of the earth because she did not have to endure the strain of cultivating it alone under harsh circumstances—she had a gardener. The Dickinson gardener, MacGregor Jenkins, provides us with an illuminating portrait of Emily Dickinson:

> One summer morning . . . Miss Emily called me. She was standing on a rug spread for her on the grass, busy with the potted plants which were all about her, . . . a beautiful woman dressed in white, with soft, fiery, brown eyes and a mass of auburn hair. . . . [S]he talked to me of her flowers, of those she loved best; of her fear lest the bad weather harm them; then, cutting a few choice buds, she bade me take them, with her love, to my mother.[20]

However, Dickinson knew that her fortunate circumstances could easily be taken away, as a nightmare she had as an adolescent reveals: she dreamed that her "Father had failed & mother said that our rye field which she & I planted, was mortgaged to Seth Nims" (*L*, 1:48, no. 16). Her father's money had bought her privileged life, and his financial failure could deprive her of it.

Because Amherst was still removed from the industrial urbanization of the Northeastern cities like Boston, Dickinson escaped the despair that Blake and Wordsworth experienced when factory smokestacks fouled London's air. Dickinson never experienced Hart Crane's horror of the subway, or T. S. Eliot's depression in the urban slums of London and New York City, or the outrage of William Carlos Williams when he discovered that the Passaic was polluted. Amherst's rivers were not yet contaminated, the air was still fresh and sweet, the streets were not lined with anonymous apartment houses and chain stores. At the same time, as Raymond Williams points out, the wealth created by industrial cities like Boston made the bucolic life of the Connecticut Valley possible.[21] Dickinson knew that it was only a matter of time before Amherst became more connected to the larger world of commerce. As we have seen, her father, who was the director of the project to bring the railroad to Amherst, finally succeeded in doing so in 1852.

Dickinson was not an apologist for a simpleminded prelapsarian ideal of a new Eden, nor did she indulge in a Romantic idealization of pastoral life. Instead, she consciously used her protected status to record the world as she saw it; her desire was to understand and to appreciate life. Her pleasure in nature was often startlingly direct: "The Frogs sing sweet—Today" (*L*, 2:406, no. 262). Most often, her perceptions were astonishingly complex and original: "A circus passed the house—still I feel the red in my mind though the drums are out" (*L*, 2:452, no. 318). Because she did not fragment her awareness, synaesthetic descriptions that interweave sounds, smells, and tastes are scattered throughout her letters: "The lawn is full of south and the odors tangle, and I hear today for the first the river in the tree," she wrote to Elizabeth Holland in May 1866 (*L*, 2:452, no. 318).

Although Dickinson appeared to affect a childlike innocence, she rejected the pastoral convention of linking rural innocence with an unblemished heart:

> The Sky is low—the Clouds are mean.
> A Travelling Flake of Snow
> Across a Barn or through a Rut
> Debates if it will go—
>
> A Narrow Wind complains all Day
> How some one treated him

> Nature, like Us is sometimes caught
> Without her Diadem.
> > (*P*, 2:760, no. 1075)

By attending to the full range of her emotions, she avoided the excesses of the cult of scenery. Nature could be wantonly destructive as well as awesome or sublime:

> Nature—sometimes sears a Sapling—
> Sometimes—scalps a Tree—
> Her Green People recollect it
> When they do not die—
>
> Fainter Leaves—to Further Seasons—
> Dumbly testify—
> We—who have the Souls—
> Die oftener—Not so vitally—
> > (*P*, 1:237–38, no. 314)

Emily Dickinson insists on responding to the entire range of experience including nature's capacity for horrible cruelty:

> Through fissures in
> Volcanic cloud
> The yellow lightning shone—
> The trees held up
> Their mangled limbs
> Like animals in pain
> > (*P*, 3:1149, no. 1694)

Dickinson was concerned with the full range of positive and negative aspects in her experience, and she remained especially fascinated by death, in the natural as well as the human world:

> Death is like the insect
> Menacing the tree,
> Competent to kill it,
> But decoyed may be.
>
> Bait it with the balsam,
> Seek it with the saw,
> Baffle, if it cost you
> Everything you are.

Then, if it have burrowed
Out of reach of skill—
Wring the tree and leave it,
'Tis the vermin's will.
     (*P*, 3:1158, no. 1716)

Cultivating a consciousness that resonated with nature's rhythms, she worked to create a poetic language that conveyed their total breadth. The ambiguity and mystery in Dickinson's poems express her understanding that language simplifies reality and is an approximation of experiential complexity. One hundred years later, Adrienne Rich was to decry the limitations of language that embody the limitations of patriarchy.

To Anne Bradstreet life was an errand into the wilderness of the New World, but Emily Dickinson was on an "errand from the heart." Whereas Bradstreet prayed for guidance through life's snares, Dickinson explored the mysteries of the human heart and nature's secrets and felt gratitude for the awesome adventure of life:

But awed beyond my errand—
I worshipped—did not "pray"—
     (*P*, 2:431, no. 564)

Emily Dickinson stands as a pivotal poet between the Puritans and the moderns. Her work refers back to the Puritan drama of salvation, which provided the scaffolding for Anne Bradstreet's poetry; it also anticipates the complexity of modern consciousness, the relativity of social, historical, and moral values, and the quest for a new society based on human need rather than religious ideals, a vision that is explored more extensively by Adrienne Rich.

TEN

"The skill of life"

Throughout her life, Emily Dickinson had very intense and sustaining friendships with women. She had a lifelong bond with her sister Lavinia, and her tie to her sister-in-law Susan Gilbert Dickinson lasted for many decades. Her early friendships with Abiah Root and Jane Humphrey were very close, as were her relationships with her cousins, Louise and Frances Norcross. In the years after her religious and romantic crises, her adult friends Mary Bowles and Elizabeth Holland were especially important to her. Nancy Cott observes that many nineteenth-century women considered their relationships with other women to be morally superior to those with men because they excluded male carnality; the "passionless" nature of these friendships was a source of intense solidarity among these women.[1] The voluntary groups and affiliative organizations that grew out of this collective identity formed the basis for the suffragist movement of the nineteenth century and the feminist movement of the twentieth century.

As an adolescent Dickinson developed her sense of self through her female friendships: "[W]hen will that hour *be* that we shall sit together and talk of what we were, and what we *are* and may be—" (*L*, 1 : 130, no. 50). Sharing a fantasy of future adventures with Susan Dickinson, she expressed her deep need to be independent and to evolve an identity that would withstand the cultural edicts against female autonomy:

> It is such an evening Susie, as you and I would walk and have such pleasant musings, if you were only here—perhaps we would have a "Reverie" after the form of "Ik Marvel," indeed I do not know why it wouldn't be just as charming as of that lonely Bachelor, smoking his cigar—and it would be far more profitable as "Marvel" *only* marvelled, and you and I would *try* to make a little destiny to have for our own. (*L*, 1 : 144, no. 56)

Reveries of a Bachelor by Ik Marvel, the pseudonym of Donald G. Mitchell (1851), was a popular sentimental narration of a bachelor's imaginary adventures,[2] but much as she enjoyed this book, Emily Dickinson was not content with vicarious travels—she wanted adventures of her own.

As a young woman, Dickinson formed the habit of retreating to her room in order to write poetry and letters to her friends. These secluded hours taught her to stay alone for long periods, and during this time she learned to develop her imaginative powers and to focus her attention on matters that were important to her. For example, she wrote to Abiah Root on August 3, 1845, "My writing apparatus is upon a stand before me, and all things are ready. I have no flowers before me as you had to inspire you. But then you know I can imagine myself inspired by them and perhaps that will do as well" (L, 1 : 15, no. 7).

While alone, the young Dickinson gave much thought to her future, and her letters to her friends indicate that she was trying to come to terms with issues of marriage and sexuality. In early June 1852, when Dickinson was twenty-one years old, she wrote to Susan Gilbert:

> How dull our lives must seem to the bride, and the plighted
> maiden, whose days are fed with gold, and who gathers pearls
> every evening; but to the *wife*, Susie, sometimes the *wife forgotten*,
> our lives perhaps seem dearer than all others in the world; you
> have seen flowers at morning, *satisfied* with the dew, and those
> same sweet flowers at noon with their heads bowed in anguish be-
> fore the mighty sun; think you these thirsty blossoms will *now*
> need nought but—*dew*? No, they will cry for sunlight, and pine for
> the burning noon, tho' it scorches them, scathes them; they have
> got through with peace—they know that the man of noon, is
> *mightier* than the morning and their life is henceforth to him. Oh,
> Susie, it is dangerous, and it is all too dear, these simple, trusting
> spirits, and the spirits mightier, which we cannot resist! It does so
> rend me, Susie, the thought of it when it comes, that I tremble lest
> at sometime I, too, am yielded up. (L, 1 : 210, no. 93)

Interestingly, Dickinson sees women represented by the flowers as colluding in their own demise by crying and pining for the searing sun even though it is damaging to them. Implicit in the diction of this paragraph is an understanding that the meaning of the word passion is "to suffer"; but Dickinson is disturbed by the one-sided suffering of women who seem to be inexorably drawn to the powerful male. Although Dickinson hopes to remain unscathed, she fears that she too will have no choice in the matter, that she too will be sacrificed on the altar of love and destroyed as a person and as a poet.[3] But as she grew older, she understood that women are not literally flowers and have no need to compulsively follow men if it is not in their self-interest to do so. Dickinson's tenacious independence contrasts with Anne Bradstreet's reluctant acceptance of the male principle as the governing force in the universe.

Lamenting the women whose lives are sacrificed to men in marriage, Dickinson sympathizes with "these simple, trusting spirits," who are overpowered by "the man of noon, [who] is *mightier*." Her underscoring of the word "mightier" emphasizes physical force, which was often cited as the basis of male dominance in the nineteenth century. In Hawthorne's *Blithedale Romance* Hollingsworth succinctly summarizes the rationale for the traditional distribution of power between the sexes: "All the separate action of woman is, and has ever been, and always shall be, false, foolish, vain, destructive. . . . man is a wretch without woman; but a woman is a monster . . . without man as her acknowledged principal! . . . I would call upon my own sex to use its physical force, the unmistakeable evidence of sovereignty, to scourge them back within their proper bounds."[4] This passage closely parallels *The Woman Question*, a diatribe against women by Orestes Brownson, which he published in his *Quarterly Review*, in October 1873: "As an independent existence, free to follow her own fancies and vague longings, her own ambition and natural love of power, without masculine direction or control, she is out of her element, and a social anomaly, sometimes a hideous monster. . . . women need a head, and the restraint of father, husband, or priest of God."[5] Echoing the accusations against Anne Hutchinson by Winthrop and Dudley, Brownson makes it clear that female assertion was seen as a breach of nature as well as an act of insubordination. Turning Brownson's tirade on its head a century later, Adrienne Rich writes, "A thinking woman sleeps with monsters."[6] From Rich's feminist perspective the monstrosity lies on the male side of the argument.

After considerable reflection about the issues of female autonomy and dependence, Emily Dickinson decided to remain single. Having achieved psychological independence at home, she was loathe to risk sacrificing her hard-won gains to a traditional marriage—male direction and control were precisely what she did not want or need. In a letter to Kate Scott Turner six years after her discourse on the man of noon, she outlined the rewards and risks of the unmarried life:

> What are your qualifications? Dare you dwell in the *East* where we dwell? Are you afraid of the Sun?—When you hear the new violet sucking her way among the sods, shall you be *resolute*? All *we* are *strangers*—dear—The world is not acquainted with us, because we are not acquainted with her. And Pilgrims!—Do you hesitate? and *Soldiers* oft—some of us victors. . . . We are hungry, and thirsty, sometimes—We are barefoot—and cold—
> Will you still come? (*L*, 2:349, no. 203)

Strangers, pilgrims, soldiers, sometimes victors—Dickinson chose words that indicate the arduousness of her struggle for independence and autonomy. This passage that echoes the language of Heb. 11 : 13 – 16 rings with militant purpose and conveys the resolution of the sisterhood of single women to survive, even to prevail, in defiance of great odds. The images of soldiers in common battle and pilgrims with a shared mission so characteristic of American thought emphasize Dickinson's determination to choose the conditions under which she would live her life.

Perhaps in agreement with Emerson's observation that "the sublime vision comes to the pure and simple soul in a clean and chaste body,"[7] Dickinson remained unmarried. In her later years Dickinson had no doubt that she had made a wise decision, declaring that she was "born for Bachelorhood." It is noteworthy that Dickinson chooses the word *bachelorhood*, which was a positive state while spinsterhood was not; Dickinson used the former because she wanted to claim for herself the privileges of the independent life. *Spinster* was a word that emerged in the nineteenth century to refer to an unmarried woman who lived in her married sister's household or who remained at home; although these women did the family spinning in order to contribute to their room and board, the word suggests a dull dependence.[8] Bachelorhood was the state enjoyed by Ik Marvel, the narrator of *Reveries*, as he sat by his fireside traveling over the world in his imagination. Although Marvel observed in the preface to the 1872 edition of his narrative that only bachelors and spinsters have the necessary detachment to observe "all phases of married life . . . which makes them intrepid in their observations,"[9] he did not grant the same liberty to women that he enjoyed himself, as demonstrated by his female protagonist, a spinster-recluse named Bella whose primary role is renunciatory and redemptive. In his typology of women Marvel describes two types of women—the "sea-coal, bituminous" or sexual woman, and the "anthracite" woman, usually a spinster who tends the sick and leaves at her death a packet of inspiring letters describing her ordeal. Like Bella, Emily Dickinson left packets of her writings, but instead of describing scenes of disease and dying she celebrated the adventure of life.

Emily Dickinson valued her experience as a single woman, even if her society did not. In addition to protecting her identity as a poet, Dickinson's decision to remain single meant that she honored the ties of kinship rather than the duties of patriarchal marriage. By staying at home, Dickinson chose to remain with her immediate family and friends—the endogamous clan; had she married, she would have had to live with her husband and his family as her own mother and her sister-in-law had been constrained to do. Exogamous—out of clan—marriage frequently caused severe homesickness and loneliness for women, especially for Emily Norcross, Emily Dickinson's mother. A letter from Lavinia Norcross to her sister shortly after the marriage of Emily Norcross to Edward Dickinson laments the disruption of their lives: "[Father] says it is foolish for me to write you so often, but I think news from home must always be desireable especially to one so homesick."[10] Social dislocation was almost as common an experience for nineteenth-century American women as it is today. The rapidly expanding industrial economy caused the fragmentation of extended families as people moved to the cities in search of employment or economic opportunity. A young wife was often compelled to leave friends she had known all her life in order to follow her husband's career. It is possible that the widespread depression and hysteria of middle-class American women in the nineteenth century resulted from being uprooted from a familiar and supportive environment as well as from the passivity enforced by the ideal of true womanhood. The shift from their father's to their husband's homes meant that wives had to relinquish their primary bonds, and Emily Dickinson was not willing to undo these ties.

Dickinson's family and friends were the center of her emotional life, and she needed them for her well-being. In addition to giving her a social identity, they provided her with a connection to the central events of life—births, marriages, and deaths. This network of friendship functioned for Dickinson as it did for many nineteenth-century women as an arena of activity that was sharply distinguished from the commercial and business world. The female sphere emphasized emotional rather than financial values; empathy and loyalty were regarded more highly than ambition or profit. A more detailed analysis of the significance of the separate sphere of women in the nineteenth century indicates that although women were isolated from the cultural mainstream, they often perceived their world as being more civilized as well as more humanly satisfying, more closely connected with the fundamental truths of life than was the business world. In recent studies of nineteenth-century domestic life, Nancy Cott and Nina Baym maintain that the female sphere provided women with a sense of "separate but equal" identities and resources.[11] When the seat of production shifted from the home to the marketplace, domestic life lost its centrality but gained a new importance as a sanctuary from the anxiety of the business world. Nina Baym observes that the female sphere included the "whole network of human attachments based on love, support, and mutual responsibility" and that "[d]omesticity [was] set forth as a value scheme for ordering all of life, in competition with the ethos of money and exploitation that is perceived to prevail in American society."[12] While Cott and Baym observe that different was not inferior, Barbara Welter and Ann Douglas view the shift in nineteenth-century social structure as an erosion of the female power base. Welter and Douglas contend that these domestic ideals of purity and piety ultimately trapped women—that the instrumental role of women promulgated by sermons, magazines, conduct books, and novels actually blinded women to the fact that they were excluded from shaping the larger society as well as economic activity.[13] As Ann Douglas has commented, the sentimentalization of the social role of women was an "inevitable part of the self-evasion of a society both committed to laissez-faire industrial expansion and disturbed by its consequences."[14] Influence, then, proved to be a poor substitute for genuine power in a society that was becoming increasingly more socially and economically stratified.

In spite of the larger political implications, the mutuality of female networks was deeply satisfying to many nineteenth-century women and the ideals of the domestic tradition were very important to Emily Dickinson. In a letter to the Norcross sisters in April 1873, Dickinson expressed the belief that women possess a deeper knowledge of life *because* they are removed from the economic and cultural mainstream:

> I hear the robins a great way off, and wagons a great way off, and rivers a great way off, and all appear to be hurrying somewhere undisclosed to me. Remoteness is the founder of sweetness; could we see all we hope, or hear the whole we fear told tranquil, like another tale, there would be madness near. Each of us gives or takes heaven in corporeal person, for each of us has the skill of life. (*L*, 2:504, no. 388)

In her view, women were more closely connected to basic life processes because, unlike men, their energies were not shaped by competition in the marketplace. As this passage suggests, distance from the commercial world enabled economically privileged women like Dickinson to enjoy the luxuries of friendship and the interior life instead of having to give priority to pragmatic considerations. Although Dickinson did not want to sacrifice her personal autonomy to marriage, she did not reject the deeper concerns of the female tradition—the commitment to a nurturing ethos.

The contrasting interpretations of Douglas and Welter and of Cott and Baym of the significance and function of the female sphere in the nineteenth century are actually two sides of the same social and economic reality. One interpretation provides an understanding of the nineteenth-century woman's reality as she experienced it subjectively; the other, by creating distance from the actual emotional experience of true womanhood, demonstrates that the cult of domesticity led women to surrender the larger cultural arena to men. Certainly Dickinson did not think that she labored under "false consciousness," or that her emphasis on the importance of friendship and a reverence for life was an evasion of social reality.

The division of social, psychological, and economic spheres according to gender is part of a larger division in Western civilization between nature and society, country and city, agriculture and industry, mind and body, subject and object, feeling and thought. This polarization of spheres that was intensified in the nineteenth century by the physical separation of the home and the marketplace parallels the bifurcation that developed in ancient Greece with the shift of social power from the countryside to the polis. In many respects, the psychological and moral struggles that characterize the lives of both Bradstreet and Dickinson are illuminated by an understanding of this ancient enmity between male and female values. Froma Zeitlin observes that during this period of Greek history there was an intense struggle between male and female values that resulted in the subordination of the chthonic mysteries of the female culture to the Olympian laws of the male world.[15] In the hierarchical system that emerged, the rural kinship patterns of an essentially female culture were eclipsed by the urban anti-family emphasis of patriarchal culture. This clash between male and female values is expressed, Zeitlin tells us, in the traditional association of men with reason, order, law, and civilization, and women with passion, chaos, ritual, and nature in the earliest forms of Western civilization.[16]

Bradstreet felt the pull of the chthonic mysteries with their emphasis on kinship, ritual, nature, generativity, the senses, and passion; however, she capitulated to Puritan rule which emphasized the primacy of the father—order, reason, and law. After struggling with her dependence on male preceptors, Dickinson resisted the male logos—her life and her poetry ultimately embraced the truths of the mother. Accepting the forces of chaos and unruliness, she did not turn away from darkness or death. Instead, she insisted on the centrality of the senses. In her fierce determination to live in harmony with cyclic time and to accept death, Dickinson uncovered the obscure mysteries of ancient female experience. Politics, that is, the activities and interests of men in the polis or *public arena*, were an absurdity to Emily Dickinson. In the last years of her life, she humorously expressed her antipathy to the male sphere: " 'George Washington was the Father of his Country'—'George Who'? That sums all Politics to me—."[17]

Home became increasingly important to Dickinson as a place that protected what she held sacred—friendship, love, nurturing values—from what she saw as the inflated importance of the male business and political world. As she grew older, her domestic life took on a sacramental quality: "Home is the definition of God," she wrote when she was forty (L, 2:483, no. 355). Not only did her attachment to her family life reflect the nineteenth-century emphasis on female domesticity, it underscored a fundamental commitment to the love of kin, to the reverence for the maternal mysteries of blood and birth, the cycles of growth and decay, and the acceptance of death. These convictions are clearly demonstrated in her correspondence with her cousins, the Norcross sisters. After the death of their mother, Lavinia Norcross, on April 17, 1860, Dickinson grieved for her aunt: "Blessed Aunt Lavinia now; all the world goes out. . . . I sob and cry till I can hardly see my way 'round the house again; . . . it is dark and strange to think of summer afterward! How she loved the summer! The birds keep singing just the same. Oh! The thoughtless birds!" (L, 2:361–62, no. 217). After her aunt's death, Dickinson assured her cousins that the maternal force that nurtures and protects life would continue. Her many letters to her cousins contain the joyous celebration of nature that characterizes her poetry. In early February 1863, she wrote: "Would it interest the children to know that the crocuses come up, in the garden off the dining-room? . . . And that we have primroses . . . and heliotropes by the aprons full, the mountain colored one—and a jessamine bud, you know the little odor like Lubin—and gilliflowers, magenta, and few mignonette and sweet alyssum bountiful, and carnation buds?" (L, 2:422, no. 279). Ten years later in April 1873, Dickinson's vision remained intact: "Spring is a happiness so beautiful, so unique, so unexpected, that I don't know what to do with my heart" (L, 2:506, no. 389).

Throughout her life Dickinson shared her intense sensory pleasure in flowers and fruit with her cousins: "I cooked the peaches as you told me, and they swelled to beautiful fleshy halves and tasted quite magic" (L, 2:471, no. 340). Almost twenty years earlier, on October 2, 1851, she had described peaches to Austin with the same intense pleasure: "[T]he peaches are very large—one side a *rosy* cheek, and the other a *golden*, and that peculiar coat of velvet and of down, which makes a peach so beautiful" (L, 1:137, no. 53). In general, the frequent exchange between Dickinson and her friends about flowers, fruits, vegetables, baked goods, and recipes expresses the deep reverence for the forces of fecundity and fruition and for the fertility of the earth which is embedded in the female tradition.

The image Emily Dickinson uses most often to express the female principle is the flower, which represents the etiolated female consciousness and female sexuality. It also symbolizes the plenitude of existence throughout all phases of growth from seed or bulb, to bud, to blossom. An analysis of the flower imagery in Dickinson's poems illuminates her evolution from passive, dependent femininity to autonomous womanhood. In an early poem, the flower represents decorative, seductive femininity; these blossoms are enticing and alluring, but their extraordinary beauty is meaningless without male approval:

I tend my flowers for thee—
Bright Absentee!
My Fuschzia's Coral Seams
Rip—while the Sower—dreams—

Geraniums—tint—and spot—
Low Daisies—dot—
My Cactus—splits her Beard
To show her throat—

Carnations—tip their spice—
And Bees—pick up—
A Hyacinth—I hid—

Puts out a Ruffled Head—
And odors fall
From flasks—so small—
You marvel how they held—

Globe Roses—break their satin flake—
Upon my Garden floor—
Yet—thou—not there—
I had as lief they bore
No Crimson—more—

Thy flower—be gay—
Her Lord—away!
It ill becometh me—
I'll dwell in Calyx—Gray—
How Modestly—alway—
Thy Daisy—
Draped for thee!

(*P*, 1:270–71, no. 339)

In contrast to the cultivated flowers, the daisy is a wildflower that grows in abundance in the fields of New England; nevertheless, this unpretentious flower also waits patiently for release. Less ornate and elaborate than the fuchsias, geraniums, carnations, hyacinths, and roses, the daisy deferentially conceals her beauty beneath her calyx—the outer series of green floral leaves as contrasted with the inner, more ornate portion—waiting passively for her "Lord." This is one of Emily Dickinson's most explicitly erotic poems; the labiate blossoms emphasize female sexual energy, but this power is nevertheless dependent on the male for completion.

A later poem demonstrates Dickinson's evolution from conflict-ridden adolescent to independent woman—here the flower is important in itself and has its own purpose. No longer is the male necessary for completion or wholeness but, as represented by the bee, is depicted as a thief and a marauder, full of pompous self-importance:

> Bloom—is Result—to meet a Flower
> And casually glance
> Would scarcely cause one to suspect
> The minor Circumstance
>
> Assisting in the Bright Affair
> So intricately done
> Then offered as a Butterfly
> To the Meridian—
>
> To pack the Bud—oppose the Worm—
> Obtain its right of Dew—
> Adjust the Heat—elude the Wind—
> Escape the prowling Bee
>
> Great Nature not to disappoint
> Awaiting Her that Day—
> To be a Flower, is profound
> Responsibility—
> (P, 2:746, no. 1058)

As a metaphor for female poetic identity, it is significant that the flowers must resist the intruders, predators, and destructive conditions—excessive heat, too much or too little moisture—in order to bloom. Recalling Dickinson's earlier association of the helpless flowers compulsively following the sun, the active verbs "pack," "oppose," "adjust," and "escape" make it clear that the focus of energy and action has shifted away from the male sun and now resides with female flowers whose responsibility it is to bloom. No longer dependent on male energy for completion, the flower is now accountable to herself. Rooted in earth, extending into the air, turning toward the sun, watered by the rain, the flower is life. By balancing the forces of nature, the flower embodies organic growth: for

Dickinson, it is also the emblem of the unfolding imagination, of the self resonating with nature.

In an even later poem, Dickinson mocks the traditional view of gender roles:

> A Bee his Burnished Carriage
> Drove boldly to a Rose—
> Combinedly alighting—
> Himself—his Carriage was—
> The Rose received his visit
> With frank tranquility
> Withholding not a Crescent
> To his Cupidity—
> Their Moment consummated—
> Remained for him—to flee—
> Remained for her—of rapture
> But the humility.
> (P, 3:925, no. 1339)

In this poem the pompous, greedy bee assaults the submissive, humble flower; his arrogant pride is contrasted with her meek modesty. Although Dickinson uses irony to convey her antipathy to the marauding male who exploits the female, a passage from Margaret Fuller's journal uses the same imagery to express rage about the abuse of female energy: "Woman is the flower, man the bee. She sighs out of melodious fragrance, and invites the winged laborer. He drains her cup, and carries off the honey. She dies on the stalk; he returns to the hive, well fed, and praised as an active member of the community." [18]

In her mature years, the bud was especially significant for Dickinson because it contains the unfolding blossom. Her niece Martha Dickinson Bianchi recalled that her aunt was fascinated by bulbs:

> [Emily Dickinson] would perhaps be by the dining-room fire, or
> better still up in her own room, forever associated with me with
> the odor of hyacinths, for the way a bulb in the sunshine had
> an uncanny fascination for her, their little pots crowding all the
> window-sills to bring a reluctant spring upon the air. From the first
> prick of the green above the earth she detected every minute sign of
> growth. [19]

As nature's midwife, Emily Dickinson fostered growth.

In addition to representing female identity—creativity and sexuality —Dickinson also associated blossoms with a full, comprehensive vision of life unrestricted by the narrowed attention of the bounded ego. Like the thousand-petaled lotus of Buddhist enlightenment, this unfolding flower represents the diverse aspects of the universe of which human beings are but a part. Inder Kher observes that Dickinson's "columnar self" is a "matrix of creation," but actually the flower best represents the complexity of her vision.[20] The center of the flower represents the basic life force and the petals the many aspects of experience; the blossom is the totality of awareness.

> This is a Blossom of the Brain—
> A small—italic Seed
> Lodged by Design or Happening
> The Spirit fructified—
>
> Shy as the Wind of his Chambers
> Swift as a Freshet's Tongue
> So of the Flower of the Soul
> It's process is unknown.
>
> When it is found, a few rejoice
> The Wise convey it Home
> Carefully cherishing the spot
> If other Flower become.
>
> When it is lost, that Day shall be
> The Funeral of God,
> Upon his Breast, a closing Soul
> The Flower of our Lord.
>   (P, 2:687, no. 945)

A meditation on the intricate relationship of the mind and the body, this poem celebrates the mysterious process of thought. Using slant rhymes and assonance—the sound of "o," emphasizing the poet's awe, is repeated throughout the poem—Dickinson makes it clear that the creative imagination is the source of vision that gives meaning to life; significantly, the blossoming spirit is not dependent on an external male agent for fertilization. Here Dickinson asserts that "the mysteries of human nature surpass the 'mysteries of redemption,' for the infinite we only suppose, while we see the finite" (L, 3:856, no. 962). Throughout her adult life Dickinson discounted the claims of formal religion: "That we are permanent temporarily, it is warm to know, though we know no more," she wrote in the same letter. Again, she emphasizes the actual—experience apprehended through the senses rather than the abstractions of metaphysics.

In Dickinson's life, the maternal nurturing tradition of women is contrasted with the logical, ordered realm of male mastery. With her women friends, Dickinson shared her acceptance of the cycle of birth and death, a cycle that could not be controlled by reason or faith: "Dear friends—we cannot believe for each other. I suppose there are depths in every Consciousness, from which we cannot rescue ourselves—to which none can go with us—which represent Mortally—the Adventure of Death" (*L*, 2:612, no. 555). An adventure is a potentially risky and dangerous but nevertheless exciting undertaking—by definition, its outcome is unknown. By describing death as an adventure, Emily Dickinson makes it clear that although its essential nature remains mysterious, it is not superseded by eternal life—"Dying is a wild Night and a new Road" (*L*, 2:463, no. 332). One of her poems, sent to Bowles in 1863, again expresses her conviction that death gives meaning to life, that the certainty of mortality imparts luminescence—a sheen to daily experience:

The Zeroes—taught us—Phosphorus—
We learned to like the Fire
By playing Glaciers—when a Boy—
And Tinder—guessed—by power
Of Opposite—to balance Odd—
If White—a Red—must be!
Paralysis—our Primer—dumb—
Unto Vitality!
(*P*, 2:532, no. 689)

In this poem, Dickinson reasons syllogistically that just as cold gives meaning to heat, so death intensifies life's vitality.

Because Emily Dickinson could finally accept death, she was able to help her friends mourn the loss of loved ones; she did not try to dilute their pain with sentimental clichés about a happier afterlife that were characteristic of the voluminous consolation letters in her time but instead gave them solace based on her own experience of loss. When Elizabeth Holland's husband died, Dickinson instructed her in the phases of mourning: "I know you will live for our sake, dear, you would not be willing to for your own. That is the duty which saves. While we are trying for others, power of life comes back, very faint at first, like the new bird, but by and by it has wings" (*L*, 3:714, no. 732). Emily Dickinson encourages Elizabeth Holland to trust the ongoing process of life, to have faith in her own strength. Having no religious certainties to comfort her, Dickinson anchored herself and her friends in the sights, sounds, and rhythms of this life. Her poem about a hummingbird, whose rapid flight is recorded by its effects on blossoms, was sent to the Norcross sisters, Helen Hunt Jackson, Mrs. Edward Tuckerman, and Mabel Loomis Todd:

A Route of Evanescence
With a revolving Wheel—
A Resonance of Emerald—
A Rush of Cochineal—
And every Blossom on the Bush
Adjusts it's Tumbled Head—
      (P, 3 : 1010, no. 1463)

The synaesthetic imagery of whirring colors ranging from intense green and silvery grays to rusty red captures the hummingbird's impermanent, fleeting aerial path.

Although Emily Dickinson rarely visited the junior Dickinsons in her later years, she did send frequent notes and gifts. There was a continual exchange of books, flowers, cookies, cakes, sometimes a roasting hen or two, between the houses. No birthday or anniversary went unnoticed. The following letter, written to her sister-in-law, makes it clear that their shared concerns based on common gender form a bulwark against death or marriage that threatens to erase female identity:

Sister,
    We both are Women, and there is a Will of God—Could the
Dying confide Death, there would be no Dead—Wedlock is shyer
than Death. Thank you for Tenderness— (L, 2 : 445, no. 312)

In 1868 Dickinson wrote: "I must wait a few Days before seeing you— You are too momentous. But remember it is idolatry, not indifference" (L, 2 : 631, no. 581). For Emily, Susan embodied female energy, recalling that of Athena, Hera, Artemis, Selene, Hecate, Aphrodite, Themis, Pandora, and Gaia.

Susan—
    Whoever blesses, you always bless—the last—and often made
the Heaven of Heavens—a sterile stimulus.
    Cherish Power—dear—
    Remember that stands in the Bible between the Kingdom and the
Glory, because it is wilder than either of them. (L, 2 : 631, no. 583)

Susan Gilbert was very supportive of Emily Dickinson's poetry writing, and the friendship between the two women was a source of artistic and emotional stimulation for Dickinson: "To miss you, Sue, is power," she wrote in September 1871. In the early 1880s Austin Dickinson became involved in a very compelling and complicated love affair with Mabel Loomis Todd,[21] and the resulting tension decreased the frequency of visits; however, Emily and Susan Dickinson remained friends, as Emily's last note to Sue in 1886 demonstrates: "Thank you, dear Sue—for every solace" (L, 3:895, no. 1030). Even when the two women had little contact, the relationship exerted an influence on Dickinson, as a letter in late 1885 reveals: "The tie between us is very fine, but a Hair never dissolves" (L, 3:893, no. 1024).

Elizabeth Holland, the wife of Josiah Gilbert Holland, the editor and founder of *Scribner's* magazine, was one of Emily Dickinson's closest friends—Emily called her "sister." Their letters are full of observations about birthdays and funerals as well as of the meaning of friendship and community. In 1856, quite early in their correspondence, which continued for thirty years until Emily Dickinson's death, Dickinson emphatically stated that love is at the core of her cosmology, and that for her, being loved by friends far surpassed power on earth or in heaven: "Pardon my sanity . . . in a world *in*sane, and love me if you will, for I had rather *be* loved than to be called a king in earth, or a lord in Heaven" (L, 2:329–30, no. 185). Here Dickinson contrasts the female tradition with its emphasis on tenderness with the male tradition that emphasizes transcendent control. For Dickinson, friendship is sacred and the only solace for mutability: "The gentian is a greedy flower, and overtakes us all. Indeed, this world is short, and I wish, until I tremble, to touch the ones I love before the hills are red—are gray—are white—are 'born again'!" (L, 2:354, no. 207). Again and again, Dickinson forged the connection between sensory and emotional experience and the purpose and pleasure of life. Seeing, touching, tasting, smelling, and feeling supersede visions of a promised land:

> Did life's penurious length
> Italicize its sweetness,
> The men that daily live
> Would stand so deep in joy
> That it would clog the cogs
> Of that revolving reason
> Whose esoteric belt
> Protects our sanity.
> (P, 3:1158, no. 1717)

Here Dickinson asserts that if there were an accurate understanding of life's parsimonious brevity, "the men" who focus on utilitarian concerns would alter their lives so radically that the extreme multiplicity of life could no longer be reduced to pragmatic goals.

While Thoreau, Emerson, Alcott, and the other transcendentalists were preoccupied by the problem of forging a heroic American mythology, Emily Dickinson and her friends shared their daily experiences.[22] While Thoreau and Emerson solemnly searched for the new Adam in America, Dickinson referred ironically to herself as "Eve, alias Mrs. Adam" and scrutinized her garden. While Emerson developed metaphors into metaphysics, Dickinson used language innovatively in her poetry to re-create her perceptions of daily life.

Dickinson's poetry focuses on a series of moments, or intense experiences, not on a mission. Her understanding of nature was not filtered through an Arcadian lens; her nature poetry was not based on the pastoral conventions of Virgil's Eclogues or Georgics. Instead, she concentrated on what *was* rather than what could be, on the life around her rather than on a literary preconception of life. Because women stayed at home, they cultivated their friendships and their gardens instead of founding empires, and Emily Dickinson clearly felt that this was a positive aspect of the domestic tradition. As she wrote to Elizabeth Holland in September 1877: "I miss my little Sanctuary, and her redeeming ways. A Savior in a Nut, is sweeter to the grasp, than ponderous Prospectives" (*L*, 2:593, no. 521). Rejecting male abstractions and theories, Dickinson chose the pleasures of female friendship rather than the challenge of the male mission. For Dickinson, solace superseded salvation, and empathic love was more important than eternal life.

Dickinson's priorities—the preservation and celebration of life—were the antithesis of the values of the increasingly economically specialized industrial world in which she lived. For Dickinson, the pleasures of friendship were more important than financial success; in her cosmology, her circle of friends replaced the community of saints. Eternal life was gained not through salvation but in the memories of the people who knew her well. Anne Bradstreet was taught that friends and family were but an intimation of God's wondrous love; for Emily Dickinson friendships were a sacred lineage based on mutual trust and care. And it was to friends that she entrusted her poems with the confidence that she would live in her art.

In late autumn 1884, Emily Dickinson wrote a letter to Elizabeth Holland expressing an urgency to communicate her understanding of life. It was as though she knew she did not have many years left and felt the need to reiterate the nature of her experience: "All grows strangely emphatic, and I think if I should see you again, I sh'd begin every sentence with 'I say unto you—' The Bible dealt with the Centre, not with the Circumference—" (*L*, 3:849–50, no. 950). Nine years earlier Dickinson had written to this same friend, "'I say unto you,' Father would read at Prayers, with a militant Accent that would startle one" (*L*, 2:537, no. 432). Sure of herself and the value of her own life, Dickinson now has the confidence to be authoritative; however, her message is dramatically different from her father's. As she tells Mrs. Holland, her life has been dedicated to discovering the alternative to the center, and she now feels that circumference deserves an assertive voice.

In her life and in her art, Emily Dickinson transmuted the patriarchal myth of the fall from grace, the expulsion from Eden, and the need to placate an angry God to gain eternal life into a female view of life as an experience that is finite but joyous, of nature as bountiful but cyclical, of experience as comprehensive totality rather than quest. Using the language and myths of the Bible, she celebrated the cycles of the seasons and of human life. Planting and harvest, birth and death replace sin and salvation, heaven and hell. As she wrote to Maria Whitney late in her life, "The sunshine almost speaks, this morning, redoubling the division, and Paul's remark grows graphic, 'the weight of glory.'" Like the saints in Revelation, Emily Dickinson wears white; her poems and letters are not hymns to a transcendent God but a celebration of "the moment immortal":

> Flowers are not quite earthly. They are like the Saints. We should doubtless feel more at Home with them than with the Saints of God.
> Were "the Great Crowd of Witnesses" chiefly Roses and Pansies, there would be less to apprehend, though let me not presume upon Jehovah's Program. (L, 2:528–29, no. 417)

When Dickinson died in May 1886, her family and friends carried her casket through fields of wildflowers to the cemetery. Eleusis had come to Amherst.

PART THREE

Adrienne Rich

"A woman with a certain mission"

I am a woman in the prime of life, with certain powers
and those powers severely limited
by authorities whose faces I rarely see.
.   .   .   .

A woman with a certain mission
Which if obeyed to the letter will leave her intact.

The Will to Change:
Poems, 1968–70, 19

Introduction

In *Of Woman Born* (1976), a collection of essays about the institution of motherhood, Adrienne Rich (1929–) describes her father as a man with pronounced opinions and elaborate theories about childhood education. She compares Arnold Rich with Bronson Alcott, the nineteenth-century transcendentalist who took his family to live in an experimental commune to subsist on fruit while he pursued his educational and social theories, and admits that, like Louisa May Alcott, she resented her father's quixotic experiments. Educated at home according to his precepts until the fourth grade, Adrienne Rich was taught to write poetry by her father who urged her to "*work, work / harder than anyone has worked before*"[1] and to strive for excellence. Like Margaret Fuller who learned under her father's tutelage to read Greek and Latin before she was five, Rich became an accomplished prosodist at an early age.

As a young woman, Rich wrote elegantly crafted, tightly rhymed, prize-winning poetry. By her mid-twenties she had published *A Change of World* (1951) and *The Diamond Cutters* (1955), which received high praise from W. H. Auden and Randall Jarrell. Married at twenty-four, with three children by the time she was thirty, Adrienne Rich discovered that cooking, cleaning, shopping, caring for the children, and entertaining her husband's colleagues left her little time to write. Overwhelmed by frustration and anger about the disparity between her professional accomplishments and aspirations and the reality of traditional domestic life, she feared that she would be deprived of selfhood altogether. In her essay, "When We Dead Awaken: Writing as Re-Vision" (1971), Rich describes the tensions of these early years of motherhood: "About the time my third child was born, I felt that I had either to consider myself a failed woman and a failed poet, or to try to find some synthesis by which to understand what was happening to me."[2] As the daughter of a respected pathologist and as the wife of an economist, Alfred Conrad, who taught at Harvard, her conditioned response was to defer to the needs of men and children. But, in addition to being a wife and mother, she was also a recognized writer. Like her twentieth-century precursors, Edna St. Vincent Millay, Hilda Doolittle, Louise Bogan, Elinor Wylie, and Marianne Moore, Adrienne Rich was influenced by the modernist struggle for literary authority as well as the tradition of romantic individualism. In contrast to many of these poets who, as Cheryl Walker has recently observed, felt that they had to deny their femininity in order to be artists, Rich has refused to accept male definitions of creativity.[3]

During the late 1950s and early 1960s, Adrienne Rich experienced extraordinary conflict between her need for love and her desire to write. While she was loathe to become a "devouring ego," traditionally the prerogative of the male artist, she was nevertheless deeply disturbed by the antithetical demands of traditional domesticity and the imagination.[4] "Snapshots of a Daughter-in-Law" (1958–60) was the first of her many poems to explore the conundrum of the female artist in a society that defines self-denial as synonymous with true womanhood. In this poem, Rich finds a connection between her own conflicts and frustrations and the lives of Mary Wollstonecraft and Simone de Beauvoir. Like these women writers, Adrienne Rich has committed herself to the understanding of the relationship between gender and culture and to creating positive, public images of women.

In the volumes from *Snapshots of a Daughter-in-Law* (1963) through *Necessities of Life* (1966), *Leaflets* (1969), and *The Will to Change* (1971), to *Diving into the Wreck* (1973), *The Dream of a Common Language* (1978), and *A Wild Patience Has Taken Me This Far* (1981), Rich has explored the pain and anger of a creative, thinking woman in a culture that has denied the most essential aspects of her experience. As she has become increasingly conscious of her deepest feelings, her poetry has reflected her growing desire to define her experience for herself and to help other women collectively to "re-vision" their lives. During the decades of the 1960s and 1970s, Rich has passed through the phases of self-analysis, individual assertion, and accomplishment to rejection of patriarchal values, feminist activism, and finally to building a woman-centered community.[5]

Adrienne Rich has tried to create a poetic web that can sustain the weight of changed consciousness and a changed life. Influenced by the open-ended writing of such poets as Ezra Pound, William Carlos Williams, and Denise Levertov as well as the confessional mode of Robert Lowell, Sylvia Plath, and John Berryman, Rich has evolved a dynamic style. She weaves a tightly woven mesh of lyrical assonance, consonance, slant rhyme, and onomatopoeia with political slogans of the antiwar and women's liberation movements of the 1960s and 1970s, literal quotations from women's diaries, letters, and essays, and startlingly discordant diction from conversation and internal monologue that captures the anger of women whose abilities have been trivialized or denied in a patriarchal society.

Although the cultural and emotional tapestry of Adrienne Rich's poetry is sometimes uneven, her work is provocative and original. Certain strands of feeling persist throughout—a commitment to lucidity, communication, community, and social change. In later volumes, the threads of revolutionary anger and political conviction have become more distinct. This unusual combination of aesthetics and activism has won her considerable praise, including the National Book Award in 1974 for *Diving into the Wreck*, as well as censure from those critics who are distressed by the political urgency of her poetry. But for Rich, poetry is not simply an aesthetic rendering of experience, but it is also a way of changing the world.

By crystallizing awareness that would otherwise be repressed or remain in a shadowy, murky region of unarticulated experience, Rich intends that her writing record "the process of going from the conflicts and strife of the unconscious into the sayable, into the actable."[6] Rich has observed that poetic form should reflect this interaction of unconscious and conscious experience: "A poem can't exist without form, but it should be the result of a dynamic or dialogue between what is coming out of the unconscious and what is coming out of experience. This dialogue is expressed through the medium of language, and everything that means—rhythm and sound and tone and repetition and the way words can ring off each other and clash against each other (*TCWM*)." As a radical feminist, Rich insists on the need to transform all relationships in an effort to create an egalitarian and humane society. This transformation of relationships requires a restructuring or re-forming, a seeing again or revisioning, of the social matrix and the linguistic generalizations that sustain symbolic and metaphysical assumptions—the very definitions of reality. Such a shift in consciousness involves exploring repressed experiences, naming these perceptions, and incorporating them into daily life by creating new clusters of awareness, new patterns of meaning. Because consciousness responds to language, Rich has committed herself to writing a poetry that will be a catalyst for social change. As she has observed: "Poetry is, among other things, a criticism of language. . . . Poetry is above all a concentration of the *power* of language, which is the power of our ultimate relationship to everything in the universe" (*LSS*, 248).

Adrienne Rich is a political poet whose ideology is rooted in early American experience. Her prophecy of the community of women and of female energy free from patriarchal repression parallels the Puritan vision of the city on a hill triumphant over Old World corruption. Women are opposed to male domination just as the colonists were opposed to the taxation and social repression of King Charles. As with the Puritans, the feminists' opposition to the existing order defines their communal boundary; external threats intensify group identity and are an important element in the dynamic of social change. The voyage to the New World was sustained, in part, by the Puritans' refusal to accept British social and economic oppression; feminism has been fueled by women's resistance to male control of their lives.

Although Rich rejects the vision of the fathers, there are striking parallels between feminist ideals and the utopian vision of the Puritans. The Puritans believed that God's elect were destined to reform the Satanic wilderness. Edward Johnson called on the community of saints to build the New World Commonwealth: *"All you the people of Christ that are here Oppressed, Imprisoned and scurrilously derided, gather yourselves together . . . and answer to your severall Names as you shall be shipped for his service, in the Westerne World, and more especially for planting the united Collonies of new England."*[7] More than three hundred years later, Rich calls for a similar dedication to the feminist vision that will bring about "the transformation of society and of our relation to all life. . . . It goes far beyond any struggle for civil liberties or equal rights— necessary as those struggles continue to be. In its deepest, most inclusive form it is an inevitable process by which women will claim our primary and central vision in shaping the future" (*LSS,* 226).

During her career, Rich has been considerably influenced by the lives and work of Anne Bradstreet and Emily Dickinson. Drawing parallels between her life and Bradstreet's, Rich has observed: "[L]ike her, I had learned to read and write in my father's library; like her, I had known the ambiguities of patronizing compliments from male critics; like her, I suffered from chronic lameness; but above all, she was one of the few women writers I knew anything about who had also been a mother" (*LSS,* 21). Although Rich has observed that she could not have chosen Dickinson's strategies for survival, she nevertheless feels a deep kinship with the reclusive poet about whom she has written three poems: "The methods, the exclusions, of Emily Dickinson's existence could not have been my own; yet more and more, as a woman finding my own methods, I have come to understand her necessities, could have been a witness in her defense" (*LSS,* 158). Neither Bradstreet nor Dickinson achieved Rich's public visibility, but they understood the fundamental relationship between writing and self-creation. As Rich has said, "When the woman writer takes pen in hand, she has been in some way, even if in only a small way, seizing power—seizing some of that male power, that logos, and saying 'I.' Both Bradstreet and Dickinson were extremely conscious of seizing power through poetry and used language to create self-hood" (*TCWM*).

In many respects Adrienne Rich's life recapitulates the lives of Anne Bradstreet and Emily Dickinson; initially, like Bradstreet, she lived within society's framework; then, like Dickinson, she set herself apart in order to define her own emotional and social territory; finally, she has struggled to overcome her historical context in an effort to change society itself. Unlike Anne Bradstreet, who ultimately capitulated to a higher authority, or Emily Dickinson, who held her own ground, Adrienne Rich has insisted on openly challenging the current social order.

As a modern woman, Adrienne Rich's life has encompassed an unusual range of experiences; as David Kalstone remarks, for Rich, "working is a jagged present, always pitched toward the future and change."[8] She has been a Radcliffe undergraduate, a wife and the mother of three sons, a widely read poet with a large audience who has received numerous awards, including the National Book Award, a university professor, a social activist and war resister, a feminist, and a lesbian. Although Rich grew up in suburban Baltimore, Maryland, she has lived most of her adult life in the Northeast—in Cambridge, Massachusetts, New York City, and most recently, near Amherst, Massachusetts. For the past thirty years, Rich has written about the separation of mind and body, the bifurcation of society into active masculinity and dependent femininity, the loss of human connection to nature, the illusion of romantic love with its promise of a protector, the lives of both extraordinary and ordinary women, the necessity of disengaging from a destructive culture, the interpenetration of art and politics as well as private and public life, and the importance of creating social and artistic forms that express women's actual experience. Like Bradstreet and Dickinson, Rich celebrates female mutuality rather than male hierarchy. Like Dickinson, she uses oxymorons to fuse the polarizations of male oppositional thought in an effort to erase the traditional subordination of women to men and nature to culture. Linking the female body with the physical landscape to create metaphors of female power, Dickinson and Rich celebrate the female dimension of nature as primary.

In our many-dimensional social universe, Adrienne Rich has lived with purpose. She has challenged traditional roles that subordinate women to men and she has evolved a social vision that is woman-centered and emphasizes the interconnection of all forms of life. She intends her personal and poetic vision to illuminate possibilities for "new human and communal relationships." Feminism is essential to her thought:

I am a feminist because I feel endangered, psychically and physically, by this society, and because I believe that the women's movement is saying we have come to an edge of history when men—insofar as they are embodiments of the patriarchal idea—have become dangerous to children and other living things, themselves included; and that we can no longer afford to keep the female principle enclosed within the confines of the tight, little post-industrial family, or within any male-induced notion of where the female principle is valid and where it is not. (*LSS*, 83)

For years, Dürer's *Melancholia* hung over Adrienne Rich's desk. Although the poet was not then familiar with the history of this depiction of melancholy, the "big, powerful, brooding woman seated among the instruments of intellectual prowess" engaged her imagination. In a description of Dürer's portrait that could be applied to her own life, Rich observes, "I created my own iconography and made her into an embodiment of the female artist, a thinker confronted with this intransigent culture" (*TCWM*).

ELEVEN

"Find Yourself and You Find the World"

Born in Baltimore, Maryland, on May 16, 1929, to Arnold Rich and Helen Jones, Adrienne Rich grew up in financially comfortable and socially advantaged circumstances. However, because her father was Jewish and Baltimore was an anti-Semitic city, the Rich family was also socially marginal. Her father, a pathologist at Johns Hopkins University, taught her to read and tutored her until the fourth grade. He encouraged her to write poetry at an early age, insisting that she should achieve metrical competence when she was still a child: "He was concerned that I should learn to write well in the sense of adhering to the established meters. I used to do little exercises in dactylic hexameter . . . and sapphics" (*TCWM*). Like Thomas Dudley and Edward Dickinson, Arnold Rich was an exacting taskmaster who set high standards for his daughter. A great believer in "formalism and strict meters," he "was offended by so-called free verse." Under his guidance, Rich read primarily Victorian writers: "Tennyson, Keats, Arnold, Rossetti, Swinburne, Carlyle, and Pater" (*TCWM*). In her early poem, "Juvenilia," Rich creates a portrait of herself as a young poet seeking her father's approval with her "sedulous lines":

> Again I sit, under duress, hands washed,
> at your inkstained oaken desk,
> . . . .
> Unspeakable fairy tales ebb like blood through my head
> as I dip the pen and for aunts, for admiring friends,
> for you above all to read,
> copy my praised and sedulous lines [1]

As a young writer, Rich's imagination was regulated by her father's standards, which she labored to meet. But even then tension between personal inclination and duty is evident.

Adrienne Rich's mother, Helen Jones, studied to be a concert pianist and composer at the Peabody Conservatory in Baltimore. After additional work in New York, she studied in Paris and Vienna and taught at girls' boarding schools to finance her lessons. During this time she was engaged to Arnold Rich who was completing medical school and establishing a career in academic medicine. Once married, her musical career gave way to domestic responsibilities. Rich observes that

> My father, brilliant, ambitious, possessed by his own drive, assumed that she would give her life over to the enhancement of his. . . . she marketed by streetcar, and later, when they could afford a car, she drove my father to and from his laboratory or lectures, often awaiting him for hours. She raised two children, and taught us all our lessons, including music. (Neither of us was sent to school until the fourth grade.) (*OWB*, 221–22)

Like Dorothy Dudley and Emily Norcross, Helen Jones devoted herself to her family. Not only did Helen Jones relinquish her musical career for marriage and motherhood, but her child-rearing responsibilities were more extensive than usual because Adrienne and her sister Cynthia, who was four years younger, received their early schooling at home.

After attending Roland Park Country School, which Rich describes as "a good old-fashioned girls' school" that "gave us fine role models of single women who were intellectually impassioned," she left her family's home to attend Radcliffe College, "where [she] did not see a woman teacher for four years" (*TCWM*) and where she learned poetic craft from the male poets she read as an undergraduate—"Frost, Dylan Thomas, Donne, Auden, MacNeice, Stevens, and Yeats" (*LSS*, 39). In 1951, Rich graduated Phi Beta Kappa from Radcliffe and published her first volume of poems *A Change of World*, which was selected by W. H. Auden for the Yale Younger Poets Series. This collection, which reveals the influence of Eliot, Lowell, Pound, Stevens, and Frost, contains artfully crafted poems about her experience and preoccupations as an undergraduate. "The Kursaal at Interlaken" demonstrates Rich's command of poetic technique as a young poet:

> The air is bright with after-images.
> The lanterns and the twinkling glasses dwindle,
> The waltzes and the croupiers' voices crumble,
> The evening folds like a kaleidoscope.
> Against the splinters of a reeling landscape
> This image still pursues us into time:
> Jungfrau, the legendary virgin spire,
> Consumes the mind with mingled snow and fire.[2]

An elaborate pattern of assonance and consonance (the repetition of the letters "l" and "i" is especially dramatic) creates vivid visual and verbal textures. Harnessing the charged excitement and anticipation of the student-explorer, the slant rhymes and elegant concluding couplet also demonstrate Rich's superb control of her craft.

Like Bradstreet, Rich was singled out by critics who praised her modesty as well as her discipline and commitment to poetry. Just as Reverend Woodbridge commended Bradstreet for her discretion in avoiding publicity, W. H. Auden, in his preface to *A Change of World*, assures the reader that Rich is not self-seeking: "Miss Rich, who is, I understand, twenty-one years old, displays a modesty not so common at that age, which disclaims any extraordinary vision, and a love for her medium, a determination to ensure that whatever she writes shall, at least, not be shoddily made" (*CW*, Preface, 9–10). Praising Rich's "versification" and her "intuitive grasp of much subtler and more difficult matters like proportion, consistency of diction and tone," Auden was especially pleased with her respectful decorum as a poet: "The poems . . . are neatly and modestly dressed, speak quietly but do not mumble, respect their elders but are not cowed by them, and do not tell fibs" (*CW*, Preface, 11).

The poems in this first volume are heavily rhymed and carefully controlled. Although, years later, Rich observed that praise for meeting traditional standards gave her the courage to be innovative and to break social and poetic conventions in her later work, the restraint of "At a Bach Concert" indicates that at this time Rich still relied on the aesthetic creed that used art as a bulwark against unruly passion:

> A too-compassionate art is half an art.
> Only such proud restraining purity
> Restores the else-betrayed, too-human heart.
>
> (*CW*, 54)

Here Rich subscribes to the traditional male aesthetic that separates pure mind and artistic creation from the lower orders of experience.

Rich traveled in Europe and England on a Guggenheim Fellowship for a year; then, in 1953, she married Alfred H. Conrad, a Harvard economist, and lived in Cambridge, Massachusetts, until 1966. As a young wife of twenty-four, Rich continued to write poetry, even though there was little social support for her artistic commitment. In spite of dramatic gains in the status of women during the early decades of the twentieth century, the 1950s in the United States was a period of intense domesticity, in which women subordinated their lives to men as did their mothers and grandmothers before them. As Rich herself observes, "[T]hese were the fifties, and in reaction to the earlier wave of feminism, middle-class women were making careers of domestic perfection, working to send their husbands through professional schools, then retiring to have large families" (*LSS*, 42). In 1955, two years after she was married, Rich gave birth to her first son, David, and published *The Diamond Cutters and Other Poems*, which received the Ridgely Torrence Memorial Award of the Poetry Society of America. Again, Rich was commended for her graceful, feminine style, her poetic decorum, and her skill in the use of metrics, scansion, and rhyme. Praising the volume, Randall Jarrell described her as "an enchanting poet," "a sort of princess in a fairy tale," and exclaimed that "she lives nearer to perfection . . . than ordinary poets do."[3] "Love in the Museum" illustrates the exquisite style of this period:

> But art requires a distance: let me be
> Always the connoisseur of your perfection.
> Stay where the spaces of the gallery
> Flow calm between your pose and my inspection,
> Lest one imperfect gesture make demands
> As troubling as the touch of human hands.[4]

Although this ironic meditation covertly challenges the view that art should not be contaminated by raw emotion, the constrained rhyme scheme controls potentially turbulent feelings.

As a young poet, wife, and mother, Rich struggled to balance her domestic and aesthetic efforts. In contrast to her later work, her early volumes, *A Change of World* and *The Diamond Cutters*, are written from the perspective of a woman who tries to conform to the demands of a traditional society and whose power is measured by her ability to attract and please men:

> She who has the power to call her man
> From that estranged intensity
> Where his mind forages alone,
> Yet keeps her peace and leaves him free,
> And when his thoughts to her return
> Stands where he left her, still his own,
> Knows this the hardest thing to learn.
> ("An Unsaid Word," *CW*, 51)

By keeping "her peace," the dutiful wife must neither distract her husband from his important work nor make demands for herself; in this poem, the poet accepts, however reluctantly, the separate spheres of men and women. This early verse is meditative; the strict meter and rhymed stanzas create the effect of muted reflection. As Albert Gelpi has commented, her first poems create a "shelter of self-preservation," and he wonders if "the artifice, no matter how skillfully wrought, may serve as the partial evasion of . . . conflicts."[5]

In 1957 and 1959, Adrienne Rich's sons Paul and Jacob were born. Rich discovered that, as a mother of three young boys, she had little time to write poetry. The demands on her energy were enormous as was the anxiety and self-doubt created by the conflict between her domestic responsibilities and her art. Although her husband did not oppose her poetry writing, he did not consider it to be equal in importance to his own career:

> My husband was a sensitive, affectionate man who wanted children and who—unusual in the professional, academic world of the fifties—was willing to "help." But it was clearly understood that this "help" was an act of generosity; that *his* work, *his* professional life, was the real work in the family; in fact, this was for years not even an issue between us. I understood that my struggles as a writer were a kind of luxury, a peculiarity of mine. . . . "Whatever I ask he tries to give me," I wrote in March, 1958, "but always the initiative has to be mine." (*OWB*, 27)

As with most marriages at that time, the implicit assumption was that a wife's nondomestic activities were less important and were expendable:

> The child (or children) might be absorbed in busyness, in his own dreamworld; but as soon as he felt me gliding into a world which did not include him, he would come to pull at my hand, ask for help, punch at the typewriter keys. And I would feel his wants at such a moment as fraudulent, as an attempt moreover to defraud me of living even for fifteen minutes as myself. (*OWB*, 23)

She felt that she was no longer in control of her life, that she was passively drifting "on a current which called itself my destiny" (*LSS*, 42). In some ways, the circumstances of her life were less conducive to writing than those of Bradstreet and Dickinson, both of whom had servants: "I did not then understand that we—the women of that academic community—as in so many middle-class communities of the period—were expected to fill both the part of the Victorian Lady of Leisure, the Angel in the House, and also of the Victorian cook, scullery maid, laundress, governess, and nurse" (*OWB*, 27).

As we have seen, Emily Dickinson had considerable leisure which she vigilantly protected. In addition to Dickinson's freedom from the de-

mands of marriage and motherhood, she was not responsible for cooking, cleaning, or other domestic maintenance, so her writing time was far
less fragmented than was Rich's during her years as a young wife and
mother. Although Bradstreet had eight children, as a governor's wife she
had a staff of servants.[6] Ironically, the ideology of the self-sufficient
housewife who operated her own washing machine, vacuum cleaner, and
electric stove actually resulted in creating more work for twentieth-
century women of the professional and middle class because modern
household technology replaced servants.[7]

During these early years of child-rearing, Rich wrote "very little, partly
from fatigue, that female fatigue of suppressed anger and loss of contact
with my own being; partly from the discontinuity of female life with its
attention to small chores, errands, work that others constantly undo,
small children's constant needs" (*LSS*, 43). After the publication of *The
Diamond Cutters*, Rich did not publish another volume of poetry for
eight years. But during this hiatus, she continued to receive awards and
honorary appointments: in 1960, she was Phi Beta Kappa poet at the
College of William and Mary; in 1961, she received an award from the
National Institute of Arts and Letters for her poetry; in 1961–62, she
won a Bollingen Foundation grant for the translation of Dutch poetry;
and in 1962–63, she was awarded an Amy Lowell Traveling Fellowship.
In 1963, *Snapshots of a Daughter-in-Law* was published and awarded
the Hokin Prize of *Poetry Magazine*. But this extraordinary professional
success did not make it easier for Rich to find enough time in her exacting
schedule to write and to read. As she observes in her essay, "When We
Dead Awaken," at this time she was "reading in fierce snatches, scrib-
bling in notebooks, writing poetry in fragments" (*LSS*, 44). A journal
entry in April 1965, when she was thirty-six, describes her feelings of
inertia, anger, and confusion:

> Paralyzed by the sense that there exists a mesh of relationships—
> e.g., between my anger at the children, my sensual life, pacifism,
> sex (I mean sex in its broadest sense, not merely sexual desire)—
> an interconnectedness which, if I could see it, make it valid, would
> give me back myself, make it possible to function lucidly and pas-
> sionately. Yet I grope in and out among these dark webs. (*LSS*, 44)

Another entry written a few months later, at 3:30 A.M., recalling Benjamin Franklin's list of resolutions, reveals Rich's determination to create
more time for poetry writing:

> Necessity for a more unyielding discipline of my life.
>   Recognize the uselessness of blind anger.
>   Limit society.

> Use children's school hours better, for work & solitude.
> Refuse to be distracted from my own style of life.
> Less waste.
> Be harder & harder on poems. (*OWB*, 31)

Although these years of child-rearing were difficult, her frustrations and conflicts as a young wife and mother gave her the basis for understanding the lives of a wide variety of women, a fact that has become increasingly important in her later poetry.

In spite of the tension between her domestic and artistic lives, Rich's publishing success provided public affirmation of her poetic identity and professional career that Emily Dickinson never had and that Anne Bradstreet experienced to a much more limited extent after the publication of *The Tenth Muse*. In addition, Rich's sense of her personal and artistic possibilities was considerably enhanced by her college education and international travel, experiences that neither Bradstreet nor Dickinson had. Clearly, as a twentieth-century American woman, Rich possessed autonomy and mobility unknown to most women in previous generations. Because of the extraordinary individual freedom she experienced as a student and young woman, Rich must have been depressed and outraged when she discovered that the general social expectation was that she would relinquish her poetic career after she was married and had children. *Snapshots of a Daughter-in-Law*, published in 1963, records her resentment and dismay about the disparity between her aspirations as an accomplished poet and the traditional social values. Rich's contemporaries, Sylvia Plath and Anne Sexton, also experienced considerable anxiety and distress due to their conflicting roles as women and as serious artists, but unlike Rich neither evolved an analytic approach that enabled them to understand the sociocultural roots of their guilt and despair. Rich's references in *Snapshots* to Mary Wollstonecraft, Simone de Beauvoir, and other autonomous women indicate that she was already working within a feminist framework that enabled her to recognize and reject self-destructive emotional responses.

Just as Anne Bradstreet began to write more openly of her personal concerns, using poetic forms more suited to her emotions after her initial publishing success, so Rich began to write in a more individual style in her third volume. In addition to breaking the bonds of traditional versification, Rich begins to probe her experiences more deeply to discover the sources of her conflict as a woman writer who is also a mother and wife. For the first time, she writes from a point of view that is clearly a woman's; Rich herself has observed that until this volume, she "had tried very much *not* to identify myself as a female poet" (*LSS*, 44). Earlier poems such as "Boundary," "An Unsaid Word," "Mathilde in Normandy,"

"Aunt Jennifer's Tigers," and "Autumn Equinox" present carefully distanced portraits of women alienated from their husbands, the community, and even themselves: for example, Aunt Jennifer spends her days embroidering tigers that "do not fear the men beneath the tree" while her own life is hopelessly constricted by custom:

> When Aunt is dead, her terrified hands will lie
> Still ringed with ordeals she was mastered by.
> The tigers in the panel that she made
> Will go on prancing, proud and unafraid.
> (CW, 19)

Again, the tight rhyme scheme serves to control the turbulent emotions that seethe beneath the surface. But the poems in *Snapshots* are less guarded in their exploration of the anger and helplessness of an artistically accomplished woman who lives in a society that demands that she be selfless and that she sacrifice her needs to the institutions of marriage and motherhood as defined by men. In a striking parallel with Bradstreet, Rich tells us that the title poem "was jotted in fragments during children's naps, brief hours in a library, or at 3 A.M. after rising with a wakeful child" (*LSS*, 44).

Written from the perspective of Coventry Patmore's "angel in the house," the title poem, "Snapshots of a Daughter-in-Law" (1958–60), explores the legacy of self-hate and wasted energy experienced by women in a society that values them to the extent that they are ornamental and able to subordinate their potential accomplishments to others:

> Sigh no more, ladies.
> Time is male
> and in his cups drinks to the fair.
> Bemused by gallantry, we hear
> our mediocrities over-praised,
> indolence read as abnegation,
> slattern thought styled intuition,
> every lapse forgiven, our crime
> only to cast too bold a shadow
> or smash the mould straight off.
> (SDL, 24)

Trapped in the ethic of self-sacrifice, the speaker in this ten-part poem has internalized the fear of being assertive in a society that trivializes or scorns woman's capacity for reason and punishes female aggression. Here Rich observes that throughout history strong women have been censured for independent thought or action, and she cites the examples of the British Queen Boadicea, who according to Tacitus led an attack against the Romans in 62 A.D., and Mary Wollstonecraft, who assailed the barriers to equal education and social rights for women; both were called "harpy, shrew, and whore."

The isolation of women in marriage is emphasized in this volume. Rich laments the tradition of economic and social dependency of women on men and protests against the polarization of emotional relationships that recurs when men and women are arbitrarily divided into providers and nurturers. The gentle cadences and carefully rhymed stanzas of the earlier work are replaced in the title poem by staccato rhythms of modern vernacular and synchronic images that connect Rich to the tradition of T. S. Eliot, Robert Lowell, Sylvia Plath, Charles Olson, and Denise Levertov. Ironically echoing the lines of Catullus and Horace, Rich points out that a woman must be "sweetly laughing; sweetly singing" to attract and hold a man who will take care of her. Here the speaker is aware of the cultural traps in which she is caught: the wife's loss of legal autonomy in marriage; the diminishing power of the aging woman in a society that values youth, not wisdom—"has Nature shown / her household books to you, daughter-in-law, / that her sons never saw?" (SDL, 23). Rich writes of the fear and guilt experienced by the woman who pierces cultural illusions: "A thinking woman sleeps with monsters. / The beak that grips her, she becomes" (SDL, 22). In "Double Monologue" (1960), anger, denied, is converted into despair and even madness or suicide.

Although more vigorous language and personal rhythms replace the careful formalism of her earlier poems, "Snapshots" is less forceful than Rich's later work. Rich herself admits that her voice is still tentative: "[The poem was written] in a longer looser mode than I'd ever trusted myself with before. It was an extraordinary relief to write that poem. It strikes me now as too literary, too dependent on allusion; I hadn't found the courage yet to do without authorities, or even to use the pronoun 'I'—the woman in the poem is always 'she'" (LSS, 44–45). Nevertheless, Adrienne Rich began to find a personal center and a poetic focus; as Albert Gelpi aptly observes, this volume marks "a penetration into experience that makes for distinguishing style."[8] Snapshots marks the beginning of a personal and political pilgrimage; subsequent works describe the stages of the journey—a journey that takes the poet into Dickinson's "plummetless well" in an effort to sound the depths of the interior self as well as into the wider world of politics and social activism. As Rich begins to become independent of the embedded values and social expecta-

tions that have previously limited her range of poetic expression, she
abandons the forms of her earlier decorative poetry:

> Since I was more than a child
>   trying on a thousand faces
> I have wanted one thing: to know
>   Simply as I know my name
> at any given moment, where I stand.
>
> How much expense of time and skill
>   which might have set itself
> to angelic fabrications! All merely
>   to chart one needle in the haymow?
> Find yourself and you find the world?
>   ("Double Monologue," *SDL*, 33)

Here her lines are more loosely structured and her ornate rhyme schemes
give way to slant rhymes that do not contain and control emotion but
express complicated ambivalences of her thought. Like Dickinson, Rich
rebels against male authorities and commits herself to the primacy of her
own perceptions, but Rich is unwilling to adopt Dickinson's stance of ostensible acceptance of a society bifurcated into passive and active spheres
in order to find a protected space in which to write. Rich's reliance on
the feminist tradition helped her avoid Dickinson's long, arduous, and
only partially successful struggle to gain control over her energies and her
life. Instead, Rich's private conflicts become the source of a wider, public
vision.

In "Snapshots of a Daughter-in-Law," Rich calls forth a woman in
command of her body, her erotic and creative energies, who celebrates
life, not death. This woman is not defined by her reproductive function;
instead she is in command of the powers of both her mind and her body:

>   Well,
>
> she's long about her coming, who must be
> more merciless to herself than history.
> Her mind full to the wind, I see her plunge
> breasted and glancing through the currents,
> taking the light upon her
> at least as beautiful as any boy
> or helicopter,
>   poised, still coming,
> her fine blades making the air wince

but her cargo
no promise then:
delivered
palpable
ours.
    (*SDL*, 24–25)

In this stanza, Rich draws on a section from Simone de Beauvoir's *The Second Sex*: "She arrives from the depths of the ages, from Thebes, Minos, Chichen Itza; she is also the totem rooted in the heart of the African bush; she is a helicopter and she is a bird; and here the greatest wonder: under her painted hair, the rustling of the leaves becomes thought and words escape from her breast."[9] Having attained a wider life as a modern woman as well as public recognition as an accomplished poet, Rich's prophecy of this new heroine takes on epic proportions, not unlike Whitman's democratic vision of the new men and women who populate the New World.

Traditionally, marriage is seen as a bulwark against social uncertainty, but as Rich rejects sacrificial womanhood, so she must give up the expectation that she will be safeguarded from anxieties and challenges traditionally experienced by men in a competitive, profit-oriented society. With the publication of *Snapshots* Rich declared her intention to move away from social forms in which she feels the lives and energy of women and men are essentially controlled by a masculine ethos that denies the intrinsic value of all but a few powerful men. As she wrote several years later,

> Patriarchy is the power of the fathers: a familial-social, ideological, political system in which men—by force, direct pressure, or through ritual, tradition, law, and language, customs, etiquette, education, and the division of labor, determine what part women shall or shall not play, and in which the female is everywhere subsumed under the male. (*OWB*, 57)

By analyzing the historical and cultural contexts of women's lives regardless of class or race, Rich hopes to achieve a comprehensive view of the relationship between gender and social values and economic reality. Whereas Dickinson undertook her explorations at home, Rich has searched for an understanding of her life that would also encompass the lives of many women. Personal anger over the circumstances of her own life fueled Rich's poetic and social vision, a vision that includes the public and historical dimensions of female experience. Rich has broadened her ground to include the lives of all women regardless of their social status or historical context. This community of women includes "the poet, the housewife, the lesbian, the mathematician, the mother, the dishwasher, the pregnant teenager, the teacher, the grandmother, the prostitute, the philosopher, the waitress."[10]

In *Necessities of Life: Poems, 1962–65*, which was published in 1966 and was nominated for the National Book Award, Rich pursues her exploration of the relationships between personal identity and the cultural context. In this collection, Rich articulates her emerging awareness that individual experience cannot be arbitrarily separated from its historic context, and there is a growing conviction that the tension she experiences between her personal values and larger social forms embodies the cultural schism between mind and body, nature and civilization, oppressor and oppressed, which she feels is the basis for patriarchal order. Many of the poems express an increasing despair with masculine territoriality as manifested in the French civil strife, the Vietnam War, and the Arab-Israeli conflicts that took place in the decade of the 1960s. "Spring Thunder" (1965) explores the human cost of war, making clear the vulnerability of the great mass of people to a military-industrial elite capable at any time of destroying life on earth:

> Thunder is all it is, and yet
> my street becomes a crack in the western hemisphere
> my house a fragile nest of grasses.
>
> The radiotelescope flings its nets
> at random; a child is crying,
> not from hunger, not from pain,
> more likely impotence. The generals are sweltering
>
> in the room with a thousand eyes.
> Red-hot lights flash off and on
> inside air-conditioned skulls.[11]

Several years later, Rich formulates an explicit cultural analysis of the concerns expressed in this poem:

> Yet it is precisely this culture and its political institutions which
> have split us off from itself. In so doing it has also split itself off from
> life, becoming the death-culture of quantification, abstraction, and
> the will to power which has reached its most refined destructive-
> ness in this century. It is this culture and politics of abstraction
> which women are talking of changing, of bringing to accountability
> in human terms. (*OWB*, 285)

In 1966, Rich was Phi Beta Kappa poet at Harvard; in the same year, she and her husband, Alfred Conrad, moved to New York City, where he taught economics at the City College of New York. In the next ten years, Rich taught at a large number of colleges and universities: in 1966–69, she held appointments at Swarthmore College and Columbia University Graduate School. In 1968–72, she taught in the open admissions and SEEK programs at the City College of New York; in 1972–73, she taught at Brandeis University as well as City College, and most recently, at Douglass College, Rutgers University. During these years of teaching in such diverse institutions as Swarthmore and City College, Rich became active in the protest against the Vietnam War; *Leaflets: Poems, 1965–68* reflects her growing awareness of the profound connection between private and public life. With her increased participation in institutional life and her growing visibility as a poet, Rich attained an identity that is dramatically different from that of Bradstreet or Dickinson. Unlike her predecessors, she has evolved a sense that she can not only shape the circumstances of her own life but that she can function as a spokeswoman for those people whose lives have not often been recorded in literature. In this regard, her prospects are more like Whitman's than Dickinson's.

In *Leaflets*, Rich writes of her desire to create public forms that are capable of meeting private needs, and she rejects traditional masculine aesthetics, which arbitrarily separates art and life. Asserting that poetry and politics are intertwined—that poetry has the power to transform lives—Rich writes, "I want to choose words that even you / would have to be changed by." [12] Having decided that she cannot merely escape into apolitical aestheticism, she calls for a reintegration of the personal and the political in order to create new forms of civilization. According to Rich, the impulse to write good poetry is an expression of the desire to reweave the fabric of our lives. Rich has said that in *Leaflets* she was "rebelling against poetic conventions" (*TCWM*), and the long caesuras in "Picnic" (1967) reflect her effort to create a more open-ended style:

Sunday in Inwood Park
              the picnic eaten
  the chicken bones scattered
                  for the fox we'll never see
  the children playing in the caves
  My death folded in my pocket
                like a nylon raincoat
  What kind of sunlight is it
              that leaves the rocks so cold?
                  (L, 36)

Here Rich is less hesitant to face the darker side of her experience; the looser line structure indicates a willingness to disturb the pattern of her perceptions and to relinquish control for the sake of achieving another angle of vision. Significantly, the male sun that enlivened Bradstreet's landscape and seared Dickinson's flowers has lost its force. Instead, this masculine element is depicted as sterile, without life-giving potency.

In this volume the poet casts her lot with the victims of war—in this instance, the Vietnam War, which is a metaphor for sexual as well as military aggression. In "Nightbreak" (1968) her personal oppression is linked with the fate of the innocent victims of war whose lives are arbitrarily destroyed:

> In the bed the pieces fly together
> and the rifts fill   or else
> my body is a list   of wounds
> symmetrically placed
> a village
> blown open   by planes
> that did not   finish the job
>   (L, 48)

Here her style becomes increasingly experimental, the spaces between the words as significant as the words themselves. The gaps between the phrases suggest a groping for understanding; the contrapuntal lines express the tension inherent in her struggle to find language that will express her growing conviction of the interconnection of all people.

Like *Necessities of Life*, *Leaflets* also documents the political upheavals of the 1960s: the turmoil of the Vietnam War, the revolt in Algeria, the student revolutions in France and the United States. For example, the third section of the collection, "Ghazals: Homage to Ghalib" (1968), evokes the dislocation created by the social and political crises of the decade. Rich experiments with the ghazal, an Arabic verse form that consists of a series of five independent but interrelated couplets, in order to convey the daily reality of the disordered and discordant world in which she lives. In her introduction to the ghazals, Rich says that "each couplet [is] autonomous and independent of the others. The continuity and unity flow from the associations and images playing back and forth among the couplets in any single *ghazal*" (L, 59). Rich uses the details of daily urban life to state her political message—conversations in Central Park represent growing dissatisfaction with American political priorities, graffiti express the anger of disenfranchised people who pay the human price of arbitrary waste of resources, unequal division of power, and

the exploitation of the mass of people through the collusion of powerful men:

> If these are letters, they will have to be misread.
> If scribblings on a wall, they must tangle with all the others.
>
> Fuck reds   Black Power   Angel loves Rosita
> —and a transistor radio answers in Spanish: *Night must fall.*
> $\qquad\qquad\qquad\qquad\qquad\qquad\qquad\qquad\qquad$ (*L,* 75)

Informal syntax, political slogans, vernacular expressions convey a sense
of the cultural fragmentation and urban dislocation and destruction.

The poems in *The Will to Change: Poems, 1968–70,* which received
the Shelley Memorial Award of the Poetry Society of America, chronicle
Rich's increasing rage at the waste of human energies, especially those of
women in patriarchal society, and continue to explore women's efforts to
define their own reality. This volume also reflects Rich's decision to change
her personal life. In 1970, she left her marriage; later the same year, Alfred Conrad, her husband, committed suicide. The fragmented lines and
images of "Shooting Script" (1970), reflect the discontinuity of her life
during this period:

> Now to give up the temptations of the projector; to see instead the
> web of cracks filtering across the plaster.
>
> To read there the map of the future, the roads radiating from the
> initial split, the filaments thrown out from that impasse.
>
> To read the instructions on your palm; to find there how the
> lifeline, broken, keeps its direction.
>
> To reread the etched rays of the bullet-hole left years ago in the
> glass; to know in every distortion of the light what fracture is.
>
> To put the prism in your pocket, the thin glass lens, the map
> of the inner city, the little book with gridded pages.
>
> To pull yourself up by your own roots; to eat the last meal in
> your old neighborhood.[13]

The familiar pattern of the poet's life has been disrupted: the words
crack, split, broken, fracture, express this fragmentation. But from the
shards of her old life comes the beginning of a new pattern; "the web of
cracks," the "filaments thrown out from that impasse" signal the poet's
intention to explore new territory.

TWELVE

"Visionary Anger Cleansing My Sight"

Adrienne Rich's effort to achieve a new understanding of her personal and political needs is perhaps best expressed in *Diving into the Wreck: Poems, 1971–72*, which was published in 1973. This volume won the National Book Award in 1974 and has been praised by Helen Vendler for its "courage in the refusal to write in forms felt to be outgrown." [1] In this volume, Rich explores the disparity between her personal experience as an active, accomplished woman and the priorities of the larger society. Many poems scrutinize the basic life events—love, sex, marriage, motherhood—from a feminist perspective; others assert the need for female collectivity—a goal of the feminist movement of the 1970s in which Rich was becoming increasingly active. In "Waking in the Dark" (1971), Rich reflects that "The tragedy of sex / lies around us, a woodlot / The axes are sharpened for." [2] In "Incipience" (1971), she explores the primordial origin of patriarchy and emphasizes the need for a female community to enable women to express their true power, which lies submerged like Dickinson's dormant volcano:

> Outside the frame of his dream we are stumbling up the hill
>   hand in hand, stumbling and guiding each other
>   over the scarred volcanic rock
>
> (*DW*, 12)

Like Dickinson, Rich turns to the community of women to sustain her as a woman and as a writer, but Rich extends her vision beyond Dickinson's select group of personal friends to women as a national, even international, collectivity. By emphasizing the need for shared female identity that transcends class and race, Rich hopes to create common ground from which an effective political vision can grow.

At the core of Adrienne Rich's feminism is the conviction that the new social order must begin with the truths of the female body as opposed to the male mind: "We must touch the unity and resonance of our physicality, the corporeal ground of our intelligence" (*OWB*, 62). In this way, Rich asserts, a gynecocentric, or woman-centered, universe would counteract and correct the antifemale bias of patriarchy. According to Rich, her poetry represents an effort to express a shift of world that may be translated into a change of language and of belief; this is where art and politics meet.

In her speech for the National Book Award ceremony for *Diving into the Wreck*, Adrienne Rich read a statement written with two other nominees, Alice Walker and Audre Lorde, accepting the award in the name of all women:

> We . . . together accept this award in the name of all women whose voices have gone and still go unheard in a patriarchal world, and in the name of those who, like us, have been tolerated as token women in this culture, often at great cost and in great pain. . . . We dedicate this occasion to the struggle for self-determination of all women, of every color, identification or derived class.[3]

Rich used this occasion intended to honor her personal achievement to give recognition to the community of women. Instead of emphasizing her individual accomplishments, she brought increased attention to the work of these black women writers. This speech underscores Rich's commitment to the ideal of cooperation among women that she feels is a necessary antidote to masculine competitiveness.

In an effort to understand her personal history more fully, the poet decides to return to her primal origins, to plunge into the depths of her psychic and cultural past. This undertaking is graphically imagined in the title poem, "Diving into the Wreck" (1972): in the depths of the sea, the origin of life, Rich explores the wreck of a ship, a multivalent metaphor for the remnants of Western culture, the poet's past, and her subconscious life. As Alicia Ostriker observes, this watery submersion is an inversion of heroic male ascents and conquests.[4] The terse cadences of the declarative sentences of the first stanza resolutely describe the preparations for the dive: the poet undertakes the descent not with a "team" but "here alone," "I put on / the body-armor of black rubber," "I go down, / Rung after rung" (*DW*, 22). This journey is necessary for the poet to confront "the wreck and not the story of the wreck / the thing itself and not the myth" (*DW*, 23).

To these oceanic depths the poet has brought artifacts of her culture to help her survive and understand her journey: the loaded camera to record her findings; the sharpened knife to defend her from deep-sea dangers. These objects represent "the book of myths" or cultural explanations that give shape to amorphous experience. Like an "insect down the ladder," she has descended alone, gradually becoming free of conventions that label reality: "there is no one / to tell me when the ocean / will begin" (DW, 23). There is no need to categorize her perceptions, to separate night from day, dusk from dawn, chaos from order, hate from love: "I have to learn alone / to turn my body without force / in the deep element" (DW, 23). According to Rich, to move "without force" but with sensitivity to the context, constitutes a female mode of perception.

Reaching the site of the wreck—psychic and cultural origins—the poet experiences the primal wholeness that predates the dualities, distinctions, and divisions of the Western psyche:

> This is the place.
> And I am here, the mermaid whose dark hair
> streams black, the merman in his armored body
> We circle silently
> about the wreck
> we dive into the hold.
> I am she: I am he
>   (DW, 24)

The mermaid and the merman must both adjust to the environment as a common denominator. Here the tensions of subject and object, mind and matter, male and female are dissolved; the poet discovers "where the spirit began" in the Judeo-Christian heritage of a divided world where light is separated from darkness, earth from water, the creatures of the air, land, and sea from one another—a world in which mind is divorced from body, spirit from matter, self from society. At the primordial center, there are no divisions between subconscious and conscious, subject and object, sacred and profane, inside and outside, good and evil, or feminine and masculine. Finally, Rich as diver-poet regains the wholeness, unimpaired by the arbitrary splits that diminish the phenomenological resonance that Dickinson so prized.

Certainly Rich and Dickinson are not the only poets to express concern with psychic and cultural integrity; for example, Blake and Whitman also wanted to create a unifying vision that would heal the social and emotional fractures, and like Rich, they realized that cultural polarities are intensified by artificial social distinctions between women and men. But in contrast to male poets, Rich is particularly concerned with the effects of gender polarity on women because women have traditionally been excluded from larger social processes. Surveying the wreck and its cargo, the poet ironically observes that she returns to this scene "by cowardice or courage," even though there is no historical connection between women and the wrecked civilization it represents—"a book of myths / in which / our names do not appear" (*DW*, 24). Nevertheless, the poet has completed the archetypal journey to reclaim her energy and to become the namer of her own experience.

Helen Vendler points out that "the forcefulness of *Diving into the Wreck* comes from the wish not to huddle wounded, but to explore the caverns, scars, and depths of the wreckage. At first these explorations must reactivate all the old wounds, inflame the old scar tissue, awaken all the suppressed anger, and inactivate the old language invented for dealing with the older self."[5] For the self to become autonomous, defining its experience, or "naming," is necessary. In the early years of the 1970s, it became important for increasing numbers of women to take charge of their lives, to free themselves from habits of dependency on men, and to interpret their own experience. In an essay written in 1971, "When We Dead Awaken: Writing as Re-Vision," Adrienne Rich has discussed the need for women to review their lives in order to examine the cultural assumptions that prevent women from having access to their most basic energies:

> Re-vision—the act of looking back, of seeing with fresh eyes, of entering an old text from a new critical direction—is for women more than a chapter in cultural history: it is an act of survival. Until we can understand the assumptions in which we are drenched we cannot know ourselves. And this drive to self-knowledge, for women, is more than a search for identity: it is part of our refusal of the self-destructiveness of male-dominated society. A radical critique of literature, feminist in its impulse, would take the work first of all as a clue to how we live, how we have been living, how we have been led to imagine ourselves, how our language has trapped as well as liberated us, how the very act of naming has been till now a male prerogative, and how we can begin to see and name— and therefore live—afresh. A change in the concept of sexual identity is essential if we are not going to see the old political order reassert itself in every new revolution. (*LSS*, 35)

The poem "Trying to Talk with a Man," written in 1971, the same year as "When We Dead Awaken," explores the breakdown of communication between men and women that results from the definition of men as dominant, masterful, and controlling and women as powerless, passive, and receptive. Deprived by the convention of submissive femininity of the opportunity to use her own emotional and intellectual resources, the poet laments to her lover that she feels "more helpless / with you than without you" (DW, 3). Rich finds a parallel between the oppression of women and the industrial destruction of the environment. For her, both are the result of the masculine need for mastery and dominance. As she writes in "Waking in the Dark," "A man's world. But finished. / They themselves have sold it to the machines" (DW, 8). And she wonders "what on earth it all might have become" (DW, 8). In "Merced" (1972), she decries the world characterized by "masculinity made / unfit for women or men" (DW, 36).

In such poems as "August" (1972), Rich confirms her need to move away from patriarchal territoriality, with its emphasis on father-right and legal paternity, toward the chthonic mysteries of the prehistoric Great Mother. According to Rich, if women are to survive the damaging effects of the culture in which they live, they must overcome "*self-trivialization, contempt for women, misplaced compassion, addiction* [to love, to depression, to male approval]; if we would purge ourselves of this quadruple poison, we would have minds and bodies more poised for the act of survival and rebuilding."[6]

Rich insists that women must no longer protect men while destroying themselves. In "A Primary Ground" (1972), she surveys the emotional topography of a conventional relationship: "And this is how you live: a woman, children / protect you from the abyss" (DW, 38). In "Translations" (1972), she describes "a woman of my time / obsessed / with Love, our subject: / we've trained it like ivy to our walls" (DW, 40). Lamenting the distortions created by the mythology of romantic love in "From a Survivor" (1972), she recognizes that genuine relationship requires mutual respect, which she feels is impossible in a society that exploits women:

> The pact that we made was the ordinary pact
> of men & women in those days
>
> I don't know who we thought we were
> that our personalities
> could resist the failures of the race
>
> (DW, 50)

In the ten-part poem, "The Phenomenology of Anger" (1972), Rich begins the arduous task of discovering complex emotional interrelationships that must be excavated to achieve the first stage of self-awareness. If these emotions are not experienced or understood, the submerged feelings express themselves in distorted and destructive ways. Denied anger, hatred, and despair become madness, murderous rage, or suicidal self-hatred. Exploring the effects of individual and social rage, this poem traces out the texture and tonality of anger—the feeling and course of the emotion: this is the phenomenology, not the epistomology of anger. Rich does not try to understand anger in order to predict its effects; instead, she is concerned with describing the process as well as the source of rage. Her approach is descriptive rather than abstract. The first two sections of the poem explore the differences between the expression and the repression of anger, between letting go and holding back the emotion: "The freedom of the wholly mad / to smear & play with her madness" is contrasted with the cold control of the machinist who limits himself to the measured boundaries of his job: "How does a pile of rags the machinist wiped his hands on / feel in its cupboard, hour upon hour?" (DW, 27). Unlike the machinist who ignores the oil-soaked rags that will smolder in the cupboard and ignite, the poet realizes that the price of mechanized routines and denied feeling is a loss of eros and a loss of a vibrant connection to life.

The next three sections of the poem correlate the emotional and sensual aridity resulting from repressed rage, which in its public form is revealed in the masculine attempt to dominate the elements with such geopolitical events as war, the technological subjugation of nature, the oppression of third-world countries. Rich asks: "Madness. Suicide. Murder. / Is there no way out but these?" In bold declarative statements she acknowledges her hatred for the patriarch who feels nothing, the death carrier who destroys himself and his world in the name of control:

> I hate you.
> I hate the mask you wear, your eyes
> assuming a depth
> they do not possess, drawing me
> into the grotto of your skull
> the landscape of bone
>
>   (DW, 29)

Then the poet decides to fight back, breaking the taboo that bound Bradstreet and Dickinson; the taboo that requires women to submerge their fury. In retaliation, she imagines herself doing battle with the man who "[guns] down the babies at My Lai / vanishing in the face of confrontation." She wants to vanquish the killer "burning the crops with some new sublimate" (DW, 29). She becomes a modern Amazon, metaphorically turning the killer's weapons against him. In a series of sibilant phrases, she uses his weapons not to destroy him but to transform him:

>   When I dream of meeting
> the enemy, this is my dream:

white acetylene
ripples from my body
effortlessly released
perfectly trained
on the true enemy

raking his body down to the thread
of existence
burning away his lie
leaving him in a new
world; a changed
man
           (DW, 28–29)

Paralleling the images of monarchs that fascinated Bradstreet and Dickinson, Rich envisions a superwoman who actively changes the world. In contrast to the indomitable queens of Bradstreet and Dickinson who reign over a fixed society, Rich's Amazon has transformative energy that can bring forth a new world.

Having dared to define the patriarchal male as the enemy and to actively and publicly resist his dominance, the poet imagines an alternative to his world. Here is a pastoral vision of a community in harmony with nature—a vision shared by many great artists male and female:

I would have loved to live in a world
of women and men gaily
in collusion with green leaves, stalks,
building mineral cities, transparent domes,
little huts of woven grass
each with its own pattern—
a conspiracy to coexist
with the Crab Nebula, the exploding
universe, the Mind—
           (DW, 30)

In contrast to the reality of a technological society, where the roar of machines is heard everywhere—in the sky, on the ground, under the ground—this community has no need to level forests, pave over plains and wetlands, erect monolithic buildings of concrete and steel.

The final stanza, recalling Hart Crane's description of the subway, conveys an apocalyptic sense of the inferno of industrial society in fierce, driving phrases:

how we are burning up our lives
testimony:
        the subway
        hurtling to Brooklyn
        her head on her knees
        asleep or drugged
la vía del tren subterráneo
es peligrosa
                (DW, 31)

The Spanish phrase that concludes the poem, literally "the way of the underground train is dangerous," is a warning about the perils of the tracks posted in every subway car in New York City. The pun on "way" also warns of the dangers of an increasingly depersonalized and mechanized society that is more concerned with profit than with the well-being of its citizens. This descent into the bowels of the industrial city documents the daily reality of the powerless. Here Whitman's mighty steed tramples human lives and Dickinson's innocent engine has become malevolent. But Rich makes it clear that it is not the machine as such that is destructive, but the misuse of technology by human beings.

The remaining poems of *Diving into the Wreck* continue to mourn the loss of resonance and wholeness in a world created by too narrow a conception of masculinity. In an analysis that is far more probing than Dickinson's, Rich protests the cultural insistence on father-right, grounded in legal possession and territoriality. Finally, in "August" (1972), the poet decides to turn away from this nightmare:

His mind is too simple, I cannot go on
sharing his nightmares

My own are becoming clearer, they open
into prehistory

which looks like a village lit with blood
where all the fathers are crying: *My son is mine!*
                (DW, 51)

Dickinson built her private world within the walls of her father's house, but Rich wants to remove herself altogether from the houses and cities of the fathers.

The final section of *Diving into the Wreck*, "Meditation for a Savage Child," is a series of poetic reflections based on *The Wild Boy of Aveyron* by Jean-Marc Gaspard Itard, a book that documents the systematic efforts of a scientist to civilize a naked child who was found wandering in the woods in 1799. Evidently, the child had never lived in society; he spoke no language and survived on acorns, roots, and berries. A rationalist, Itard was convinced that consistent training would eradicate all traces of primitive behavior. Instead of demonstrating the efficacy of his methods, however, Itard's account makes it clear that it is almost impossible to extinguish the profound connection between human and natural cycles. Itard's narrative reveals that the capacity for reason constitutes only a fraction of human consciousness:

> If . . . a stormy wind chanced to blow, if the sun behind the clouds showed itself suddenly illuminating the atmosphere more brightly, there were loud bursts of laughter, an almost convulsive joy, during which all his movements backwards and forwards very much resembled a kind of leap he would like to take, in order to break through the window and dash into the garden.[7]

Distressed by the boy's "constant tendency to trot and gallop," Itard dressed the child in a suit and tried to teach him European social conventions. Rich deplores Itard's ethnocentric efforts to teach the boy "names / for things / you did not need." The artifacts of civilization, "muslin shirred against the sun / linen on a sack of feathers / locks, keys / boxes with coins inside" do not affect the boy as deeply as a storm or a sunset.

The scientist observed that he never saw the boy weep until one day he threatened to throw the child out of the window. Itard reports that he "drew near him with every appearance of anger and seizing him forcibly by the haunches held him out of the window, his head directly turned toward the bottom of the chasm. . . . Afterwards he went and threw himself on his bed and wept copiously."[8] In her poetic version of this episode, Rich asks, "why should the wild child / weep / for the scientists / why" (DW, 62). Rich draws a parallel between Itard's efforts to discipline the boy and those of men to control women:

> At the end of the distinguished doctor's
> lecture
> a young woman raised her hand:
>
> > *You have the power*
> > *in your hands, you control our lives—*
> > *why do you want our pity too?*
> > (DW, 62)

In contrast with *Snapshots of a Daughter-in-Law*, published a decade earlier, *Diving into the Wreck* represents a major shift in attitude. During the interval between the publication of the two volumes, Rich's poetry became less ironic and instead concentrated on emotional awareness and forceful self-presentation. *Snapshots of a Daughter-in-Law* is written from the perspective of an outsider—a daughter-in-law—who observes but does not affect the world around her. The voice in the poems of *Diving into the Wreck* is strong and resolute; Rich has abandoned the indirect strategies of Bradstreet and Dickinson in order to engage in direct, public confrontation. This volume expresses the concerns of the increasingly visible feminist movement of the 1970s.

In *Diving into the Wreck*, Rich has learned to use anger as a source of energy: "my visionary anger cleansing my sight" ("The Stranger" [1972], *DW*, 19). In a conversation with Barbara and Albert Gelpi, Rich has stated: "I think anger can be a kind of genius if it's acted on."[9] Anger releases the poet from social forms that no longer fit her experience, and as she indicates in "Song" (1971), her rage sustains her during her solitary journey toward personal and cultural origins:

> If I'm lonely
> it's with the rowboat ice-fast on the shore
> in the last red light of the year
> that knows what it is, that knows it's neither
> ice nor mud nor winter light
> but wood, with a gift for burning
>
> (*DW*, 20)

The image of wood or logs representing the potential for illumination occurs frequently in Rich's poetry; in her early poems, the logs are "half rotten" or dead, while in her later work, as she comes to understand and act on her anger, the logs burn with a fierce intensity. As Rich has repeatedly observed, anger is a creative force that women have not been permitted to experience:

> Women's survival and self-respect have been so terribly dependent on male approval. I almost think that we have a history of centuries of women in depression: really angry women who could have been using their anger creatively. . . . And therefore it's not only that there are unwritten books, but many of the books that were written are subdued, they're like banked fires—they're not what they might have been. (*ARP*, 111)

Rich's explication of anger counteracts the romantic mythology that sustained Dickinson's "Master" letters in which internalized rage became groveling humiliation and abject depression. In addition, Rich suggests that women as a group have not had access to their full powers because their fury has been converted into self-hate and despondency. Anger, then, should be empowering, not the cause of paralysis.

In 1974, the same year that Adrienne Rich received the National Book Award for *Diving into the Wreck*, Allen Ginsberg was also honored for *The Fall of America*. Dedicated to Walt Whitman and "manly friendship," this volume is the counterculture male's response to patriarchy. Like Rich, Ginsberg decries the senseless destruction of innocent people and the poisoning of the planet: "Oh awful Man! What have we made of the World! Oh man / capitalist exploiter of Mother Planet!" [10] In his acceptance speech for the award, delivered by Peter Orlovsky, Ginsberg admits that he too has contributed to the "debacle" of "materialist brutality we have forced on ourselves and the world" with "aggression and self-righteousness." Concluding with the declaration that "there is no longer any hope of the salvation of America proclaimed by Jack Kerouac and others of our Beat Generation," he retreats to "the vast empty quiet space of [his] own consciousness." [11] Just as feminists were evolving a collective political identity, Ginsberg was sounding the death knell of the male counterculture.

The contrast between the lives and careers of Adrienne Rich and Allen Ginsberg illuminates the disparity between male and female gender roles that has been the basis for feminist protest. Adrienne Rich spent most of her twenties and thirties trying to come to terms with her domestic responsibilities and her life as an American woman poet, while Ginsberg spent those years in pursuit of spiritual illumination, a quest that took him through Mexico, Tangiers, Europe, India, Africa, the Arctic, Chile, Bolivia, Peru, the Amazon, Cuba, the Soviet Union, Poland, and Czechoslovakia. Although Rich traveled in Europe during these years, the difference in the extent of their mobility and personal freedom is reminiscent of home-bound Dickinson and roving Whitman. While Rich was frantically writing poetry between household chores or in the middle of the night after comforting a restless child, Ginsberg was "waking mid-afternoon, day wasted idly—weeks passing idly." [12]

Although the Beats abused alcohol and psychedelics and experimented with orgies and meditation in order to achieve egolessness, their poetry and politics often remained egocentric. For example, Ginsberg's "Footnote to Howl" is a series of pronouncements that reinforce the poet's position at the center of the universe: "The world is holy! The soul is holy! The skin is holy! The navel is holy! The tongue and cock and hand and asshole holy!" [13] In 1965, when Rich was reviewing the essentials of her life, "I am gliding backward away from those who knew me / as the moon grows thinner and finally shuts its lantern" ("Moth Hour" [1965],

NL, 47), Ginsberg playfully proclaimed, "I do declare that I am God!," and asserted himself as Whitman's heir in his intention to "sing my Prophecy before / the Nations!" [14] In the early 1970s, when Rich was calling for feminist revision of cultural values based on motherhood and the female body, Ginsberg said, "Sperm is art, poetry, music, yoga. Sperm is *Kundalini,* serpent power." [15] In 1974, when Rich was writing about relationship, mutuality, and the interdependence of human life, "The decision to feed the world / is the real decision. No revolution / has chosen it," [16] Ginsberg was writing: "I want to be the most brilliant man in America." [17] In spite of unprecedented freedom gained by women since the 1920s, there are still dramatic inequities in privileges and prerogatives between male and female poets. In general, the difference in poetic style between Dickinson and Whitman is echoed in Rich and Ginsberg. Ginsberg's phallocentric poetry is characterized by declaration and projective egocentricity while Rich's work is concerned with internal process and relationship.

Poems: Selected and New, published in 1975, includes a sixteen-part poem, "From an Old House in America" (1974), in which a country house provides a metaphor for the lives of the women who lived in it: the woman who planted the narcissus flower beds; the woman whose postcards, sent to her from Norway, Holland, and Corsica, were thumbtacked to the wall. Like Anne Bradstreet and Emily Dickinson, the major events of the lives of these women occurred at home; their existence was shaped by the social and economic paradigm of differentiated spheres of female domesticity and male commerce. The poem attempts to recapitulate the complex and varied history of American women with a montage of voices from the past that recalls the women who first came to America across the Bering Strait, and then with the Puritans; like Anne Bradstreet, these women followed their men:

> I am washed up on this continent
> shipped here to be fruitful
>
> my body a hollow ship
> bearing sons to the wilderness
>
> sons who ride away
> on horseback, daughters
>
> whose juices drain like mine
> into the *arroyo* of stillbirths, massacres [18]

The women of the Massachusetts Bay Colony and other Puritan settlements, the African women brought as slaves to the American South, and the women of the mining camps and frontier settlements of the West had the power to survive harsh conditions:

> I am not the wheatfield
> nor the virgin forest
>
> I never chose this place
> yet I am of it now
>
> In my decent collar, in the daguerreotype
> I pierce its legend with my look
>
> my hands wring the necks of prairie chickens
> I am used to blood
>
> When the men hit the hobo track
> I stay on with the children
>
> My power is brief and local
> but I know my power
> (*PSN,* 239)

In this poem, elegantly crafted lyrical lines celebrate the coexistence of women and nature: "striated iris stand in a jar with daisies / the porcupine gnaws in the shed" (*PSN,* 239). Their daily routine centered "in plain and ordinary things" contrasts with the abstract edicts of the fathers: "he with fingers frozen around his Law / she with her down quilt sewn through iron nights" (*PSN,* 240).

The final stanzas of this poem reach back through American and Western European history to prehistory, evoking a mythology in which female power is not domesticated: "Their terror of blinding / by the look of her who bore them" (*PSN,* 243). In place of the sterile law of the fathers, Rich calls forth "The Erinyes," the Greek goddesses of vengeance who inhabit netherworld caves, to demand reparation for the damage done to women in Western civilization in the name of reason, logic, and intellect. Signaling a need for a new cultural direction, Rich recasts Donne's phrase: "Any woman's death diminishes me." In an effort to redress centuries of misogyny, Rich now places women at the center of history.[19]

"From an Old House in America" blends a variety of styles, from portraiture ("in my decent collar, in the daguerreotype") to historical commentary ("I am an American woman: / I turn that over") to fragments of monologue ("*I will live for others, asking nothing / I will ask nothing, ever, for myself*"). The poem combines direct, even blunt, lines ("*will you punish me for history* / he said / *what will you undertake* / she said") with highly lyrical phrases that again intricately mesh assonance and consonance:

> fireflies beat and simmer
>
> caterpillars begin again
> their long, innocent climb
>
> the length of leaves of burdock
> or webbing of a garden chair.
>   (*PSN*, 239–40)

A pattern binding past with present can be discerned in this patchwork of the faces, voices, and stories of American women:

> yet something hangs between us
> older and stranger than ourselves
>
> like a translucent curtain, a sheet of water
> a dusty window
>
> the irreducible, incomplete connection
> between the dead and the living
>
> or between man and woman in this
> savagely fathered and unmothered world.
>   (*PSN*, 237)

Moving back and forth between past and present, these lines attempt to bridge the gaps between lucidity and darkness, isolation and community, suffering and reparation, primal power and its terrors. This excavation of prehistory is a process that parallels the function of consciousness-raising on a personal level. Just as the release of repressed memories increases the self-awareness of individual women, so the unearthing of ancient cultural forms opens up new social possibilities. This revisioning of the chthonic past, American history, and feminist ideals signals a change of emotional and poetic center for Adrienne Rich.

THIRTEEN

"A Whole New Poetry Beginning Here"

Since the publication of *Diving into the Wreck*, Rich has increasingly devoted her energy to recording women's history and to understanding the ancient and contemporary forms of female relationships. In *Of Woman Born: Motherhood as Experience and Institution* (1976), an extended analysis of the ways in which patriarchal institutions deny women control over their bodies and their lives, Rich searches the past for historical clues that can help women envisage a viable future. Attempting to recover the lost history of women, Rich examines the mythic and anthropological prehistory of motherhood in Western culture, the modern domination of the birth process by male physicians, the psychological roots of "matrophobia," and the nature of the mother-daughter bond—issues that were especially important to American feminists in the 1970s.[1]

Throughout *Of Woman Born*, Rich cites specific incidents from her life to illustrate her analysis. Candid comments about her complicated feelings toward her own mother and her children, as well as astute historical analysis, are interspersed with quotes from her diaries and journals, such as the following August 1958 entry: "I write this as the early rays of sunlight light upon our hillside and eastern windows. Rose with [the baby] at 5:30 A.M. and have fed him and breakfasted. This is one of the few mornings in which I haven't felt terrible mental depression and physical exhaustion" (*OWB*, 28). By including observations from her personal experience, Rich achieves an unusual blend of subjective insight and objective analysis, undercutting male genre hierarchies that accord more importance to the philosophical treatise than the diary. This combination of private and public discourse in order to eliminate arbitrary stylistic categories parallels her refusal to accept the traditional distinction between politics and poetry.

Protesting the ontological hierarchies that have subordinated women to men and nature to civilization, Rich observes that patriarchal culture has cut itself off from the source of all life. In an effort to demonstrate the historical process by which the "primacy of the mothers" was subsumed by the "kingdom of the fathers," Rich reviews the archaeological and anthropological theories of James Mellart, Erich Neumann, Robert Brieffault, J. J. Bachofen, G. Rachel Levy, and Elizabeth Gould Davis, which suggest that women were of primary importance to the "Neolithic, pre-Columbian, Cypriot, Cycladic, Minoan, predynastic Egyptian" societies (OWB, 94). To counteract the misogynist images and metaphors of American public life, Rich feels it is important to examine those cultures that honor female power and provide myths of independent and powerful women. In prehistoric Crete and Eleusis, the earth was called "mother" because it was the source of food.[2] Later, the goddess Gaia-Ge represented the powers of mother earth and was often depicted as rising from under the ground bearing a cornucopia of fruit and a child; sometimes she was represented by the fruit-bearing tree. Rich points out that traces of this mother worship can be seen in the close relationships between the words *mother* and *matter* in most languages: *mutter, madre, mater, materia, moeder* (OWB, 108). In such totemistic societies as Minoan Crete, there was no sharp distinction between human, plant, or animal life; a woman bore a child as the fruit of her womb, just as the tree bore fruit, or the ground, corn. The connection between the menstrual cycle and the lunar cycle, as well as the fertility cults that revered the transformative power of childbearing and birth, were central mythic elements. All plants and animals were sacred, and religion was a collective worship of nature's forms. Seasonal changes were marked by the phases of planting, germination, and harvest: growth and decay, represented by the snake coiled around a fruit tree, were accepted as an inevitable part of this process; the omphalos, or sacred earth mound, was a fertility symbol marking dissolution and death as well as the regeneration of life.

With the shift to patriarchal religion, the gods were located on Olympus rather than in groves and gardens; the hero proved his prowess by killing the sacred snake; the omphalos was replaced by phallic towers; and sharp distinctions were made between mind and matter as well as human and nonhuman life. Social life moved from the family, the domain of women, to the marketplace; the tribe was replaced by the polis, and the pluralistic deities of earlier religions were fused into one God who offered believers the reward of eternal life. As Jane Harrison points out, this shift from the belief that all life is sacred to the emphasis on human immortality "is really the denial of life, for life is change."[3]

In the Hellenic and Judeo-Christian cosmology, the female body is controlled by the male will; its connection to nature's cycles is displaced by the definition of woman as a lower order of being rather than an awesome force, as she had been in earlier societies. Reviewing the evidence of fear of woman's power and the splitting off of the "good" or nurturing mother from the terrible mother in *Of Woman Born*, Rich connects matrophobia with the efforts of modern medicine to control women's bodies. As pregnancy and childbirth became the province of male control following the invention of the forceps that gave precedence to male technology over the midwives' hands, an expectant mother was perceived as a passive object in the birth process; in contrast to the midwife who assisted the laboring woman, the doctor directed the process of birth. In a chapter entitled "Alienated Labor," Rich analyzes the gradual control of all phases of reproduction by male doctors: current controversy about abortion, contraception, methods of delivery, and gynecological surgical procedures indicates that women are still denied the right to make their own decisions about their sexual and procreative processes. In *Of Woman Born*, the medical control of women's bodies becomes a paradigm for the domination of women in other areas of society.

In the chapter "Motherhood and Daughterhood" in *Of Woman Born*, Rich states that the "cathexis between mother and daughter—essential, distorted, misused—is the great unwritten story." Exploring the legacy of self-hate and repression passed on from mother to daughter, Rich says:

> Matrophobia can be seen as a womanly splitting of the self, in the desire to become purged once and for all of our mothers' bondage, to become individuated and free. The mother stands for the victim in ourselves, the unfree woman, the martyr. Our personalities seem dangerously to blur and to overlap with our mothers'; and, in a desperate attempt to know where mother ends and daughter begins, we perform radical surgery. (*OWB*, 236)

This alienation of mother and daughter is a modern version of the separation of Demeter and Kore. Rich observes that the Eleusinian celebration of the reunion of Demeter and Kore is an antidote to the distortion of the relationship between mother and daughter in male-dominated society; she insists that this celebration must be translated into modern experience as a need for "courageous mothering." Emphasizing the importance of a mother's struggle to "create liveable space around her, demonstrating to her daughter that these possibilities exist" (*OWB*, 247), Rich calls for a female bonding that will recognize the strength and diversity of women's abilities and powers. Like Dickinson, Rich is sustained by her relationships with women, but instead of being limited to the private circle of female friendships, Rich develops her personal experience into public discourse and social vision.

"Sibling Mysteries" (1976) is a six-part tour de force that uses the relationship between two sisters to illuminate the themes of chthonic mysteries, the primordial origins of the family, the denial of female power, and the longing to return to the mother. Throughout the poem, the refrain "Remind me" is used to recapture the prehistoric past:

> Remind me how the stream
> wetted the clay between our palms
> and how the flame
>
> licked it to mineral colors
> how we traced our signs by torchlight
> in the deep chambers of the caves
>   (DCL, 47)

An elaborate interweaving of assonance and consonance—especially the intricate patterning of the e's and l's—emphasizes the bond shared by the sisters with their mother, a bond that transcends their individual separateness: "our lives were driven down the same dark canal" (DCL, 51). The rhythms of this poem move easily, and the lines are graceful yet controlled: "Remind me how we loved our mother's body / our mouths drawing the first / thin sweetness from her nipples" (DCL, 48). The images are vivid and resonant, appealing to sight and touch: "smelling the rains before they came / feeling the fullness of the moon / before moonrise" (DCL, 47). In a complex texture of sound and sense—"and how we drew quills / of porcupines between our teeth / to a keen thinness" (DCL, 47–48)—Rich recreates the realm of women's primordial power, a world that Dickinson was also trying to revive.

Recalling the myth of Demeter and Kore, the second section laments the daughter's separation from the mother and celebrates the nurturing and healing power of "woman's flesh": "our faces dreaming hour on hour / in the salt smell of her lap / Remind me / how her touch melted childgrief" (DCL, 48). In the pre-Homeric legends, Kore is the maiden who initiates the annual growth cycle, and Demeter, her mother, represents the generativity of the earth. In the shift from the growth-centered religions of the Great Mother to the male religions emphasizing control and mastery, Demeter's daughter, Kore, is robbed of her power to initiate life. In the Homeric myth of Demeter, Kore (Persephone) is raped by Hades and abducted to the underworld: this rape and abduction of Persephone symbolizes the male usurpation of female agency and power. In the pre-Homeric myths, Persephone was associated with cyclic flux, and the inevitable rhythms of birth, growth, and decay, but once she has become a captive in Hades, she rises to earth only with the permission of Hades and Zeus. Demeter grieves because her daughter has been physically violated and abducted and because now men possess women and control seasonal change.

When Demeter mourned the abduction of Kore, she grieved not only for the loss of her daughter but for the loss of their shared vision of life. In her sadness and anger, Demeter made the earth barren as a demonstration of her power; not until she was reunited with Kore did nature again flourish. But Demeter and Kore could not resume their former lives; Kore had to return to Hades for a part of each year. Observing that marriage entails sacrifice and maturity requires suffering, some critics have interpreted Kore's enforced exile to Hades as a necessary renunciation that enabled her to attain womanhood.[4] But Demeter grieves because her daughter has become the captive of Hades and is no longer autonomous. The world of abundance and growth has been diminished by Kore's abduction, and the blight of winter symbolizes this loss of Demeter's connection to Kore.

In patriarchal society, the rape of Persephone carries with it the message that women must be ravished to experience womanhood, whereas the pre-Hellenic myths honor women's powers to cultivate the earth and give birth to children. When Demeter gave birth to Kore, she completed the phases of her life as maiden and mother; in her daughter, this cycle was to be perpetuated. The rape of Persephone gave men the symbolic power to control women's sexuality. In the original myth, fertility, reproduction, and death are intrinsic to life, and male and female sexuality are part of a fundamental process that produces offspring just as the combination of a seed, earth, and water produces corn.

In "Sibling Mysteries," Rich depicts the conflict caused by having to live in "two worlds / the daughters and the mothers / in the Kingdom of the sons" (DCL, 49). However, the memory of the mother creates a fundamental bond that cannot be severed: "Sister gazed at sister / reaching through mirrored pupils / back to the mother" (DCL, 50). Rich sees this bond between the two sisters and between the daughters and their mother as the primary social relationship, and this poem attempts to bring this deeply rooted pattern to consciousness:

> the daughters were to begin with
> brides of the mother
>
> then brides of each other
> under a different law
>
> (DCL, 52)

Dickinson's description of her bond to her sister Lavinia as "early, earnest, insoluble" and her observation that "without [Lavinia] life were fear, and Paradise a cowardice, except for her inciting voice" (L, 3 : 779, no. 827) parallels the relationship celebrated in Rich's poem.

In her analysis of the bonding patterns of mothers and daughters, Nancy Chodorow observes that the psychosocial developmental process for women in our culture creates a female psyche that is "relational" and a male psyche that is comparatively self-contained.[5] As Chodorow argues, women are mothered by women and then required to transfer this love to their fathers in order to develop heterosexually; therefore, they have a tendency to perceive themselves in terms of relationships and are more bisexually oriented than men.[6] Recent anthropological studies indicate that in prehistoric societies and contemporary hunter-gatherer groups the mother-child bond is the strongest social force.[7]

As in *Of Woman Born*, Adrienne Rich's subsequent volumes of poetry, *The Dream of a Common Language* and *A Wild Patience Has Taken Me This Far*, attempt to reverse the classification of women and nature with the lower orders of being. *The Dream of a Common Language* is divided into three sections, each having a different emphasis: the poems in the first group, "Power," are concerned with the outstanding achievements of individual women; the second group, "Twenty-One Love Poems," is a lyrical testimony of female eros and the shared lives of women; the third group, "Not Somewhere Else, But Here," explores the effects of the past on the present, analyzing natural, social, and personal history in order to discover its implications for contemporary women's lives.

The Dream of a Common Language articulates Rich's belief in the need for a community of women based on shared values and goals. "Origins and History of Consciousness," written over a two-year period from 1972 to 1974, excavates the experience of the modern woman who is no longer bound by the narrow emotional range of socially defined female self-images. Having won her freedom from *"the hunter, / the trapper / the wardens of the mind,"* Rich has decided that survival in an alien society is not enough. Insisting on the need for communication as the basis of companionship and of community, she declares, "No one sleeps in this room without / the dream of a common language" (DCL, 8).

In "Natural Resources" (1977), Rich again reminds her readers of the common fabric of women's daily lives:

> the loving humdrum acts
> of attention to this house
> transplanting lilac suckers,
> washing panes, scrubbing

> wood-smoke from splitting paint,
> sweeping stairs, brushing the thread
> of the spider aside,
> and so much yet undone
> a woman's work
>
> (DCL, 71)

The onomatopoeic cataloging of household tasks—scrubbing, washing, sweeping—and the allusion to the phrase "a woman's work is never done" underscore the poet's acceptance of life as a process of repeated and renewed effort through time.

Both *The Dream of a Common Language* and *Of Woman Born* are concerned with the suffering of women separated from community, the power of cooperation, the need to understand and name one's experience. In the title poem of the first section, "Power" (1974), Marie Curie's extraordinary achievement illustrates the paradoxical conditions of many women's lives in a patriarchal society:

> Today I was reading about Marie Curie:
> she must have known she suffered   from radiation sickness
> her body bombarded for years   by the element
> she had purified
> It seems she denied to the end
> the source of the cataracts on her eyes
> the cracked and suppurating skin   of her finger-ends
> till she could no longer hold   a test-tube or a pencil
>
> She died   a famous woman   denying
> her wounds
> denying
> her wounds   came   from the same source as her power
>
> (DCL, 3)

Although she was a brilliant and innovative scientist, the very nature of the work she was doing deprived her of life itself. The long caesuras between phrases of the final sentence underscore the difficulty of Marie Curie's struggle—a triumph that, ultimately, killed her.

This implosion of female energy exists in direct contrast with the joyful explosion in "Phantasia for Elvira Shatayev." Shatayev was the leader of the women's team that climbed Russia's Lenin Peak in August 1974; all of the women were killed in a storm. Like Curie, Shatayev and her team died in their effort, but the women climbers were aware of the risks and dangers of their undertaking:

<pre>
                    we stream
    into the unfinished   the unbegun
    the possible
</pre>

                                (DCL, 5)

In this poem, the caesuras do not isolate the phrases from each other, but indicate, instead, the resistance to be overcome. The silences are meditative and indicate possibilities, not limitations: "We could have stitched that blueness together like a quilt" (DCL, 5). Here the pause makes possible the sharing of syntactic resources and meanings that express the women's collective effort. Together, they confront the sky and the mountain, bringing their separate skills to the task; at the same time, their common cause unites them. The play on the word "together" emphasizes the power of this community of women. Outlined against the sky, their long climb is compared to sewing a quilt; each woman's skillful maneuvers bring the team closer to the mountaintop, just as the separate squares stitched by individual women help to complete the final pattern of the quilt. This analogy underscores the tradition of cooperative female activities.

In "Hunger" (1974–75), a four-part poem dedicated to Audre Lorde, Rich imagines what it would be like if a community of women used their collective intelligence and emotional resources to transform society:

> of what it could be to take and use our love,
> hose it on a city, on a world,
> to wield and guide its spray, destroying
> poisons, parasites, rats, viruses—
> like the terrible mothers we long and dread to be.
>
> (DCL, 13)

The modern Amazon of "The Phenomenology of Anger" is joined by other women who wish to transform the community; the collective commitment of the female community has replaced the resolute anger of one woman.

The second part of The Dream of a Common Language is entitled "Twenty-One Love Poems" (1974–76). The declarative, unadorned, sometimes flat lines of these poems focus on the simple details of everyday experience:

> I wake up in your bed. I know I have been dreaming.
> Much earlier, the alarm broke us from each other,
> You've been at your desk for hours.
>
> (DCL, 25)

In contrast to the tradition of Dante, Petrarch, and Shakespeare, the tone of these poems is conversational, sometimes colloquial; the mood is lyrical, and there is no yearning for escape. Instead, the words weighted with consonance affirm the ordinariness of the present moment: "the scrubbed, sheenless wood of the dressing table / cluttered with our brushes, books, vials in the moonlight—" (DCL, 33). These are poems of ecstasy but not of flight. Behind the simple, proselike stanzas is Rich's commitment to reveal her erotic relationship with another woman. She asserts that private attachment must exist in the context of wider public life. Risking the possible censure of homophobic readers and critics, Rich refuses to settle for a closeted, secret existence.

The love poems are remarkably direct. There is no need to construct a myth of the mysterious other; instead, there is tender intimacy, unobscured by elaborate metaphors or opaque references:

> But we have different voices, even in sleep,
> and our bodies, so alike, are yet so different
> and the past echoing through our bloodstreams
> is freighted with different language, different meanings—
> though in any chronicle of the world we share
> it could be written with new meaning
> we were two lovers of one gender,
> we were two women of one generation.
> (DCL, 30)

This is not an easy love; there are obstacles both external and self-generated, particularly for two people who are committed to equality. The poet does not indulge in the illusion that her passionate involvement will eliminate the need for struggle in daily life:

> If I could let you know—
> two women together is a work
> nothing in civilization has made simple,
> two people together is a work
> heroic in its ordinariness
> (DCL, 35)

The intricacy of the feelings and responses of two people requires "fierce attention" in order to achieve mutuality without sacrificing selfhood.

"Twenty-One Love Poems" explores emotional complexity and ambivalence in addition to the pleasures and joys of a relationship, and

these poems acknowledge the loneliness and separation that come from
failed love:

> and I discern a woman
> I loved, drowning in secrets, fear wound round her throat
> and choking her like hair. And this is she
> with whom I tried to speak, whose hurt, expressive head
> turning aside from pain, is dragged down deeper
> where it cannot hear me,
> and soon I shall know I was talking to my own soul.
>
> (DCL, 35)

Although the poet's lover is unable to acknowledge the relationship publicly, these poems affirm shared love while accepting pain, anger, and
fear:

> this we were, this is how we tried to love,
> and these are the forces they had ranged against us,
> and these are the forces we had ranged within us,
> within us and against us, against us and within us.
>
> (DCL, 34)

The litany of repeated phrases describes the internal and external tensions that defeat the relationship. In contrast to the utter dependence
on the beloved expressed in Bradstreet's and Dickinson's love poetry,
Adrienne Rich writes from the perspective of mutuality rather than the
traditional romantic scheme of masculine dominance and feminine submission. Monique Wittig suggests that the word "lesbian" describes
women who are not economically or ideologically dependent on men;
similarly for Rich, lesbian love is a paradigm of female sexuality that is
neither defined by men nor exploited by a phallocentric political system.[8]

In an essay, "Compulsory Heterosexuality and Lesbian Existence,"
published in 1980, Rich issues a radical challenge to the cultural definition of lesbianism as deviant or perverse. She asks why "species-survival,
the means of impregnation, and emotional / erotic relationships should
have become so rigidly identified with each other; and why such violent
structures should be found necessary to enforce women's total emotional,
erotic loyalty and subservience to men."[9] Challenging these traditional
assumptions, Rich observes that stereotyped sexuality deprives individuals of a range of choices; institutionalized heterosexuality "strips women
of their autonomy, dignity and sexual potential, including the potential
of loving and being loved by women in mutuality and integrity."[10] Rich

emphasizes the fact that the nature of female sexuality is defined by men, who use shame and guilt as a means of controlling women's behavior: "heterosexuality is a beach-head for male dominance."[11] Insisting that female sexuality no longer be defined by males, Rich draws the distinction between indoctrination and free choice; she maintains that "sexual slavery" exists whenever women cannot change the conditions of their lives. As we have seen, Emily Dickinson deliberately resisted marriage which she saw as threatening to destroy her life as a poet. Paralleling Anne Hutchinson's insistence on spiritual freedom, Adrienne Rich demands that freedom of sexual choice be granted as a fundamental human right.

"Not Somewhere Else, But Here," the third section of the volume, contains poems written over the three-year period 1974–77. The material in *The Dream of a Common Language* is not organized chronologically or even thematically. Themes and images reappearing throughout all the sections of the book create ever-widening spirals of intensified meaning. The need for relationship, for community, for the power of women is explored throughout the volume. The title poem of this section, written in 1974, serves as the companion poem to "Origins and History of Consciousness." Lamenting the failure of love to achieve fusion, the poem grieves for "Spilt wine   The unbuilt   house the unmade life." Staccato rhythms with long pauses between each phrase underscore the loss of connection, isolation, and fear: "the blood shrinks to the heart / the head severed it does not pay to feel." The broken, halting phrases of the poem express the poet's effort to understand her pain instead of repressing it:

> Her face   The fast rain tearing   Courage
> to feel this   To tell of this   to be alive
> trying to learn   unteachable lessons
> 　　　　　　　(DCL, 39–40)

The structure of these poems is no longer restrained by convention but reflects the poet's struggle to probe the depths of consciousness. The language, intense yet lyrical, is often punctuated by silences as weighted as the words. For example, the following poem expresses Rich's determination to give shape to her deepest emotions with images that sear the darkness of repressed hopes and possibilities denied:

> The fugue   Blood in my eyes   The careful sutures
> ripped open   The hands that touch me   shall it be said
> I am not alone
> Spilt love   seeking its level   flooding other

> lives   that must be lived   not somewhere else
> but here   seeing through blood   nothing is lost
> $(DCL, 40)$

Misery is not masked or refined by elaborate metaphors or ornamental images; instead, the phrases explode against each other. Because the poet experiences the full extent of her suffering, she does not blunt or cripple her capacity to feel love again. The poem speaks of the difficulty of communication, the pain of failed love. Although there is grief and intense pain in this poem, the abnegation and despair of Dickinson's "Master" poems are absent, as are the elaborate conceits and metaphors of Bradstreet's love poems. Instead, there is a direct, open expression of sorrow—undisguised and unmitigated.

Historical monologue and portrait are used in "Paula Becker to Clara Westhoff" (1975–76) to further explore female relationships. Paula Becker, a painter, and Clara Westhoff, a sculptor, met in an artists' colony near Bremen, Germany, in 1899. In 1901, Clara Westhoff married Rainer Maria Rilke, and Paula Becker married Otto Modersohn; the women continued to be close friends until Paula Modersohn-Becker died in childbirth, murmuring, "What a pity!" Using fragments of Becker's diaries, Rich pays tribute to the supportive friendship of two women artists who have been largely ignored by Americans until their recent rediscovery by feminist art historians. In the poem, Becker speaks of the pledge of these two friends "trying to create according to our plan / that we'd bring, against all odds, our full power / to every subject. Hold back nothing / because we were women" $(DCL, 44)$.

The yonic images of "Natural Resources" (1977) again link the landscape with the female body: "The core of the strong hill: not understood: the mulch-heat of the underwood." The repetition of the vowel "o" sounds the depth of unexplored caverns. The central metaphor of the poem is that of a miner; it describes the effort of a woman to explore the crevices of her mind, a psychological excavation likened to the tasks that confront a subterranean laborer. There is much work yet to be done, and the poet expresses anger at those men who threaten to interfere with the process of female discovery—men who misuse words like "humanism" and "androgyny." She warns against a male "passivity we mistake / —in the desperation of our search— / for gentleness," and she calls forth the active nurturing power in women "to help the world deliver." In contrast to its use in heroic narratives, here "deliver" means to assist in the birth process, not to rescue, set free, or aim at a destination, or to produce expected results:

> My heart is moved by all I cannot save:
> so much has been destroyed
>
> I have to cast my lot with those
> who age after age, perversely,
>
> with no extraordinary power,
> reconstitute the world.
>
> (DCL, 67)

Rich's tough yet lyrical lines do not passively contemplate suffering and loss; instead, the poet commits herself to active restoration of the world. This lost world is not Eden—a paradise where sickness and death are absent and roses have no thorns—but diurnal existence that requires constant effort and care.

The final poem in the volume, "Transcendental Etude" (1977), is a sustained vision of a woman whose energies are balanced between the self and the world around her. In this poem, Rich honors the fertility of the earth and the complexity of nature: "Later I stood in the dooryard, / my nerves singing the immense fragility of all this sweetness." The poem conveys an appreciation of the plenitude of the landscape before her:

> I've sat on a stone fence above a great, soft, sloping field
> of musing heifers, a farmstead
> slanting its planes calmly in the calm light,
> a dead elm raising its bleached arms
> above a green so dense with life,
> minute, momentary life—slugs, moles, pheasants, gnats,
> spiders, moths, hummingbirds, groundhogs, butterflies—
> a lifetime is too narrow
> to understand it all, beginning with the huge
> rockshelves that underlie all that life.
>
> (DCL, 73)

This is a long poem that is not broken into sections; the lyrical language flows without pause or interruption as Rich finds her full poetic voice: "a whole new poetry beginning here / Vision begins to happen in such a life." Rich is not concerned with "the striving for greatness, brilliance," but "only with the musing of a mind / one with her body." This poem expresses reverence for "the many-lived, unending / forms" in which she finds herself as well as a calm acceptance of the complex life processes. The perspective in this poem is not fragmented or partial. Instead of focusing on flowers, trees, or meadows, Rich takes in the entire landscape and does not sacrifice the whole to any part because she understands that the countryside before her involves an elaborate balance of relationships.

In contrast to the acceptance of the life cycle in "Transcendental Etude" the following passage from Samuel Sewall's description of the seventeenth-century New England landscape articulates the Puritan conviction that the purpose of human life was to prepare for eternal existence, to transcend corporeality to become "Saints in Light":

> As long as Plum Island shall faithfully keep the commanded post;
> Notwithstanding all the hectoring Words, and hard Blows of the
> proud and Boisterous ocean; As long as any Salmon, or Sturgeon
> shall swim in the streams of Merrimack; Or any Perch, or Pickerel,
> in Crane-Pond; . . . As long as Cattel shall be fed with the Grass
> growing in the Meadows, which do humbly bow down themselves
> before Turkie-Hill; As long as any Sheep shall walk upon Old
> Town Hills, and shall from thence pleasantly look down upon the
> River Parker, and the fruitfull Marshes lying beneath; . . . So long
> shall Christians be born there; and being first made meet, shall
> from thence be Translated, to be made partakers of the Inheritance
> of the Saints in Light. [12]

Although Sewall clearly appreciates nature, his desire to be "translated" to heaven bifurcates his experience in such a way that nature is merely a harbinger of everlasting life. In contrast to Sewall, Rich does not dismiss earthly life to arrive at a heavenly destination, nor does she engage in the Puritan effort to tame and control nature in the name of God's elect. Like Dickinson, she accepts the cycle of birth, growth, and death and celebrates generativity.

Comparable to Anne Bradstreet's "Contemplations" in its deep appreciation of nature's beauty, there is no progress from earth to heaven in "Transcendental Etude," but rather an acceptance of life for its own sake. Rejecting ontological hierarchy, Rich's poem does not attempt to rise above ordinary experience. In contrast to Anne Bradstreet, Adrienne Rich does not feel a need to find a prime mover to explain the diverse interdependence before her, and the stratified universe of Bradstreet's poetry is replaced by an intricate web of interrelated life forms. "Transcendental Etude" emphasizes the connections between past, present, and future, nature and civilization, self and other. As in past poems, the themes that most concern Rich in this poem are the life-destroying drive for mastery; the old house through which generations have passed; the distress of the modern woman in a patriarchal culture; the difficulty of mothering in a society that does not prize nurturing; the necessity of cooperation. Rich stresses the importance of reverence toward life in its many forms, human and natural. The title of the poem is double-edged because Rich, like Dickinson, wants to be grounded in life, not released from it. For Rich, transcendence means the dissolution of artificial categories that obscure the multidimensionality of experience; moreover, transcendence also means the possibility of living in harmony with nature, a commitment to growth, not destruction—life, not death. This understanding and acceptance of the profound connection between nature and human life permits a vision that overcomes the habitual separation of mind and body, self and other:

> *I am the lover and the loved,*
> *home and the wanderer, she who splits*
> *firewood and she who knocks, a stranger*
> *in the storm*
>
> (DCL, 76)

Echoing and answering Yeats, this sustained lyric affirms the interconnection between nature and culture, past and present. Reintegrating consciousness that has been fragmented by masculine hierarchical thought, this poem captures the fluidity, simultaneity, and multiplicity of experience instead of subordinating one perception or state of being to another. The past is not jettisoned in this poem; instead, it is a basis for the future. Like the "rockshelf" that provides the foundation for life in nature, the past supports present and future lives.

FOURTEEN

"A Wild Patience Has Taken Me This Far"

Adrienne Rich's collection of essays, *On Lies, Secrets, and Silence: Selected Prose, 1966–78* (1979), is an extensive exploration of the feminist concerns that inform her poetry. In her essay, "Conditions for Work" (1976), Rich explores the meaning and future of feminism:

> Feminism begins but cannot end with the discovery by an individual of her self-consciousness as a woman. It is not, finally, even the recognition for her reasons for anger, or the decision to change her life, go back to school, leave a marriage (though in any individual life such decisions can be momentous and require great courage). Feminism means finally that we renounce our obedience to the fathers and recognize the world they have described is not the whole world. . . . Feminism implies that we recognize fully the inadequacy for us, the distortion, of male-created ideologies, and that we proceed to think, and act, out of that recognition. (*LSS*, 207)

This analysis summarizes the development of Rich's work and the direction of her life for the past twenty years. *A Wild Patience Has Taken Me This Far: Poems, 1978–81*[1] continues to celebrate the accomplishments of women, extraordinary and ordinary, in an effort to create positive, public female images. There are portraits of Willa Cather, Simone Weil, and Ethel Rosenberg, as well as of Rich's grandmothers—Mary Gravely Jones and Hattie Rice Rich, all of whom are remembered for their ability to endure hardship or to excel in spite of negative circumstances.

"Culture and Anarchy" (1978), with a title taken from Matthew Arnold's collection of essays first published in London in 1869, is a long poem that presents the female version of his pledge to "use ideas freely," to be "nourished not bound" by them. In contrast to Arnold's emphasis on the civilization that men have made, Rich sustains the lyrical celebration of nature and the power of women begun in "Transcendental Etude." The opening stanza evokes the vibrance of full summer, too abundant to be contained:

Leafshade stirring on lichened bark
                                        Daylilies
run wild, "escaped" the botanists call it
from dooryard to meadow to roadside

Life tingle of angled light
                        late summer
sharpening toward fall, each year more sharply

This headlong, loved, escaping life
                        (WP, 10)

The insistent rise and fall of the lines, the dropped word or phrase set below the primary line, create a sense of the inevitable movement of life toward death. Like the nineteenth-century suffragettes quoted in the poem, the poet lives in finite time that ultimately becomes history; the poem juxtaposes past and present in order to provide a comprehensive portrait of female friendship, female community, and female vision. Excerpts from the diaries, letters, memoirs, essays, and speeches of Susan B. Anthony, Jane Addams, Elizabeth Barrett Browning, Ida Huston Harper, and Elizabeth Cady Stanton are set in iambic pentameter with no breaks or spaces between the lines to emphasize the vigor and vision of these women and to dramatize the relevance of their experience to the lives of contemporary women.

A central focus of the poem is the tradition of female friendship, reflected in the deeply felt connection of Susan B. Anthony to Elizabeth Cady Stanton, Elizabeth Barrett to Miss Mitford, Emily to Charlotte Brontë, and Adrienne Rich to Michelle Cliff to whom the poem is dedicated. These friendships are at life's core, as the quotation from Elizabeth Cady Stanton to Susan B. Anthony demonstrates:

> *I should miss you more than any other*
> *living being from this earth . . .*
> *Yes, our work is one,*
> *we are at one in aim and sympathy*
> *and we should be together . . .*
>   (WP, 15)

Like Emily Dickinson and Elizabeth Holland, Anthony and Stanton depended on each other's support and wrote to each other often. By incorporating portions of their letters and diaries in this poem, Rich emphasizes the importance of women's love for each other not only in her own life but as a major social and literary influence.

Arrayed against the shared love and work of these women stand the controls ranging from social exclusion to rape that support patriarchal culture. These evils perpetrated against women are contrasted with the poet's delight in nature:

> I slice the beetroots to the core,
> each one contains a different landscape
> of bloodlight filaments, distinct rose-purple
> striations like the oldest
> strata of Southwestern canyon
> an undiscovered planet laid open in the lens
> (WP, 15)

Quiet observation, careful attention to small details—this concentration of energy on coexistence with nature, like the sustained attentiveness and caring of a supportive friendship, is a true act of civilization.

This emphasis on the quotidian is found once again in the five-part poem, "The Spirit of Place" (1980), a lyrical homage to the precise details of the New England countryside in which Anne Bradstreet and Emily Dickinson formed their poetic images:

> The mountain laurel in bloom
> constructed like needlework
> tiny half-pulled stitches piercing
> flushed and stippled petals
>
> here in these woods it grows wild
> midsummer moonrise turns it opal
> the night breathes with its clusters
> protected species
> (WP, 41)

Again, a tightly woven web of assonance and consonance—the repeated l's are especially effective—sustains the lyrical description of the landscape. Acknowledging her affinity with Emily Dickinson, Rich pulls away from her presence to confront her own life:

> This place is large enough for both of us
> the river-fog will do for privacy
> this is my third and last address to you
>
> With the hands of a daughter I would cover you
> from all intrusion   even my own
> saying   rest to your ghost

with the hands of a sister I would leave your hands
open or closed as they prefer to lie
and ask no more of who or why or wherefore

With the hands of a mother I would close the door
on the rooms you've left behind
and silently pick up my fallen work

(WP, 43)

Finally, the poet recommits herself to the present and to natural cycles:

force nothing, be unforced
accept no giant miracles of growth
by counterfeit light

trust roots, allow the days to shrink
give credence to these slender means
want without sadness and with grave impatience

(WP, 44)

As with Dickinson, there is a commitment to daily life, to the nurturing ethos. A similar reverence for the commonplace appears in "For Memory" (1979):

The past is not a husk   yet change goes on

Freedom. It isn't once, to walk out
under the Milky Way, feeling the rivers
of light, the fields of dark—
freedom is daily, prose-bound, routine
remembering. Putting together, inch by inch
the starry worlds. From all the lost collections.

(WP, 22)

Rejecting the romantic exaltation in freedom from daily concerns, Rich creates a version of liberty that emphasizes the importance of choosing to sustain life on a daily basis.

"The Images" (1976–78) contrasts the violent and pornographic images of Manhattan street life with the lost forms of ancient civilizations represented by the Cretan sculptures of the ancient goddess: the "violence and woman loathing" expressed by the graffiti of contemporary society is contrasted with the sentience and many-aspected power of the Great Mother:

When I saw hér face, she of the several faces
  Staring, indrawn,   in judgment,   laughing for joy
her serpents twisting,   her arms raised
    her breasts gazing
  when I looked into hér world
I wished to cry loose my soul
    into her, to become
      free of language   at last.
            (*WP*, 5)

This poem struggles with the growing awareness that the values of a society have a profound impact on its images and symbols. According to
Rich, a misogynist culture produces violent pornography, which con-
dones and even encourages the exploitation and rape of women; in contrast, those civilizations that honor women, such as the Cycladic and Minoan cultures, celebrate female social, sexual, and emotional power.

Emphasizing that women must fight to preserve fragments of those
past cultures that affirm their power, Rich continues to urge them to insist resolutely on the right to describe and define their own experiences in
order to bring into being a world of their own. Observing that patriarchal language has produced a world of oppositions, violent conflict, and
global pollution, she characterizes its consequences with the metaphor of
rape—rape of women by men, of third-world peoples by Western imperi-
alism, and of the earth by industrial society. As we have seen, both Bradstreet and Dickinson went to great lengths to portray themselves as too
insignificant to be worthwhile targets. In a male-dominated society,
women are fair game if they stray beyond their proper sphere; once
women enter the public arena, they can be hunted. By objectifying
women, pornography marks them as prey. Rich refuses to use diminu-
tives to describe herself. She has observed that although the ethical, political, historical, and economic impact of the debased images of women
is "profoundly angering and disturbing," understanding the process by
which women are debased is a necessary concomitant to social change:
"Yes it is all of this, and more. And I need to know it all."[2]

Insisting that women must find the appropriate syntax, images, and
metaphors to create their realities, Rich asserts that women must actively
work to create a vision that captures their organic connection to the
deepest forms of life. And she feels that the conflict between feminist and
patriarchal perspectives runs so deep that it affects the most basic perceptions of the human body and the environment: "this is the war of images." Rich states that "language is power" and that poetry can be "used
as a means of changing reality" (*TCWM*). Since poetry gives voice to our

deepest experiences, it can change reality, but, as Rich observes, it must be a poetry that "will dare to explore, and to begin exploding, the phallic delusions which are now endangering consciousness itself" (*LSS*, 116).

Rich's perspective is supported by a recent anthropological study of broad cross-cultural patterns linking sex roles, social institutions, and the prevalence of rape. Peggy Reeves Sanday correlates the incidence of rape in a society with the fundamental images of male and female behavior.[3] She observes that rape-prone societies tolerate violence, encourage men and boys to be aggressive, and give women little or no role in public decision making. Other societies give much greater weight to nurturance, fertility, and cooperation. Interestingly, Sanday reports that many rape-prone societies have endured scarce resources and harsh circumstances, and she speculates that male dominance may have helped the societies to survive. However, when the environment changes, continuing cultural images of the world as dangerous, and of people as inherently aggressive, perpetuate male dominance even though it no longer contributes to social survival. In contemporary American society, where the media and political institutions continuously emphasize images of danger, competition, and violence at personal, social, and international levels, the incidence of rape is among the highest in the world. Rich's celebration of female power and nurturance is an attempt to reformulate the images by which our culture defines itself and to reverse the destructive impact of distorted and exploitative views of women.

Several of the poems in *A Wild Patience Has Taken Me This Far* forge new language to celebrate nature and female experience. For example, "Coast to Coast" (1978) contains an extraordinary portrait in which a woman's face and body and the words she speaks are fused with the landscape in a sensory collage:

> Seeing through the prism   Your face, fog-hollowed   burning
> cold of eucalyptus hung with butterflies
> lavender of rockbloom
> O and your anger uttered in silence word and stammer
> shattering the fog   lances of sun
> piercing the grey Pacific   unanswerable tide
> carving itself in clefts and fissures of the rock
> Beauty of your breasts   your hands
> turning a stone a shell a weed a prism   in coastal light
> traveller and witness
> the passion of the speechless
> driving your speech
> protectless
>   (*WP*, 6–7)

Rich combines deep emotion with startling and paradoxical images. Like Dickinson, Rich makes extensive use of oxymorons—"burning cold," "fog-hollowed"—replacing conventional divisions with extraordinary fullness of perception. The surging rhymes, the swirling words give voice to the ocean's tides ceaselessly beating against the rocks. The word "protectless," here as in past poems, refers to energy unbounded and uncategorized by conventional patterns of perception that would separate the poet from her poem. The woman in this poem is not portrayed as an object of desire or wrenched from her resonant context. The woman and the place she inhabits are inseparable, just as heat and cold, light and opacity, silence and sound, action and observation are interconnected, interdependent.

The title of this volume comes from the first line of "Integrity" (1978): "A wild patience has taken me this far." This poem presents another portrait of a woman and her landscape. Again, the poem is concerned with wholeness. Prefaced with Webster's definition of the word, "the quality or state of being complete; unbroken condition; wholeness; entirety," the poet takes a solitary journey that in some respects parallels her earlier exploration of emotional and cultural origins in "Diving into the Wreck." However, this time the anger that impelled the poet to penetrate psychic and social depths has been replaced by "wild patience"—an untamed steadfastness—that enables her to find a mooring in the facts of her own experience. Again, antithetical emotions are yoked indicating the fullness and complexity of the poet's evolution. No longer does the poet passively gaze at "anagrams of light" as in her early poem "For the Conjunction of Two Planets." The "veridical light" of "Focus" has become "critical"—unsparing yet essential—and the poet uses this light for her own purposes:

> The length of daylight
> this far north, in this
> forty-ninth year of my life
> is critical.
>
> (WP, 8)

The fear and uncertainty of "Diving into the Wreck" has become the quiet strength of a woman who knows herself and accepts the diversity of her experience:

> Anger and tenderness: my selves.
> And now I understand they breathe in me
> as angels, not polarities.
> Anger and tenderness: the spider's genius

> to spin and weave in the same action
> from her own body, anywhere—
> even from a broken web.
>
> (WP, 9)

Using the image of the spider to describe her poetic process, Rich, like Dickinson, rejects emotional polarization; refusing to accept the narrow range of ritualized consciousness, she expresses the totality of responses. Anne Bradstreet thought of herself as either a saint or a sinner; by recording a wide range of emotional states, Emily Dickinson ultimately overcame the dichotomy between "empress" and "daisy"; and Adrienne Rich understands that she is the sum of all her experiences. Again, the poems in this volume do not avoid complexity, ambivalence, or confusion. For example, "Rift" (1980) describes a painful disagreement:

> When language fails us, when we fail each other
> there is no exorcism. The hurt continues. Yes, your scorn
> turns up the jet of my anger Yes, I find you
> overweening, obsessed, and even in your genius
> narrow-minded—I could list much more—
> and absolute loyalty was never in my line
> once having left it in my father's house—
> but as I go on sorting images of you
> my hand trembles, and I try
>
> (WP, 49)

Words with harsh consonants: "rift," "fail," "exorcism," "hurt," "scorn," "jet," "anger" underscore the poet's alienation and resolution to be tough-minded in spite of her obvious distress.

In "Turning the Wheel" (1981), the eight-part poem that concludes the volume, the nature of female power is again explored and again Rich insists that it is to be found in the lives of particular women, not in idealized images or projections:

> So long as you want her faceless, without smell
> or voice, so long as she does not squat
> to urinate, or scratch herself, so long
> as she does not snore beneath her blanket
> or grimace as she grasps the stone-cold
> grinding stone at dawn
> so long as she does not have her own peculiar
> face, slightly wall-eyed or with a streak

of topaz lightning in the blackness
of one eye, so long as she does not limp
so long as you try to simplify her meaning
so long as she simply symbolizes power
she is kept helpless and conventional

(*WP*, 56)

In the romantic tradition, women do not "squat," "urinate," "snore," "grimace," or "limp"; this portrait insists on those realistic details.

In 1982 Rich completed "Sources," a twenty-three part poem that is among the most probing of her autobiographical and cultural explorations.[4] Composed in a variety of styles from short lyrical stanzas and conversational phrases to staccato dialogue and long prose paragraphs, this poem contains characteristic images from past work—the blooming milkweed, Queen Anne's lace, the old country house. Questions of power, authority, the interior life versus the quest, phenomenological versus theoretical rendering of experience, and the importance of place versus abstraction resurface in this work. As in past poems, there are passages that capture the beauty of the New England landscape in an elegant mesh of assonance, consonance, and internal rhyme:

collapsed shed-boards gleam like pewter in the dew
the realms of touch-me-not   fiery with tiny tongues

cover the wild ground of the woods

(*Sources*, 3)

As in past poems, there are blunt declarations, searching questions that permit no evasion:

From where does your strength come, you
Southern Jew
Split at the root, raised in a castle of air?

(*Sources*, 3)

While acknowledging the influence and importance of New England's culture and geography on her life and work, for the first time Rich explores the influence of her Jewish heritage. Her father was an assimilated southern Jew who, although he had great admiration for the Jewish intellectual tradition, disconnected from his ethnic roots in order to be part of the dominant culture—"a citizen of the world." In this extended meditation on her early relationship to her father, Rich questions his "rootless ideology." Similarly, she challenges her Jewish, Brooklyn-born husband's sardonic and defensive reduction of his culture to a matter of "food and humor." Although Arnold Rich and Alfred Conrad are portrayed as emotionally guarded—her father emerges as a stern, exacting disciplinarian, whose daughter became angry and rebellious, and her husband is depicted as a private, brooding person—there is compassion and love for these men who have been damaged by the patriarchal equation of masculinity with invulnerability, as well as by anti-Semitism itself. Driven by the injunction to be self-sufficient and independent, both men cut themselves off from the past, from the sources of emotion and identity that might have sustained them.

The poet ponders her own rootlessness, her involvement with "New" Englanders even to the extent of "believing their Biblical language / their harping on righteousness" (*Sources*, 9). Then she acknowledges another biographical thread—that part of her related to the southern Jews of Vicksburg and Birmingham, and to extend the connection, that part of her connected to the Ashkenazi, the *halutzot*, the Jews destroyed in the pogroms of World War II. Rejecting notions of special destiny—whether it be the Jews as "chosen people" or the Puritan "elect"—that have inspired repeated missions to build a city on a hill from Jerusalem to the New World, she dedicates herself to an "end to suffering" and vows to bring her intelligence and understanding to bear on her existence:

> I mean knowing the world, and my place in it,
> not in order to stare with bitterness or
> detachment, but as a powerful and womanly
> series of choices: and here I write
> the words, in their fullness: powerful   womanly.
>
> (*Sources*, 26)

This poem outlines a female counter-quest—the mission is not to abandon the past in order to control the future but to remain connected to specific circumstances of experience while making personal choices that also shape the larger world.[5] For Rich, vision means being able to see present life clearly as well as to imagine future possibilities.

From the disintegration of Rich's old life has come a new synthesis based on a commitment to write of women's actual lived experience. Choosing the particularities of everyday life over metaphysical imperatives, her emphasis on the quotidian and on nurturance constitutes a female response to the zealous elitism of the Puritan saints and the egotistical subjectivity of the male romantics.

FIFTEEN

"A New Relation to the Universe"

Adrienne Rich's poetry serves a prophetic function by articulating the history and ideals of the feminist struggle. By recalling the ancient chthonic mysteries of blood and birth, by reconnecting daughters with their mothers, by drawing parallels between women today and their historical counterparts, and by envisioning the women of the future who will emerge from the feminist struggle, her poetry celebrates women's strength and possibilities. Elaborating her vision, Rich brings a nurturing ethos to her analysis of social priorities:

> I simply believe that human society is capable of meeting the fundamental needs of all human beings: we can give them a minimum standard of living, we can give them an education, we can create an environment which is more healthy to live in, and we can give people free medical care. We can provide these things for everybody in the society. We're not doing it, and I don't think there is any male system that is going to do that. (*TCWM*)

Like Virginia Woolf, who asked, "Where in short is it leading, this procession of the sons of educated men?," [1] Rich finds that "masculine ideologies are the creation of masculine subjectivity; they are neither objective, nor value-free, nor inclusively 'human'" (*LSS*, 207), and she regards feminism as a corrective to distortions of patriarchal ideologies.

In contrast to the monotheistic Judeo-Christian traditions, Rich defines feminism as a pluralistic ethos that cuts across divisions of race, caste, and nationality:

> If we conceive of feminism . . . as an ethics, a methodology, a
> more complex way of thinking about, thus more responsibly acting
> upon, the conditions of human life, we need a self-knowledge
> which can only develop through a steady, passionate attention to
> *all* female experience. I cannot imagine a feminist evolution leading

to radical change in the private/political realm of gender that is not rooted in the conviction that all women's lives are important; that the lives of men cannot be understood by burying the lives of women; and that to make visible the full meaning of women's experience, to reinterpret knowledge in terms of that experience, is now the most important task of thinking. (*LSS*, 213)

This emphasis on making women's reality and values "visible" echoes the Puritan injunction to externalize faith. Like the Puritans who became "visible saints" through spiritual preparation for the day God called them, women "name" themselves by analyzing their experience and understanding the meaning of their lives:

And it means the most difficult thing of all: listening and watching in art and literature, in the social sciences, in all the descriptions we are given of the world, for the silences, the absences, the nameless, the unspoken, the encoded—for there we will find the true knowledge of women. And in breaking those silences, naming our selves, uncovering the hidden, making ourselves present, we begin to define a reality which resonates to *us*, which affirms *our* being . . . to take ourselves, and each other, seriously: meaning, to begin to take charge of our lives. (*LSS*, 245)

In addition to shared rhetorical patterns, there are structural parallels in Puritan reformation and feminist transformation: both envision the creation of a new world and both are threatened by external forces—Puritanism by Old World corruption and Satanic guile, feminism by sexist oppression and patriarchal exploitation. Puritans scrutinized their souls for sin and moral lapses; feminists "raise" consciousness to eliminate male-identified values. Just as Puritans experienced conversion from an unregenerate to a regenerate state, so feminists reject patriarchal values and become woman-identified. Similarly, the community of women corresponds to the commonwealth of God, and Puritan fears of the apocalypse are paralleled by feminist concern about the threat of global pollution and technological destruction. Although extensive damage has been done to the environment as a result of industrialization and technology, Mary Douglas and Aaron Wildavsky suggest that discussion of these very real and distressing problems also performs the ritual function of creating community cohesion.[2]

Like the Puritans, the feminists accept struggle as a necessary part of the effort to create a new society. In *Wonder-Working Providence of Sions Saviour in New-England* (1654), Edward Johnson warned that victory requires strenuous effort: "you that long so much for it, come forth and fight: who can expect a victory without a battle?"[3] Echoing Johnson in "The Spirit of Place" (1980), Rich calls to her readers to struggle:

Are we all in training for something we don't name?
to exact reparation for things
done long ago to us and to those who did not

survive what was done to them   whom we ought to honor
with grief   with fury   with action

(WP, 45)

Further parallels in Puritan and feminist thought can be seen in controversies in both groups over ideological priorities. For example, as we have seen, in the Massachusetts Bay Colony, there was considerable contention between the preparationists (or legalists) and the spiritists, who believed in the inner light, and there was much discussion about the threat of the antinomian and Arminian heresies as well as possible contamination by familism and Brownism. Similarly, there has been controversy in the feminist community between those who advocate a pluralistic, diverse approach to the study of gender and culture and those who feel that it is imperative to focus more rigorously on the female response to a society that is inimical to the values of women. Like the inner-light advocates, the feminist pluralists stress the importance of individual conviction and personal inclination while the antipluralists, like the legalists, believe that this ideological permissiveness creates the potential for capitulation to the patriarchal establishment.[4] In addition, the debates in the American feminist community in the mid-1970s between lesbian and heterosexual feminists over the question of allegiance to the cause of women paralleled the Puritan controversies about the nature of true faith at the time of the Half-Way Covenant. Like Puritanism, feminism fits the larger pattern inherited from Protestantism in which the concept of reformation has been pivotal ever since Martin Luther hammered his theses on the church door.

Although feminism in the United States shares the Puritan millennial orientation, there are major differences between the two perspectives. As an international sociocultural movement, feminism is far less proscriptive than Puritanism; feminism is not concerned with a narrow range of beliefs but with ways to achieve social equality for women and men. As Adrienne Rich has concluded, "Radical feminism is about transforming all relationships and about the creation of a human society in which human needs are met, and in which there is no exploitation of one group of human beings by another, beginning with women" (TCWM). Historians and social theorists have repeatedly observed that this conflict between opposing systems of social thought results in a dialectic that creates social change. Rich insists that this process must be inclusive, that categories must not harden into permanent oppositions:

> [F]eminism—woman's consciousness—ultimately has to break down that dichotomy [between masculine power and feminine powerlessness]. Once you stop splitting inner and outer, you have to stop splitting all these other dichotomies, which I think proceed from that. Yourself-other, head-body, psyche-politics, them-us. The good society would be one in which those divisions would be broken down, and there was much more flow back and forth. (*ARP*, 119)

Demanding that the social dialectic include women, Rich writes: "The repossession by women of our bodies will bring far more essential change to human society than the seizing of the means of production by workers" (*OWB*, 285). Because women constitute such a large portion of the population, any movement that mobilizes them has potential for substantial social change.

The necessity for a change of language to create a more complete awareness of women's experience is central to Adrienne Rich's poetic and political vision. In order to break the hold of patriarchal restrictions on women's lives, the linguistic universe that supports it must be "decentered"; embedded habits of language need to be displaced, old words must be resounded, new meanings must be discovered, and a new order must be designed.[5] Adrienne Rich has observed that "poetry is, among other things, a criticism of language. . . . Poetry is above all a concentration of *power* of language, which is the power of our ultimate relationship to everything in the universe" (*LSS*, 248). Because consciousness responds to metaphors, it is necessary to insist that speech encompass the full range of female perceptions. It is this understanding of the relationship between language and what we call reality that informs Rich's activism and poetry.

Rich's work clearly attempts to fuse some of the dichotomies embedded in patriarchal speech: "I am she: I am he." Here Rich takes the traditional dichotomies of female and male roles and permits herself to experience both states of mind simultaneously. Because her awareness is not bifurcated, the full range of human experience becomes more accessible to her.[6] By allowing herself to be both active and passive, Rich reclaims the active part of herself that is usually assigned to men and sees herself as the source of her own creativity. For example, in "Transcendental Etude," the a priori expectation that women will wait while their men

wander, is shattered: "I am the lover and the loved / home and the wan-
derer." The prescriptive code that defines women as receptive and men as
agentic no longer accords with the poet's experience as a woman. The
word *androgyny*, combining the Greek words for male and female, implies a range of nonpolarized perceptual and behavioral options. Emphasizing this emotional and social continuum rather than antithetical sex
roles, many feminists have suggested androgynous behavior as a synthesis
of traditional masculine and feminine responses.[7] Recently, Rich has opposed the use of the word *androgyny* because she feels it is grounded in opposition and does not adequately express the fluidity and variety of experience; she argues that the word *lesbian* more accurately describes a
woman who commands her own energy.

As we have seen, Rich repeatedly observes throughout her work that
women have not traditionally been permitted control over their lives. Because women have been defined as passive, they have often been denied
the reality of their most primal experiences. Rich points out that anti-
abortion laws do not allow women to decide whether or not to have children; the male medical profession has discouraged women from determining the circumstances of their children's births; discrimination
against women in the labor market has denied women equal pay for
equal work; property laws have often prohibited women control of their
financial resources; the possibility of assault or rape threatens women's
mobility in public places; and pornographic images of women objectifying them as objects of male sexual gratification rob women of positive
images of themselves. Rich explains that in such a world women feel
dominated, embattled, tyrannized, and victimized. As many feminist critics have observed, women often internalize this cultural bias as self-
hatred or depression. Feminists have attempted to define a reality of their
own, in which anger is not internalized as depression, rape is no longer
excused as feminine surrender, female self-sacrifice is not rationalized as
the redemption of men, and the horror of war is not justified as a need to
protect national interest.

Rich's poetry attacks patriarchal consciousness for narrowing perception to the part rather than the whole and for insisting on dominance at
the expense of the multiplicity of experience. By substituting abstractions
for actual experience, it is possible to pollute the earth because the connection between human existence and other forms of life is lost. Rape is
condoned or tolerated because empathy for the victim is reduced or non-
existent. War is perceived in terms of victory or loss and not in terms
of human devastation and suffering or the destruction of precious resources. Rich rejects not men, but destructive masculinity. *Of Woman
Born* concludes with a visionary injunction:

> We need to imagine a world in which every woman is the presiding genius of her own body. In such a world women will truly create new life, bring forth not only children (if and as we choose) but the visions, and the thinking, necessary to sustain, console, and alter human existence—a new relationship to the universe. Sexuality, politics, intelligence, power, motherhood, work, community, intimacy will develop new meanings; thinking itself will be transformed. (*OWB*, 285–86)

In her work, Rich attempts to portray female-centered or gynecocratic consciousness, which she views as comprehensive, cooperative and collective, empathic and sensory; its focus is to nurture and honor life in all its forms. As Rich writes: "To acknowledge a cyclic change of events (that birth is followed by death, . . . that tides ebb and flow, winter alternates with summer, the full moon with the dark of the moon) is to acknowledge that process and continuity embrace both positive and negative events" (*OWB*, 108). Building on the romantic tradition, this feminist cosmology replaces mastery with mystery; certainty with empathy; control with understanding; division with connection; product with process; abstraction with texture; and predictability with variety. Insisting that women should have an opportunity to participate fully in the historical process and to use their powers to set cultural as well as personal priorities, Rich feels a nurturing ethos is a necessary antidote to patriarchy. And if the larger society refuses to listen to women's voices, Rich urges them to save themselves:

> I think women have a mission to survive . . . and to be whole people. I believe that this can save the world, but I don't think that women have a mission to clean up after men's messes. I think we have to save the world by doing it for ourselves—for all women—I don't mean some narrow, restricted notion of who women are, only white women or only middle-class women and only Western women. (*TCWM*)

Three hundred years ago, also acting on the desire to save themselves, the Puritan settlers reached the New World. Like the feminists, they wanted to create new cultural forms that would better fit their inner lives. As Anne Bradstreet's father wrote: "We are not like those which have dispensations to lie; but as we were free enough in Old England to turn our insides outwards, sometimes to our disadvantage, very unlike it is that now, being *procul a fulmine* [far from the lightning bolt], we should be so unlike ourselves."[8] However, the feminists, unlike the Puritans, want to save all women rather than a small band of the faithful. Articulating the feminist vision, Rich has said, "we speak for the right of every woman to live without fear of sexual and racial violence, and to conduct her life and, if she chooses, to raise children in some level of decency and peace, to respect and love herself and other women, to choose how she shall use her body and her mind."[9] In her attempt to create new forms of thought, language, and culture that express women's concerns, Rich recognizes that no formula is adequate and that any solution must grow from the complex, paradoxical details of life itself. In "What Is Possible" (1980), she observes:

> A clear night. But the mind
> of the woman imagining all this   the mind
> that allows all this to be possible
> is not clear as the night
> is never simple   cannot clasp
> its truths as the transiting planets clasp each other
> does not so easily
>   work free from remorse
> does not so easily
>   manage the miracle
> for which mind is famous
>   or used to be famous
>
> does not at will become abstract and pure
>
> this woman's mind
>
> does not even will that miracle
> having a different mission
>   in the universe
>   (WP, 23)

In contrast to the New England Puritans whose rhetoric has influenced the forms of her thought, Adrienne Rich rejects the metaphysical imperatives with which they sought to achieve their millennial ideals. For her, there is no distinction between the conditions of daily life and projected goals just as there is no disjunction between mind and body or civilization and nature. Rejecting the Puritan heritage of the city on a hill as well as the Jewish legacy of a chosen people, Rich concentrates on the lived experiences of women in the hope that feminist consciousness can foster an increasingly democratic, egalitarian society. For most of her career, Adrienne Rich has been involved in an ongoing public debate about the nature of gender that is at least as old as the *Querelle des Femmes* initiated by Christine de Pisan in the early fifteenth century. Like feminist writers from Judith Sargent Murray and Mary Wollstonecraft to Margaret Fuller and Virginia Woolf, Adrienne Rich has attempted to create positive, public images of women to counteract the distortions wrought by the subjection of the female mind and the objectification of the female body in patriarchal society.

From *Snapshots of a Daughter-in-Law* (1963), *Necessities of Life* (1966), *Leaflets* (1969), *The Will to Change* (1971), *Diving into the Wreck* (1973), *The Dream of a Common Language* (1978) to *A Wild Patience Has Taken Me This Far* (1981), Rich's poetry has evolved from the perceptions of a woman dependent on men for her social and sexual identity and economic support to the discoveries and difficulties experienced by a woman who has become autonomous and self-directing. Because she has increasingly trusted her own experience and rejected male authority, Adrienne Rich is part of the tradition that links her to Anne Bradstreet and Emily Dickinson. In addition, Rich has been empowered by the romantic legacy of individualism as well as the modernist and feminist struggles for literary and social autonomy. As a contemporary woman who has inherited a tradition of social and artistic protest, Rich has been able to explore and, finally, to reject the conflict, ambivalence, and torment of a female psyche divided against itself by a tradition that does not permit women to perceive themselves as the source of their own energy.

Building on the tradition of such women poets as H.D., Millay, Moore, Plath, and Levertov as well as Bradstreet and Dickinson, Rich has evolved a female aesthetic-ethic based on shared relationship, emotional reciprocity, and empathic identification—concerns that Carol Gilligan has recently argued are characteristic of women's development.[10] Finally, Rich has written poetry that suggests alternatives to the city on a hill, the virgin land, and the machine in the garden, metaphors that have been used by writers and literary historians to describe the American experience. As a writer, as an activist, Rich has tried to bring a nurturing ethos to the larger society: as she writes in "Hunger" (1974–75), "I'm alive to want more than life, want it for others starving and unborn" (*DCL*, 14). Anne Bradstreet ultimately saw heaven as her home; Emily Dickinson thought that her home *was* paradise; Adrienne Rich has tried to envision a society in which all women can be at home.

Notes

✻ ✻ ✻ ✻ ✻ ✻ ✻ ✻ ✻ ✻ ✻ ✻ ✻

INTRODUCTION

1. In the tradition of Perry Miller, Sacvan Bercovitch has analyzed the influence of Puritan eschatology on American character and culture in *The Puritan Origins of the American Self* (New Haven: Yale University Press, 1975). Also see Sacvan Bercovitch, *The American Jeremiad* (Madison: University of Wisconsin Press, 1979), for an illuminating analysis of the linguistic structures that sustained the Puritan ideology. Other studies of the influence of Puritanism on American millennial or utopian impulses are: Charles Sanford, *The Quest for Paradise* (Urbana: University of Illinois Press, 1961); Roderick Nash, *Wilderness and the American Mind* (1967; 3d rev. ed., New Haven: Yale University Press, 1982).

Michael Kammen, *People of Paradox* (New York: Alfred A. Knopf, 1972), and John Seelye, *Prophetic Waters: The River in Early American Life and Literature* (New York: Oxford University Press, 1977), are concerned with the pluralistic nature of the American experience. Larzer Ziff, *Puritanism in America: New Culture in a New World* (New York: Viking Press, 1973), and Richard Slotkin, *Regeneration through Violence: The Mythology of the American Frontier, 1600–1860* (Middletown, Conn.: Wesleyan University Press, 1973), analyze economic motives underlying millennial ideas.

Also see Henry Nash Smith, *Virgin Land: The American West as Symbol and Myth* (Cambridge, Mass.: Harvard University Press, 1950), and Leo Marx, *The Machine in the Garden: Technology and the Pastoral Ideal in America* (New York: Oxford University Press, 1964).

More exclusively literary in focus, the following books have analyzed the cultural continuities underlying American literature and experience: R. W. B. Lewis, *The American Adam: Innocence, Tragedy, and Tradition in the Nineteenth Century* (Chicago: University of Chicago Press, 1955), focuses on the function of American myth for Emerson and his contemporaries; Richard Chase, *The American Novel and Its Tradition* (Garden City, N.Y.: Doubleday and Co., 1957); Leon Howard, *Literature and the American Tradition* (Garden City, N.Y.: Doubleday and Co., 1960); Roy Harvey Pearce, *The Continuity of American Poetry* (Princeton: Princeton University Press, 1961); Edwin Fussell, *Frontier: American Literature and the American West* (Princeton: Princeton University Press, 1965); Alan Trachtenberg, *Brooklyn Bridge: Fact and Symbol* (New York: Oxford University Press, 1965); Leslie Fiedler, *The Return of the Vanishing American* (New York: Stein and Day, 1968); and Albert Gelpi, *The Tenth Muse* (Cambridge, Mass.: Harvard University Press, 1975).

2. See Kate Millett, *Sexual Politics* (Garden City, N.Y.: Doubleday and Co., 1970); Vivian Gornick and Barbara K. Moran, eds., *Woman in Sexist Society: Studies in Power and Powerlessness* (New York: Basic Books, 1971); Carolyn Heilbrun, *Toward a Recognition of Androgyny* (New York: Alfred A. Knopf, 1973); Patricia Meyer Spacks, *The Female Imagination* (New York: Alfred A. Knopf, 1975); Ellen Moers, *Literary Women* (Garden City, N.Y.: Doubleday and Co., 1976); Ann Douglas, *The Feminization of American Culture* (New York: Alfred A. Knopf, 1977); Elaine Showalter, *A Literature of Their Own: British Women Novelists from Brontë to Lessing* (Princeton: Princeton University Press, 1977); Nina Auerbach, *Communities of Women: An Idea in Fiction* (Cambridge, Mass.: Harvard University Press, 1978); Nina Baym, *Woman's Fiction: A Guide to Novels by and about Women in America, 1820–1870* (Ithaca: Cornell University Press, 1978); Judith Fetterley, *The Resisting Reader: A Feminist Approach to American Fiction* (Bloomington: Indiana University Press, 1978); Sandra Gilbert and Susan Gubar, *The Madwoman in the Attic: The Woman Writer and the Nineteenth-Century Literary Imagination* (New Haven: Yale University Press, 1979).

3. A range of American women poets is discussed in Suzanne Juhasz, *Naked and Fiery Forms: Modern American Poetry by Women, a New Tradition* (New York: Harper and Row, 1976); Emily Stipes Watts, *The Poetry of American Women from 1632 to 1945* (Austin: University of Texas Press, 1977); Sandra Gilbert and Susan Gubar, eds., *Shakespeare's Sisters: Feminist Essays on Women Poets* (Bloomington: Indiana University Press, 1978); and Cheryl Walker, *The Nightingale's Burden: Women Poets and American Culture before 1900* (Bloomington: Indiana University Press, 1982).

4. For an early exploration of cultural frameworks resulting in subordination of female nature to the male mind, see Sherry B. Ortner, "Is Female to Male as Nature Is to Culture?," in Michelle Zimbalist Rosaldo and Louise Lamphere, eds., *Woman, Culture, and Society* (Stanford: Stanford University Press, 1974), 67–87. Also see Susan Griffin, *Woman and Nature: The Roaring Inside Her* (New York: Harper and Row, 1978); Evelyn Fox Keller, "Gender and Science," *Psychoanalysis and Contemporary Thought* 1 (1978): 409–33, and "Feminism and Science," *Signs* 7, no. 3 (Spring 1982): 589–602; Carol P. MacCormack and Marilyn Strathern, eds., *Nature, Culture, and Gender* (New York: Cambridge University Press, 1980); and Carolyn Merchant, *The Death of Nature: Women, Ecology, and the Scientific Revolution* (San Francisco: Harper and Row, 1980).

5. For an excellent study of H. D.'s self-affirming transformation of the mythology of the quest, see Susan Friedman, *Psyche Reborn: The Emergence of H. D.* (Bloomington: Indiana University Press, 1981). Sylvia Plath's poetic evolution is the focus of Mary Lynn Broe's *Protean Poetic: The Poetry of Sylvia Plath* (Columbia: University of Missouri Press, 1980). Also see Bonnie Costello, *Marianne Moore: Imaginary Possessions* (Cambridge, Mass.: Harvard University Press, 1982); Nancy Mitford's definitive study of Edna St. Vincent Millay is forthcoming.

PART ONE: INTRODUCTION

1. Anne Bradstreet, "Letter to my Dear Children," in John Harvard Ellis, ed., *The Works of Anne Bradstreet in Prose and Verse* (Charlestown, Mass.: Abram E. Cutter, 1867), p. 99 (hereafter cited in the text as *Works*, followed by page number). This is a variorum edition drawn primarily from the second edition of Bradstreet's *Poems* (printed in Boston in 1678), which contains her additions and corrections of the 1650 edition of *The Tenth Muse* printed in London. When there are substantial differences in the texts of the first and second editions, I will so note. Josephine K. Piercy has edited a facsimile of the original (1650), *"The Tenth Muse" and from the Manuscripts, "Meditations Divine and Morall," Together with Letters and Occasional Pieces*, by Anne Bradstreet (Gainesville, Fla.: Scholars' Facsimiles and Reprints, 1965). A modern edition can be found in Jeannine Hensley, ed., *The Works of Anne Bradstreet* (1967; reprint, Cambridge, Mass.: Harvard University Press, 1980).

2. See Robert Richardson, "The Puritan Poetry of Anne Bradstreet," in *Texas Studies in Language and Literature* 9 (Autumn 1967): 317, 331, and William J. Irvin, "Allegory and Typology 'Imbrace and Greet': Anne Bradstreet's 'Contemplations,'" in *Early American Literature* 10 (Spring 1975): 44. Both Richardson and Irvin argue that this poem presents Bradstreet's successful struggle to attain Puritan moral imperatives. In his chapter on Anne Bradstreet in *God's Altar: The World and the Flesh in Puritan Poetry* (Berkeley: University of California Press, 1978), Robert Daly observes that this struggle allowed the Puritan "to wean the affections from the unmixed love of such creatures, to convince himself finally the world he loved was subordinate to its creator" (86).

3. In "Anne Bradstreet—Dogmatist or Rebel?," *New England Quarterly* 34 (September 1966): 388, Ann Stanford notes the clash of "feeling and dogma" in Bradstreet's poetry. Stanford elaborates this analysis in *Anne Bradstreet: The Worldly Puritan* (New York: Burt Franklin, 1975). In *Anne Bradstreet: "The Tenth Muse"* (New York: Oxford University Press, 1971), Elizabeth Wade White observes that Bradstreet "could be possessed by a sort of mental rage that might, if once allowed to break out from the intellectual discipline under which she kept it, have caused irreparable damage" (177).

4. Thomas Shepard, *God's Plot: The Paradoxes of Puritan Piety, Being the Autobiography and Journal of Thomas Shepard*, ed. Michael McGiffert (Amherst: University of Massachusetts Press, 1972), 69, 70.

CHAPTER ONE

1. For biographies of Anne Bradstreet, see Elizabeth Wade White, *Anne Bradstreet: "The Tenth Muse"*; Josephine K. Piercy, *Anne Bradstreet* (New York: Twayne Publishers, 1965); and Ann Stanford, *Anne Bradstreet: The Worldly Puritan*.

2. "The Charlestown Records," in Alexander Young, ed., *Chronicles of the*

First Planters of the Colony of Massachusetts Bay (Boston: Charles C. Little and James Brown, 1846), 378–79.

3. The three major biographies of Bradstreet—by Piercy, White, and Stanford (see n. 1 above)—all discuss the literary influences on her work.

4. Kenneth Silverman, ed., *Colonial American Poetry* (New York: Hafner Publishing Co., 1968), 32.

5. See Cotton Mather, "The Life of Thomas Dudley," in *Magnalia Christi Americana* (1702) (Hartford: S. Andrus, 1953–55), Book 2, p. 16.

For an elaborate discussion of the books available to Bradstreet in both the earl's library and her father's personal library, see White, *Anne Bradstreet*, pp. 61–70. White observes that references in Bradstreet's poetry demonstrate that she also read Josuah Sylvester's English translation of Guillaume du Bartas's *Divine Weekes and Workes*, Sir Walter Raleigh's *History of the World*, Helkiah Crooke's *Microcosmographia or a Description of the Body of Man*, Sidney's *Arcadia* and *Astrophel and Stella*, John Speed's *Historie of Great Britaine*, and William Camden's *Britannia*, which was translated from the Latin in 1610. Probably the library at the Sempringham manor house also contained Burton's *Anatomy of Melancholy*, Bacon's *Essays* and *The Advancement of Learning*, and Captain John Smith's *General History of Virginia, New England, and the Summer Isles*. The Geneva Bible and Foxe's *Actes and Monuments* were staples of Puritan reading, and the works of Aristotle, Hesiod, Homer, Ovid, Pliny, Plutarch, Seneca, Thucydides, Virgil, and Xenophon were generally in the libraries of educated people.

6. White, *Anne Bradstreet*, 42–70; Piercy, *Anne Bradstreet*, 22.

7. Raymond Williams, *The Country and the City* (New York: Oxford University Press, 1973). In *Puritanism in America: New Culture in a New World* (New York: Viking Press, 1973), Larzer Ziff, building on Raymond Williams's economic and historical analysis, says that Puritanism was a compensatory response to "the threatening conditions of masterlessness and landlessness in sixteenth-century England" (x).

8. Because he was orphaned at nine and adopted by Lord Compton, Dudley's social background is not certain; however, White points out that in his will of 1653 he used the prestigious single-tailed lion of the Sutton-Dudleys, denoting the younger son of a baronial household (*Anne Bradstreet*, 11). For further discussion of Dudley's early life and education, see ibid., 29–41.

9. Anne Bradstreet, "Religious Experiences and Occasional Pieces," in *Works*, 4.

10. For an analysis of the impact of Puritan eschatology on New World society and American culture, see Perry Miller, *Errand into the Wilderness* (Cambridge, Mass.: Harvard University Press, 1956). For a more recent analysis of this theme, see Sacvan Bercovitch, *The Puritan Origins of the American Self* (New Haven: Yale University Press, 1975), and *The American Jeremiad* (Madison: University of Wisconsin Press, 1979). Bercovitch analyzes the Puritan belief that the settling of the New World was the "fulfillment of scriptural prophecy" (136).

11. John Winthrop, "Journal," in *Winthrop Papers*, 5 vols. (Boston: Massachusetts Historical Society, 1929–47), 2:259.

12. Thomas Dudley, "Letter to the Countess of Lincoln," in Young, ed., *Chronicles of the First Planters*, 311–12.

13. Ibid., 304.

14. Ibid., 325.

15. Ibid., 255.

16. Young, ed., *Chronicles of the First Planters*, 381.

17. Mather, *Magnalia Christi Americana*, Book 1, p. 71.

18. See George Dow, *Domestic Life in New England in the Seventeenth Century* (New York: Benjamin Blom, 1925) 7, 17–18, for a discussion of the colonial diet that included a wide variety of fruits and vegetables as well as meat and seafood. Edmund Browne, one of the founders of Boston, cataloged the food available to many of the colonists: "strawberries, raspberries, gooseberries, red and green, most large grapes . . . and [an] abundance of plum trees," as well as melons, pears, and apples. In addition to venison, rabbit, pork, mutton, turkey, pigeons, partridge, quail, goose, duck, and veal, he mentions sturgeon, salmon, cod, bass, mackerel, oysters, and lobsters. See "Letter of Edmund Browne to Sir Simonds D'Ewes," September 7, 1638, in Everett Emerson, ed., *Letters from New England: The Massachusetts Bay Colony, 1629–1638* (Amherst: University of Massachusetts Press, 1976), 227–28.

19. Dow, *Domestic Life in New England*, 1.

20. Ibid., 9–11, 36–48.

21. None of this finery could be afforded by servants, laborers, and other working-class people who wore leather and rough fabrics for the most part. See Dow, *Domestic Life*, 24–25.

22. Winthrop, "Journal," in *Winthrop Papers*, 3:183.

23. Mather, *Magnalia Christi Americana*, Book 2, p. 17.

24. In *The Visible Saints: The History of a Puritan Idea* (New York: New York University Press, 1963), Edmund Morgan discusses these preparatory stages of conversion, which he describes as "the morphology of conversion."

25. William Perkins, *A Golden Chaine: or, The Description of Theologie*, in *Workes* (London: John Legatt, 1612–13), 1:21.

26. John Donne, Sonnet XIV, in Herbert Grierson, ed., *Metaphysical Lyrics and Poems of the Seventeenth Century* (London: Oxford University Press, 1921), 88.

27. George Herbert, "Perseverance," in Grierson, ed., *Metaphysical Lyrics and Poems*, 103.

CHAPTER TWO

1. Mather, *Magnalia Christi Americana*, Book 2, pp. 578–79, quoted in Bercovitch, *The Puritan Origins of the American Self*, 65.

2. Edmund Spenser, *The Shepherd's Calendar and Other Poems*, ed. Philip Henderson (London: J. M. Dent & Sons, 1932), 32.

3. Ibid., 330–31.

4. Peter N. Carroll, *The Puritans and the Wilderness: the Intellectual Signifi-

cance of the New England Frontier, 1629–1700 (New York: Columbia University Press, 1969), observes that the rhetoric of Puritan sermons, letters, diaries, and tracts reveals an increasing hostility to nature as a wild and unruly force. In *The Lay of the Land: Metaphor as Experience and History in American Life and Letters* (Chapel Hill: University of North Carolina Press, 1975), Annette Kolodny contends that the Puritans perceived nature as unregenerate, a force that needed to be subdued and tamed just as female sexuality needed to be contained.

5. This process of deforestation and cultivation in the New World paralleled the development of civilization elsewhere; for example, Crete was once a rain forest but excessive clearing caused a change of climate in addition to a loss of topsoil. What was once a lush, fertile place is now arid and rocky. Throughout the world, soil erosion is now a serious problem. An elaborate scientific discussion of nature's balance and environmental reform can be found in J. E. Lovelock, *Gaia: A New Look at Life on Earth* (New York: Oxford University Press, 1979).

6. See Cecelia Tichi, *New World, New Earth: Environmental Reform in American Literature from the Puritans through Whitman* (New Haven: Yale University Press, 1979), for a discussion of the Puritan imperative to reform nature in an effort to impose God's order on the environment.

7. See Jane Harrison, *Themis: A Study of the Social Origins of Greek Religion* (1912; reprint, London: Merlin Press, 1963). This is a detailed scholarly discussion of the shift from chthonic to Olympic religions and social order. I am indebted to Harrison's illuminating analysis in my discussion of pre-Hellenic civilization and matriarchal values. Also see Jane Harrison, *Prolegomena to the Study of Greek Religion* (1903; reprint, New York: Arno Press, 1975), and *Ancient Art and Ritual; Epilegomena to the Study of Greek Religion* (Cambridge: Cambridge University Press, 1921).

8. For a discussion of the historic roots of the Protestant views of nature, see Herbert N. Schneidau, *Sacred Discontent: The Bible and Western Tradition* (Berkeley: University of California Press, 1976).

9. See White, *Anne Bradstreet*, 67, for a discussion of the sources of this poem. Also see Stanford, *The Worldly Puritan*, 65–66, for a detailed discussion of the parallels with Raleigh.

CHAPTER THREE

1. Edward Taylor, "Meditation 1:40," in *Preparatory Meditations*, 2:3–6. For a discussion of Taylor's excremental and scatological imagery, see Karl Keller, *The Example of Edward Taylor* (Amherst: University of Massachusetts Press, 1975), 191–211.

2. Sir John Davies, "Of the Soule of Man, and the Immortalitie thereof," in *Nosce Teipsum: The Poems of Sir John Davies*, ed. Robert Kruger (London: Oxford University Press, 1975), 15.

3. Andrew Marvell, "A Dialogue between the Soul and Body," in Grierson, ed., *Metaphysical Lyrics and Poems*, 163.

4. Ibid., 159.

5. Ibid., 161.

6. John Winthrop, *Journal: History of New England, 1630–1649*, ed. James Kendall Hosmer, 2 vols. (New York: Charles Scribner's Sons, 1908), 1:230.

7. See Norman Petit, *The Heart Prepared: Grace and Conversion in Puritan Spiritual Life* (New Haven: Yale University Press, 1966). Petit elaborates the importance of introspection as preparation for being called to God to become a saint, that is, one of the elect. Nevertheless, as Petit observes, "no matter how much they prepared, no matter how thoroughly they searched beneath the surface of human appearances, God's mercy could be denied in the end" (19).

8. Shepard, *God's Plot*, 392.

9. Perry Miller, *The New England Mind: From Colony to Province* (Cambridge, Mass.: Harvard University Press, 1953), and *Errand into the Wilderness* (Cambridge, Mass.: Harvard University Press, 1956); Sacvan Bercovitch, *The Puritan Origins of the American Self* (New Haven: Yale University Press, 1975), and *The American Jeremiad* (Madison: University of Wisconsin Press, 1979).

10. White, *Anne Bradstreet*, 67.

11. John Winthrop, "Religious Experience," in *Winthrop Papers*, 3:342.

12. Ibid., 3:340.

13. As I have pointed out, suffering was no guarantee of salvation. Edmund Morgan remarks, "Not every member of the visible church was destined for salvation, for not every man who professed belief would actually possess the true belief, the saving faith necessary for redemption" (*The Visible Saints*, 3). In addition, Morgan's chapter, "The Morphology of Conversion," is very helpful in illuminating this process.

14. Winthrop, "Religious Experience," in *Winthrop Papers*, 3:343.

15. Thomas Shepard, "Thomas Shepard's Memoir of Himself," in Young, ed., *Chronicles of the First Planters*, 509. See also Thomas Shepard, "The Autobiography of Thomas Shepard," *Publications of the Colonial Society of Massachusetts* 27 (1930): 362.

16. Cotton Mather, *Diary*, 7 vols. (Boston: Massachusetts Historical Society, 1878–82), 7:437–38; also quoted in Kenneth Murdock, *Literature and Theology in Colonial New England* (Cambridge, Mass.: Harvard University Press, 1949), 110.

17. Cotton Mather, *Diaries of Cotton Mather*, 2 vols. (New York: Frederick Ungar, 1957), 2:87, 349–50, 631–39.

18. Thomas Hooker, *The Soules Preparation for Christ; or, A Treatise of Contrition* (London: A. Crooke, 1632), 177–80.

19. For a detailed discussion of the relationship of church membership and Puritan politics in the Massachusetts Bay Colony, see David D. Hall, *The Faithful Shepherd: A History of the New England Ministry in the Seventeenth Century* (Chapel Hill: University of North Carolina Press, 1972).

20. See Bercovitch, *The American Jeremiad*, passim.

CHAPTER FOUR

1. Winthrop, *Journal*, ed. Hosmer, 2:225.

2. Ibid.

3. Thomas Parker, *The Copy of a Letter Written . . . to His Sister* (London, 1650), 13.

4. Letter from Stephen Winthrop to John Winthrop, Jr., March 27, 1646, in *Winthrop Papers*, 5:70.

5. Transcript of MS records of the First Church in Boston, 1630–87, at Massachusetts Historical Society, Boston, Mass., 1:24.

6. Letter of Benjamin Keayne to Thomas Dudley, March 18, 1646, in *Winthrop Papers*, 5:144.

7. Edward Johnson, *Wonder-Working Providence of Sions Saviour in New-England* (London: Nathaniel Brooke, 1654); reprinted by Scholars' Facsimiles and Reprints (New York: Delmar, 1974), 95–96.

8. John Winthrop, *A Short Story of the Rise, Reign, and Ruine of the Antinomians, Familists, and Libertines, That Infected the Churches of New England* (London: R. Smith, 1644), reprinted in Charles Francis Adams, ed., *Antinomianism in the Colony of Massachusetts Bay* (Boston: The Prince Society, 1894), vi.

9. John Wheelwright, "A Sermon Preached at New England upon a Fast Day the XVIth of January, 1636," *Massachusetts History Society Proceedings*, 1st ser. 9 (1867): 266–68.

10. Winthrop, *Antinomians, Familists, and Libertines*, 326.

11. Ibid., 83.

12. See Hall, *The Faithful Shepherd*, 72–75, and passim.

13. See Winthrop, *Journal*, ed. Hosmer, 1:195–96.

14. For a report and transcription of Hutchinson's trial, see Thomas Hutchinson, *History of the Colony and Province of Massachusetts Bay* (Boston, 1767). For additional material, see *Anne Hutchinson and Other Papers* (White Plains, N.Y.: Westchester County Historical Society, 1670). A documentary account of the antinomian controversy as well as transcripts of Hutchinson's trial can be found in David Hall, ed., *The Antinomian Controversy, 1636–1638: A Documentary History* (Middletown, Conn.: Wesleyan University Press, 1968). For further discussion of Anne Hutchinson and the antinomian controversy, see George E. Ellis, "Life of Anne Marbury Hutchinson," in Jared Sparks, ed., *Library of American Biography* (New York: Harper, 1848) vol. 15; Charles Francis Adams, ed., *Antinomianism in the Colony of Massachusetts Bay, 1636–1638* (Boston: Prince Society, 1894); and Edmund S. Morgan, "The Case against Mrs. Anne Hutchinson," *New England Quarterly* 10 (1937): 675–97. Emery Battis, *Saints and Sectaries: Anne Hutchinson and the Antinomian Controversy in the Massachusetts Bay Colony* (Chapel Hill: University of North Carolina Press, 1962), provides a detailed discussion of the subject.

15. "A Report on the Trial of Mrs. Anne Hutchinson before the Church in Boston" (March 1638), in the *Massachusetts History Society Proceedings*, 2d ser. 4 (1889): 190–91. Also in Winthrop, *Antinomians, Familists, and Libertines*, 336.

16. Thomas Hooker, *A Survey of the Summe of Church Discipline* (London, 1648), unpaged; this quote can also be found in Thomas Hutchinson, *The History of Massachusetts* (Boston, 1795), 1:61–63.

17. See *A Conference Mr. John Cotton Held at Boston with the Elders of New England* (London, 1646).

18. Winthrop, *Antinomians, Familists, and Libertines*, 83.

19. Winthrop, *Journal*, ed. Hosmer, 1:264.

20. Ibid., 1:277. Also see Edith Curtis, *Anne Hutchinson: A Biography* (Cambridge, Mass.: Washburn and Thomas, 1930).

21. Winthrop, *Journal*, ed. Hosmer, 1 : 267.

22. Winthrop, *Antinomians, Familists, and Libertines*, 14.

23. Richard Sibbes, *Soules Conflict* (London, 1638), 176.

24. Edward Reynolds, *Treatise of the Passions and Faculties of the Soul of Man* (London, 1658), 904–5.

25. Richard Baxter, *Christian Directory* (1830), quoted in Sacvan Bercovitch's *The Puritan Origins of the American Self*, 17. For an illuminating discussion of the relationship between the concept of self and Puritanism, see Bercovitch, ibid., 16–20.

26. Kai T. Erikson, *The Wayward Puritans* (New York: John Wiley, 1966).

27. Sacvan Bercovitch observes, "Decline in church membership after the mid-1650's followed at least partly from the *seriousness* with which children responded to the demands of the fathers. Their sense of inadequacy, their hesitations about professing sainthood, suggest intensity of belief, not indifference" (*The Puritan Origins of the American Self*, 97). Emory Elliott discusses this interpretation in considerable detail in *Power and the Pulpit in Puritan New England* (Princeton: Princeton University Press, 1975).

28. Cotton Mather, *A Family Well-Ordered* (Boston, 1669), 3; also quoted in Morgan, *The Visible Saints*, 88.

29. John Cotton, *A Meet Help; or, A Wedding Sermon* (Boston, 1699), 21.

30. Winthrop, *Journal*, ed. Hosmer, 1:299. Although Puritan codes regarding women's participation in church organization were repressive, there were women who participated in public life by running their own businesses or in partnerships with their husbands or by representing their husbands in court. For an extensive bibliography of the economic activities of colonial women, see Eugenie Andruss Leonard, Sophie Hutchinson Drinker, and Miriam Young Holden, *The American Woman in Colonial and Revolutionary Times* (Philadelphia: University of Pennsylvania Press, 1962). It is important to understand that during this period of economic development, all able people, including children, were expected to work. Puritan women were excluded from positions of power and influence in the church much more than they were in the marketplace.

CHAPTER FIVE

1. Stanford, *Anne Bradstreet*, 118.

2. John Calvin, *Institutes of Christian Religion*, 2 vols. (Philadelphia, 1960),

2:41–43; also quoted in Page Smith, *Daughters of the Promised Land* (Boston: Little, Brown and Co., 1970), 41.

3. See Edmund S. Morgan, *The Puritan Family: Essays on Religion and Domestic Matters in Seventeenth-Century New England* (1944; rev. ed., New York: Harper and Row, 1966); Levin L. Schucking, *The Puritan Family: A Social Study from the Literary Sources* (London: Routledge and Kegan Paul, 1969); John Demos, *A Little Commonwealth: Family Life in Plymouth Colony* (New York: Oxford University Press, 1970); and Philip Greven, *The Protestant Temperament: Patterns of Child-rearing, Religious Experience, and the Self in Early America* (New York: Alfred A. Knopf, 1977). For a discussion of all social institutions as being part of a covenant with God, see Perry Miller, *The New England Mind: The Seventeenth Century* (New York: Macmillan Co., 1939), 365–491.

4. John Cotton, *A Practical Commentary; or, An Exposition with Observations, Reasons, and Uses Upon the First Epistle Generall of John* (London, 1656), 193.

5. Ibid.

6. Benjamin Wadsworth, *The Well-Ordered Family or Relative Duties* (Boston: Printed by B. Green, 1712), 12.

7. Rosemary M. Laughlin, "Anne Bradstreet: Poet in Search of Form," *American Literature* 42 (1970): 4–5, asserts that "the slow alexandrines . . . suggest that resignation to God's will was a heavy thing for the poet to bear, especially since the slight irregularity of the meter produces a somewhat tortured hesitation." See also Ann Stanford, *Anne Bradstreet*, 386. In *God's Altar*, Robert Daly argues that Bradstreet accepts "the child's untimely death [as] a clear act of providence, not merely a regrettable part of the order of nature" (112).

8. Ben Jonson, "On My First Son," in Ben Jonson, *Selected Works*, ed. Harry Levin (New York: Random House, 1938), 874.

9. Piercy, *Anne Bradstreet*, 99, 101. See also Alan H. Rosenfeld, "Anne Bradstreet's 'Contemplations': Patterns of Form and Meaning," *New England Quarterly* 43 (March 1970): 79–96.

10. Calvin, *Institutes*, 1:xiv, 20–21.

11. For a discussion of the emblematic connection of the divine and temporal spheres, see Roy Harvey Pearce, *The Continuity of American Poetry* (Princeton: Princeton University Press, 1961); Murdock, *Literature and Theology in Colonial New England*; and Silverman, ed., *Colonial American Poetry*.

12. Piercy, *Anne Bradstreet*, 353.

13. Bradstreet, *Works*, lxiv.

PART TWO: INTRODUCTION

1. Thomas H. Johnson and Theodora Ward, eds., *The Letters of Emily Dickinson*, 3 vols. (Cambridge, Mass.: Harvard University Press, 1958), 1:197 (hereafter cited in the text as *L*, followed by volume, page, and letter number).

2. Sandra Gilbert and Susan Gubar, *The Madwoman in the Attic: The Woman Writer and the Nineteenth-Century Literary Imagination* (New Haven: Yale Uni-

versity Press, 1979), 583. Gilbert also uses the line from Dickinson's poem no. 605, "A Woman white," in the title of her chapter on Emily Dickinson.

3. Barbara Mossberg, *Emily Dickinson: When a Writer Is a Daughter* (Bloomington: Indiana University Press, 1982). This study provides important insights into Dickinson's relationship with her family. Mossberg explores in detail Dickinson's anger toward her father for denying her rights that he granted her brother Austin as well as her fury with her mother for being inadequate both as a nurturer and role model.

4. Adrienne Rich, "Vesuvius at Home: The Power of Emily Dickinson," *Parnassus: Poetry in Review* 5, no. 1 (1976): 49–74, reprinted in Adrienne Rich, *Selected Prose, 1966–1978* (New York: W. W. Norton, 1979), 161.

5. David Porter, *Dickinson: The Modern Idiom* (Cambridge, Mass.: Harvard University Press, 1981).

6. Joanne Feit Diehl, *Dickinson and the Romantic Imagination* (Princeton: Princeton University Press, 1981), passim; and Margaret Homans, *Women Writers and Poetic Identity: Dorothy Wordsworth, Emily Brontë, and Emily Dickinson* (Princeton: Princeton University Press, 1980), 36.

7. Karl Keller, *The Only Kangaroo among the Beauty: Emily Dickinson and America* (Baltimore: Johns Hopkins University Press, 1979), 133–34.

CHAPTER SIX

1. Adrienne Rich, "I Am In Danger—Sir—," in *Necessities of Life* (New York: W. W. Norton, 1966), 33.

2. Richard Chase, *Emily Dickinson* (New York: William Sloane, 1951), 9. Other critical studies include George Frisbee Whicher, *This Was a Poet: A Critical Biography of Emily Dickinson* (New York: Charles Scribner's Sons, 1939); Charles Anderson, *Emily Dickinson's Poetry: Stairway of Surprise* (New York: Holt, Rinehart, and Winston, 1960); William R. Sherwood, *Circumference and Circumstance* (New York: Columbia University Press, 1968); Klaus Lubbers, *Emily Dickinson: The Critical Revolution* (Ann Arbor: University of Michigan, 1968); Denis Donoghue, *Emily Dickinson* (Minneapolis: University of Minnesota Press, 1969); Robert Weisbuch, *Emily Dickinson's Poetry* (Chicago: University of Chicago Press, 1972).

3. Edward Dickinson, *Celebration of the Two Hundredth Anniversary of the settlement of Hadley, Massachusetts* (Northampton, 1859), 77, quoted in David Higgins, *Portrait of Emily Dickinson: The Poet and Her Prose* (New Brunswick, N.J.: Rutgers University Press, 1967).

4. Jay Leyda, *The Years and Hours of Emily Dickinson*, 2 vols. (New Haven: Yale University Press, 1960), 1:171.

5. Emily Dickinson, Seminary Journal, January 3, 1843, quoted in Whicher, *This Was a Poet*, 73.

6. Thomas Johnson, *Emily Dickinson: An Interpretive Biography* (Cambridge, Mass.: Harvard University Press, 1955), 36.

7. Thomas Johnson, ed., *The Poems of Emily Dickinson*, 3 vols. (Cambridge,

Mass.: Harvard University Press, 1951) (hereafter cited in the text as *P*, followed by volume, page, and poem number).

8. Leyda, *Years and Hours of Emily Dickinson*, 1:172.

9. Harriet Martineau, *Retrospective of Western Travel*, quoted in ibid., 1:29.

10. It was widely believed that there was an inverse relationship between the womb and the brain. See G. J. Barker-Benfield, *The Horrors of the Half-Known Life: Male Attitudes toward Women and Sexuality in Nineteenth-Century America* (New York: Harper and Row, 1976), 45–61, for a discussion of medical literature on the subject.

11. See Jack L. Capps, *Emily Dickinson's Reading, 1836–1886* (Cambridge, Mass.: Harvard University Press, 1966), for an extensive survey of the books in the Dickinson library.

12. Leyda, *Years and Hours of Emily Dickinson*, 1:10.

13. This letter is dated January 3, 1838. Ibid., 1:38.

14. This letter is dated January 9, 1838. Ibid., 1:40.

15. This letter is dated February 16, 1838. Ibid., 1:44.

16. This letter is dated May 19, 1844. Ibid., 1:86.

17. Ibid., 1:30.

18. Ibid., 1:18. This speech printed in the *Hampshire Gazette* was presented to the Committee of Household Manufacturers.

19. Ibid., 2:450.

20. Whicher, *This Was a Poet*, 55.

21. Carroll Smith-Rosenberg, "The Hysterical Woman: Sex Roles and Role Conflict in Nineteenth-Century America," *Social Research* 29 (Winter 1972): 652–78, argues that the invalidism of Victorian women was a result of repressed anger and enforced passivity.

22. For a discussion of the common nervous disorders of middle-class women in the nineteenth century see Ann Douglas, "The Fashionable Diseases: Women's Complaints and Their Treatment in Nineteenth-Century America," *Journal of Interdisciplinary History* 4, no. 1 (Summer 1973): 25–52. Also see Barbara Ehrenreich and Deirdre English, *Complaints and Disorders: The Sexual Politics of Sickness* (Old Westbury, N.Y.: Feminist Press, 1973).

An extended analysis of anger expressed as disease can be found in Patricia Branca, *The Silent Sisterhood: Middle-class Women in the Victorian Home* (Pittsburgh: Carnegie Mellon University Press, 1975); Jean Strouse, *Alice James: A Biography* (Boston: Houghton Mifflin Co., 1980); and Ruth Yeazell, ed., *The Death and Letters of Alice James* (Berkeley: University of California Press, 1980).

23. Useful additional background and discussion of nineteenth-century medical views of women can be found in Barker-Benfield, *The Horrors of the Half-Known Life*.

Also see Carroll Smith-Rosenberg, "Puberty to Menopause: The Cycle of Femininity in Nineteenth-Century America," *Feminist Studies* 1 (1973): 25; John S. Haller and Robin M. Haller, *The Physician and Sexuality in Victorian America* (Urbana: University of Illinois Press, 1974).

These studies indicate that many doctors believed that female sexuality was intrinsically pathological; menstruation, menopause, and pregnancy were god-given female burdens and the cause of the inherent weakness of women.

24. Elaine Showalter, *A Literature of Their Own: British Women Novelists from Brontë to Lessing* (Princeton: Princeton University Press, 1976), 274–75.

25. Leyda, *Years and Hours of Emily Dickinson*, 1:16.

26. See Martha Vicinus, ed., *Suffer and Be Still: Women in the Victorian Age* (Bloomington: Indiana University Press, 1972). This collection of essays explores the effects of enforced passivity and self-denial on Victorian women.

27. Millicent Todd Bingham, *Emily Dickinson's Home: Letters of Edward Dickinson and His Family* (New York: Harper and Brothers, 1955).

28. See Richard Sewall, *The Life of Emily Dickinson*, 2 vols. (New York: Farrar, Straus and Giroux, 1974).

29. Mossberg, *Emily Dickinson*, also discusses Dickinson's resentment of her brother's privileged position in the family. Mossberg's analysis of Emily's jealousy of Austin's prerogatives as the only son is especially illuminating.

30. Letter from Mrs. Jameson to her son Frank, May 16, 1886, in Leyda, *Years and Hours of Emily Dickinson*, 1:471.

31. Letter from Mrs. Todd to her parents, May 16, 1886, in ibid., 1:472.

32. R. D. Laing, *The Politics of the Family* (New York: Pantheon Books, 1971). See "Family Scenarios," 77–87, and "Mapping," 117–24.

33. Letter from Mabel Loomis Todd to T. W. Higginson, July 9, 1891, in Leyda, *Years and Hours of Emily Dickinson*, 2:224.

34. Ibid.

35. Ibid., 2:283.

36. Dickinson is spelled Dickenson. This spelling error seems to have been overlooked by most scholars to date.

CHAPTER SEVEN

1. There has been extraordinary critical controversy about the nature of Dickinson's romantic attachments. For many years, critics thought that Emily Dickinson was in love with Charles Wadsworth. See Thomas Johnson, *Emily Dickinson: An Interpretive Biography*. Theodora Ward, *The Capsule of the Mind: Chapters in the Life of Emily Dickinson* (Cambridge, Mass.: Harvard University Press, 1961), states that the identity of Emily Dickinson's lover is still unknown.

Ruth Miller and David Higgins have argued convincingly that Samuel Bowles was the man to whom Dickinson's love poems and letters were written. See Ruth Miller, *The Poetry of Emily Dickinson* (Middletown, Conn.: Wesleyan University Press, 1968), 101–28, and Higgins, *Portrait of Emily Dickinson: The Poet and Her Prose*. Higgins compares similarities of language and imagery in a "Master" letter (Johnson and Ward, eds., *Letters of Emily Dickinson*, 2:374) and a letter to Bowles (ibid., 2:393).

Rebecca Patterson, in *The Riddle of Emily Dickinson* (Boston: Houghton Mifflin Co., 1951), asserted that Dickinson was in love with Kate Scot Anthon, and John Cody, in *After Great Pain: The Inner Life of Emily Dickinson* (Cambridge, Mass.: Harvard University Press, 1971), writes that Dickinson suffered from a conflict in her sexual attraction to both men and women.

2. George S. Merriam, *The Life and Times of Samuel Bowles* (New York: Century Company, 1885), 271. Bowles's friendship with Maria Whitney was especially troubling to Mary Bowles who expressed her anxiety to her son. See Leyda, *Years and Hours of Emily Dickinson*, 1:129–30, 142, 172.

3. Millicent Todd Bingham, *Emily Dickinson: A Revelation* (New York: Harper and Brothers, 1954), 8, also quotes Austin as saying that she did not love Wadsworth.

4. There has been considerable controversy about the dating and ordering of these letters. Johnson and Ward, eds., *Letters of Emily Dickinson*, 2:375, indicate that the date and ordering of some of the letters have been determined by handwriting style.

5. *The Love Letters of Charlotte Brontë to Constantin Heger* (London: Printed for Private Circulation Only, 1914), 30.

6. Helene Moglen, *Charlotte Brontë: The Self Concerned* (New York: W. W. Norton, 1976), 51.

7. Sandra M. Gilbert and Susan Gubar, "Strength in Agony: Nineteenth-Century Poetry by Women," in *The Madwoman in the Attic*, 539–650.

8. See Adrienne Rich, "Vesuvius at Home: The Power of Emily Dickinson," 49–74, and Joanne Feit Diehl, "'Come Slowly—Eden': The Woman Poet and Her Muse," in *Dickinson and the Romantic Imagination*, 13–33.

Also see Millicent Todd Bingham's statement in *Ancestor's Brocades: The Literary Debut of Emily Dickinson* (New York: Harper and Brothers, 1945) that "Emily was more interested in her poems than in any man" (322). In "A Mystical Poet," in Archibald MacLeish, ed., *Emily Dickinson: Three Views: Archibald MacLeish, Louise Bogan, Richard Wilbur* (Amherst: Amherst College Press, 1960), Louise Bogan also asserts that Dickinson was most interested in "her progress as a writer, and as a person" (32).

9. Margaret Fuller Ossoli, *Woman in the Nineteenth Century and Kindred Papers* (Boston: John Jewett and Co., 1855; reprint, New York: W. W. Norton, 1971), 176–77.

10. Ibid., 121.

11. In his essay, "Literature as an Art," *Atlantic Monthly* 20 (December 1867): 753, Higginson observed that it was "no discredit to Walt Whitman that he wrote *Leaves of Grass* only that he did not burn it afterwards."

12. Johnson and Ward, eds., *Letters of Emily Dickinson*, 2:403.

13. In *The Poetry of Emily Dickinson*, Ruth Miller argues that Dickinson very much wanted Higginson's approval for publication as she did Bowles's approval, passim. But Bingham, in *Emily Dickinson's Home*, quotes Dickinson as saying, "How can you print a piece of your soul?," 166.

14. *Atlantic Monthly* 68 (October 1891): 453.

15. Leyda, *Years and Hours of Emily Dickinson*, 2:302.

16. Clark Griffin, *The Long Shadow: Emily Dickinson's Tragic Poetry* (Princeton: Princeton University Press, 1964), says that Dickinson "stood in *dread* of

everything masculine" (24). This is much too simple an interpretation of her complex relationships to men; clearly, her bantering irony indicates that she does not dread Higginson.

17. Merriam, *The Life and Times of Samuel Bowles*, 217.

18. Letter from Maria Whitney to her sister Lizzie, March 10, 1868, in Leyda, *Years and Hours of Emily Dickinson*, 2:129–30.

19. See ibid., 2:173, 177, 178.

20. Ibid., 2:602. In *The Life and Times of Samuel Bowles*, George Merriam observes that Bowles was attracted to "women of a characteristic New England type . . . who inherit a fine intellect, an unsparing conscience, a sensitive nervous organization; whose minds have a natural bent towards the problems of the soul and the universe" (215).

21. For further discussion of Dickinson's relationship to Lord, see Bingham, *Emily Dickinson: A Revelation*.

22. Johnson, ed., *Poems of Emily Dickinson*, 3:1054, cites the last quatrain as a later variant of the poem. The original version read:

If Aims impel these Astral Ones
The ones allowed to know
Know that which makes them is forgot
As Dawn forgets them—now—

23. Letter of Mrs. Jameson to her son, John, October 14, 1883, in Leyda, *Years and Hours of Emily Dickinson*, 2:406.

24. This is a fragment written on the back of a letter to Sue Dickinson in October 1884. See Johnson and Ward, eds., *Letters of Emily Dickinson*, 3:919.

25. See Whicher, *This Was a Poet*, 170–71, for a discussion of Dickinson's "Yankee wit."

CHAPTER EIGHT

1. Millicent Todd Bingham's *Ancestor's Brocades* provides a narration of the preparation of Dickinson's poems for posthumous publication. Additional details about the publication of Dickinson's poems can be found in the following biographies: Thomas Johnson, *Emily Dickinson: An Interpretive Biography*, and Ralph William Franklin, *The Editing of Emily Dickinson: A Reconsideration* (Madison: University of Wisconsin Press, 1967).

2. The following poems were published in the *Springfield Republican*: no. 3, "Sic transit gloria mundi," titled "A Valentine," on February 20, 1852; no. 214, "I taste a liquor never brewed," titled "The May-wine," on May 4, 1861; no. 216, "Safe in their alabaster chambers," titled "The Sleeping," on March 30, 1864; no. 228, "Blazing in gold and quenching in purple," titled "Sunset," on March 30, 1864; no. 986, "A narrow fellow in the grass," titled "The Snake," on February 14, 1866. "Some keep the sabbath going to church" (no. 324), titled "My Sabbath," appeared in *The Round Table*, March 12, 1864; "Success is counted sweetest" (no. 67), titled "Success," appeared in *A Masque of Poets*, November 1878.

3. Albert Gelpi, *Emily Dickinson: The Mind of the Poet* (Cambridge, Mass: Harvard University Press, 1965), 59.

4. Chase, *Emily Dickinson*, 124, equates Emily Dickinson's sudden "illumina-tions" with Puritan grace. Gelpi, *Emily Dickinson*, places Dickinson in the religious tradition that began with Bradford, Winthrop, and Edwards, and extends through Emerson and Dickinson to Eliot and Frost.

5. Clara Newman Turner, "My Personal Acquaintance with Emily Dickinson," in Sewall, *The Life of Emily Dickinson*, 1:269.

6. Leyda, *Years and Hours of Emily Dickinson*, 1:171.

7. F. B. Sanburn, ed., *Familiar Letters of Henry David Thoreau* (Boston and New York: Houghton Mifflin Co., 1894), 7–9.

8. Ralph Waldo Emerson, "Experience," in *The Essays of Ralph Waldo Emerson* (New York: Modern Library, 1944), 245.

9. Emerson, "The Poet," in *Essays*, 232.

10. David Porter, *Emerson and Literary Change* (Cambridge, Mass.: Harvard University Press, 1979). Porter describes Emerson's technique as a "linear" progression from experience to "truth," the expression of insight in "binary" form, and a resistance to immediate experience as "digression." Porter also observes that Emerson has a tendency to rely heavily on pastoral conventions in his poetry; however, Emerson is credited with a loosening of the poetic form that Whitman and Dickinson use to write their strikingly original poems.

11. See Joel Porte, *Representative Men: Ralph Waldo Emerson and His Time* (New York: Oxford University Press, 1979).

12. Emerson, "Experience," in *Essays*, 246.

13. The two modes of human consciousness have been explored by Robert Ornstein, Michael Gazzaniga, Arthur Deikman, G. William Domhoff, Jerome Bruner, Roger Sperry, and others in recent years. See Robert E. Ornstein, *The Psychology of Consciousness* (New York: Harcourt Brace Jovanovich, 1977); Michael S. Gazzaniga, "The Split Brain in Man," *Scientific American*, August 1967, 24–29; Arthur Deikman, "Bimodal Consciousness," *Archives of General Psychiatry* 25 (December 1971): 481–89; Arthur Deikman, "King's Right in the First Place?," *Psychoanalytic Review* 56 (1969–70): 586–96; Jerome Bruner, *On Knowing: Essays for the Left Hand* (New York: Atheneum, 1965); Roger W. Sperry, "The Great Cerebral Commissure," *Scientific American* (January 1964), 142–52; Roger W. Sperry, "Lateral Specialization in the Surgically Separated Hemispheres," in Frances O. Schmidt and Frederic Waden, eds., *The Neurosciences: Third Study Program* (Cambridge, Mass.: MIT Press, 1974); Robert Ornstein, ed., *Symposium on Consciousness* (New York: Viking Press, 1976).

14. As Margaret Homans observes, Emily Dickinson challenges "the oppressive structure [of] hierarchy in language . . . at the heart of male supremacy. The desire to be at the center generates hierarchical thinking." In *Women Writers and Poetic Identity: Dorothy Wordsworth, Emily Brontë, and Emily Dickinson*, Homans's deconstructionist analysis of Emily Dickinson's poetry supports my emphasis on Dickinson's nonhierarchical consciousness (36).

15. Emerson, "The Poet," in *Essays*, 227.

16. Emerson, "Self Reliance," in *Essays*, 34.

17. For discussions of traditional social roles and responsibilities of women in the nineteenth century, see Barbara Welter, *Dimity Convictions: The American Woman in the Nineteenth Century* (Athens, Ohio: Ohio University Press, 1976); Nancy F. Cott, *The Bonds of Womanhood: "Woman's Sphere" in New England, 1780–1835* (New Haven: Yale University Press, 1977); and Ann Douglas, *The Feminization of American Culture* (New York: Alfred A. Knopf, 1977).

18. Leyda, *Years and Hours of Emily Dickinson*, 1:88.

19. Whicher, *This Was a Poet*, quotes Professor John Burgess as saying: "The social leader of the town was Mrs. Austin Dickinson, a really brilliant and highly cultivated woman of great taste and refinement, perhaps a little too aggressive, and a little too sharp in wit and repartee, and a little too ambitious for social prestige, but, withal, a woman of the world in the best sense" (34).

20. Cody, *After Great Pain*, passim. Cody's analysis does not take into account the pleasures of solitude or the demands of art. Johnson, *Emily Dickinson: An Interpretive Biography*, 51. In general, the transcendentalists felt that excessive sociability dulled the mind.

21. Virginia Woolf, *To the Lighthouse* (London: Hogarth Press, 1927), 249.

22. See Nancy Chodorow, "Family Structure and Feminine Personality," in Michelle Zimbalist Rosaldo and Louise Lamphere, eds., *Women, Culture, and Society* (Stanford: Stanford University Press, 1974), 43–66. Chodorow suggests that men are trained to think "oppositionally" while women are taught to respond "relationally." This bifurcation is explored more extensively in Nancy Chodorow, *The Reproduction of Mothering: Psychoanalysis and the Sociology of Gender* (Berkeley: University of California Press, 1978).

23. For a discussion of the influence of Elizabeth Barrett Browning's poetry, especially "Aurora Leigh," on Dickinson's metaphors, see Ellen Moer's *Literary Women* (New York: Doubleday and Co., 1976), 55–62. Gilbert and Gubar, *Madwoman in the Attic*, 582–86, discusses the influence of the plot of "Aurora Leigh" on Dickinson's life and work.

24. Suzanne Juhasz, "'A Privilege So Awful': Emily Dickinson as Woman Poet," in *Naked and Fiery Forms: Modern American Poetry by Women, A New Tradition* (New York: Harper and Row, 1976), asserts that "sitting in the world of her room, of her mind," Dickinson "gently mock[s] the traditional woman's restricted life and self in comparison with her own" (31). In "Emily Dickinson," in *Interpretations of American Literature*, ed. Charles Feidelson, Jr., and Paul Brodtkorb, Jr. (New York: Oxford University Press, 1959), 197–211, Allen Tate observes that Dickinson's "life was one of the richest and deepest ever lived on this continent. . . . When she went upstairs and closed the door, she mastered life by rejecting it" (202). Inder Kher observes that Dickinson's insistence on privacy was a way of contending with society, in *The Landscape of Absence: Emily Dickinson's Poetry* (New Haven: Yale University Press, 1974), passim.

25. See Cott, *The Bonds of Womanhood*, and Nina Baym, *Woman's Fiction: A Guide to Novels by and about Women in America, 1820–1870* (Ithaca: Cornell University Press, 1978), for a discussion of the traditional woman's experience of domestic life in the nineteenth century.

26. See Wendy Martin, ed., *The American Sisterhood: Writings of the Feminist*

Movement from Colonial Times to the Present (New York: Harper and Row, 1972), and Gail Parker, *The Oven Birds: American Women and Womanhood, 1820–1920* (Garden City, N.Y.: Doubleday and Co., 1972), for collections of feminist writing protesting the confinement of women to the domestic sphere in the nineteenth century.

27. See Elaine Showalter, ed., *These Modern Women: Autobiographical Essays from the Twenties* (Old Westbury, N.Y.: Feminist Press, 1978), which contains essays by accomplished professional women describing the challenges and conflicts of combining career and marriage.

CHAPTER NINE

1. Lawrence Buell, *Literary Transcendentalism: Style and Vision in the American Renaissance* (Ithaca: Cornell University Press, 1973), observes that "well before Yeats and Joyce invented private mythologies as a substitute for orthodox Christianity, Melville, Whitman, and Emily Dickinson had begun to devise for themselves esoteric vocabularies and symbolic systems" (141).

2. William Carlos Williams, "How to Write," Linda Welshimer Wagner, ed., *Interviews with William Carlos Williams* (New York: New Directions, 1961), 100.

3. Walt Whitman, "A Noiseless Patient Spider," in *Leaves of Grass* (Philadelphia: David McKay, 1891–92), 343.

4. Ibid., 358–59.

5. For the details of the railroad connection between Amherst and Belchertown, see Bingham, *Emily Dickinson's Home*, 215–43.

6. Ibid., 72.

7. See Harold Bloom, *The Anxiety of Influence: A Theory of Poetry* (New York: Oxford University Press, 1975). Bloom discusses the anxiety generated by the individual artist's need to break free of precursors. But nineteenth-century American artists did not have an elaborate established literary tradition to contend with; instead, they had to break free from religious values, which meant standing apart from God. For a discussion of the conflict and anxiety of the nineteenth-century woman writer, see Gilbert and Gubar, *Madwoman in the Attic*.

8. See M. H. Abrams, *The Mirror and the Lamp: Romantic Theory and the Critical Tradition* (New York: Oxford University Press, 1953), and *Natural Supernaturalism: Tradition and Revolution in Romantic Literature* (New York: W. W. Norton, 1973), for a discussion of the romantic tradition. For a discussion of the romantic impulse to transcend immediate experience, see Donald Stone, *The Romantic Impulse in Victorian Fiction* (Cambridge, Mass.: Harvard University Press, 1980).

9. Selma Bishop, *Isaac Watts, Hymns and Spiritual Songs, 1707–1748: A Study in Early Eighteenth-Century Language Changes* (London: Faith Press, 1962), 236–37.

10. Ibid., 56.

11. See William Carlos Williams, "On Measure," in Wagner, ed., *Interviews with William Carlos Williams*, 66–69.

12. See Lois Cuddy's detailed discussion in "The Influence of Latin Poetics on Emily Dickinson's Style," *Comparative Literature Studies* 13 (September 1976): 214–29, and in "The Latin Imprint of Emily Dickinson's Poetry: Theory and Practice," *American Literature* 50 (March 1978): 74–84.

13. Solomon Stoddard and Ethan Allen Andrews, *A Grammar of the Latin Language: For the use of Schools and Colleges* (Boston, 1843), listed in Capps, *Emily Dickinson's Reading, 1836–66*. Also see Johnson and Ward, eds., *Letters of Emily Dickinson*, 1:208, no. 92, for Dickinson's own reference to "Stoddard and Andrews."

14. Quoted in Griffin, *The Long Shadow*, 273. Griffin uses this passage to demonstrate that Emily Dickinson associated time with masculine images—her father and God, for example. Griffin contends that Dickinson attempted to escape effects of temporal process by retreating into her father's house. Like many male critics, he argues that fear was her dominant emotion.

15. Sharon Cameron, "'A Loaded Gun': Dickinson and the Dialect of Rage," *Publications of the Modern Language Association* 93 (May 1978): 423–37, argues that Dickinson "has rage toward all that is temporal, all that has a history whose requirement is sacrifice and choice." In *Lyric Time: Dickinson and the Limits of Genre* (Baltimore: Johns Hopkins University Press, 1979), Cameron elaborates her analysis.

16. Johnson, ed., *Poems of Emily Dickinson*, Introduction, 1:xxxiii–xxxiv.

17. Ibid.

18. Higgins, *Portrait of Emily Dickinson*, describes Dickinson's drafts as "the scrap basket of Emily's workshop" (6–7).

19. See Franklin, *The Editing of Emily Dickinson*. Miller, *The Poetry of Emily Dickinson*, argues that the principle behind the fascicles is dramatic. "Each is a dramatic structure designed to recreate the experience of the woman as she strives for acceptance or knowledge, is rebuffed or fails because of her limitations" (186). Nina Baym, Review of *The Life of Emily Dickinson* by Richard B. Sewall, *The Landscape of Absence: Emily Dickinson's Poetry* by Inder Nath Kher, *Emily Dickinson's Poetry* by Robert Weisbuch, in *Journal of English and Germanic Philology* 75 (Jan.–Apr. 1976): 301–7, has observed that "more work should be done on the analytic questions raised by the texts: the variants, for example, or the arrangement of her poems within the sewn packets" (307).

20. Leyda, *Years and Hours of Emily Dickinson*, 2:240. Also see MacGregor Jenkins, *Emily Dickinson, Friend and Neighbor* (Boston: Little, Brown, 1930).

21. Raymond Williams, *The Country and the City* (New York: Oxford University Press, 1973).

CHAPTER TEN

1. See Nancy F. Cott, "Passionlessness: An Interpretation of Victorian Sexual Ideology, 1790–1850," *Signs* 4, no. 2 (Winter 1978): 219–36. For a discussion

254 · Notes to Pages 149–54

of nineteenth-century female friendship networks, see Carroll Smith-Rosenberg, "The Female World of Love and Ritual: Relations between Women in Nineteenth-Century America," *Signs* 1, no. 1 (1975): 1–29.

2. Donald G. Mitchell [Ik Marvel], *Reveries of a Bachelor; or a Book of the Heart* (New York: Baker and Scribner, 1851).

3. Albert Gelpi notes that Dickinson's emphasis on the sun's power to "scorch" and "scathe" as well as the passive "yielded up" suggests sacrifice rather than choice (*The Tenth Muse: The Psyche of the American Poet* [Cambridge, Mass.: Harvard University Press, 1975], 225). Commenting on the elaborate imagery of male power and female powerlessness, Sandra Gilbert points out that the flower "must helplessly trace [the sun's] course" (Gilbert and Gubar, *Madwoman in the Attic*, 596–97).

4. Nathaniel Hawthorne, *The Blithedale Romance* (Boston: Ticknor and Fields, 1852), 262.

5. Orestes A. Brownson, "The Woman Question" (1873), quoted in Martin, ed., *The American Sisterhood*, 4.

6. Adrienne Rich, "Snapshots of a Daughter-in-Law," in *Snapshots of a Daughter-in-Law: Poems, 1954–1962* (New York: W. W. Norton, 1963), 22.

7. Emerson, "The Poet," in *Essays*, 233.

8. Sandra Gilbert suggests that Dickinson's celibacy signifies "power instead of weakness" and represents the boon of "androgynous wholeness, autonomy, self-sufficiency" (Gilbert and Gubar, *Madwoman in the Attic*, 617).

9. Mitchell, *Reveries of a Bachelor*, 6.

10. Leyda, *Years and Hours of Emily Dickinson*, 1:6.

11. Cott, *The Bonds of Womanhood*; Baym, *Woman's Fiction*.

12. Baym, *Woman's Fiction*, 27.

13. Welter, *Dimity Convictions*; Douglas, *The Feminization of American Culture*, passim.

14. Douglas, *The Feminization of American Culture*, 12.

15. See Froma L. Zeitlin, "The Dynamics of Misogyny: Myth and Mythmaking in the *Orestia*," *Arethusa* 2, nos. 1–2 (Spring/Fall, 1978): 149–81, for a detailed discussion of the changes in social structure that occur with the shift from matriarchal to patriarchal values.

16. Zeitlin, ibid., observes that the following dichotomies are characteristic of the fundamental conflict:

Male	*Female*
Logos	Repetition
Apollo	Erinyes
Olympian	Chthonic
Marriage (non-kin)	Kinship
Law (court)	Ritual
Culture	Nature
Order	Chaos
Rule	Unruly (misrule)
Active	Passive
Reason	Unreason (passion)

Light	Dark
Clarity (plain speaking)	Obscurity (riddle)
Intellect	Senses, representation

17. Leyda, *Years and Hours of Emily Dickinson*, 2:435.

18. Margaret Fuller, "Life Without and Life Within," quoted in Belle Gayle Chevigny's *The Woman and the Myth: Margaret Fuller's Life and Writings* (Old Westbury, N.Y.: Feminist Press, 1976), 349.

19. Leyda, *Years and Hours of Emily Dickinson*, 2:413.

20. Kher, *The Landscape of Absence*, 273.

21. See Sewall, *Life of Emily Dickinson*, vol. 2, for a detailed and insightful discussion of this affair.

22. Robert Richardson, Jr., *Myth and Literature in the American Renaissance* (Bloomington: Indiana University Press, 1978), documents the transcendentalists' search for mythologies in Greek and Latin epics and Indian legends to buttress the identity of the new nation.

PART THREE: INTRODUCTION

1. Adrienne Rich, *Sources* (Woodside, Calif.: Heyeck Press, 1984), 14 (hereafter cited in the text as *Sources*).

2. Adrienne Rich, "When We Dead Awaken: Writing as Re-Vision," *College English* 34, no. 1 (October 1972): 18–25, reprinted in Adrienne Rich, *On Lies, Secrets, and Silences* (New York: W. W. Norton, 1979), 42 (hereafter cited in the text as *LSS*).

3. Cheryl Walker, *The Nightingale's Burden: Women Poets and Culture before 1900* (Bloomington: Indiana University Press, 1982), 150.

4. Adrienne Rich, *Of Woman Born: Motherhood as Experience and Institution* (New York: W. W. Norton, 1976), 43 (hereafter cited in the text as *OWB*).

5. For additional discussion of the evolution of Rich's style, see Wendy Martin, "From Patriarchy to the Female Principle: A Chronological Reading of Adrienne Rich's Poems," in Barbara Charlesworth Gelpi and Albert Gelpi, eds., *Adrienne Rich's Poetry* (New York: W. W. Norton, 1975), 175–89, and Wendy Martin, "Adrienne Rich's Poetry," in Leonard Unger, ed., *American Writers* (New York: Charles Scribner's Sons, 1979).

6. Adrienne Rich, taped conversation with Wendy Martin, May 1978 (hereafter cited in the text as *TCWM*).

7. Edward Johnson, *Wonder-Working Providence of Sions Saviour in New-England* (London: Nathaniel Brooke, 1654), reprinted by Scholars' Facsimiles and Reprints (New York: Delmar, 1974), 2.

8. David Kalstone, *Five Temperaments: Elizabeth Bishop, Robert Lowell, James Merrill, Adrienne Rich, and John Ashbery* (New York: Oxford University Press, 1977), 129.

CHAPTER ELEVEN

1. Adrienne Rich, *Snapshots of a Daughter-in-Law: Poems, 1954–1962* (New York: W. W. Norton, 1963), 32 (hereafter cited in the text as *SDL*).

2. Adrienne Rich, *A Change of World* (New Haven: Yale University Press, 1951; reprint, New York: Arms Press, 1971), 26 (hereafter cited in the text as *CW*).

3. Randall Jarrell, "New Books in Review," *Yale Review* 46, no. 1 (September 1956): 100–103.

4. Adrienne Rich, *The Diamond Cutters and Other Poems* (New York: Harper and Brothers, 1955), 89–90 (hereafter cited in the text as *DC*).

5. Albert Gelpi, "Adrienne Rich: The Poetics of Change," in Robert B. Shaw, ed., *American Poetry since 1960* (Cheshire, England: Carcanet Press, 1973), 123–43, reprinted in Gelpi and Gelpi, eds., *Adrienne Rich's Poetry*, 140–48.

6. For an elaborate discussion of the domestic lives of seventeenth-century New England women, see Laurel Thatcher Ulrich, *Goodwives: Image and Reality in the Lives of Women in Northern New England, 1650–1750* (New York: Alfred A. Knopf, 1982).

7. See Ruth Cowan, "Two Washes in the Morning and a Bridge Party at Night: The American Housewife between the Wars," *Women's Studies* 3, no. 2 (1976): 147–71.

8. Albert Gelpi, "The Poetics of Change," in Shaw, ed., *American Poetry since 1960*, 122–43; and in Gelpi and Gelpi, eds., *Adrienne Rich's Poetry*, 133.

9. Simone de Beauvoir, *Le Deuxième Sexe*, 2 vols. (Paris: Gallimard, 1949), 2:574; translation mine.

10. Adrienne Rich, "Acceptance Speech for the National Book Award," in Gelpi and Gelpi, eds., *Adrienne Rich's Poetry*, 204 (hereafter cited in the text as *ARP*).

11. Adrienne Rich, "Spring Thunder," in *Necessities of Life: Poems, 1962–1965* (New York: W. W. Norton, 1966), 44.

12. "Implosions," in Adrienne Rich, *Leaflets: Poems, 1965–68* (New York: W. W. Norton, 1969), 42 (hereafter cited in the text as *L*).

13. Adrienne Rich, *The Will to Change: Poems, 1968–70* (New York: W. W. Norton, 1971), 67 (hereafter cited in the text as *WC*).

CHAPTER TWELVE

1. Helen Vendler, "Ghostlier Demarcations, Keener Sounds," *Parnassus: Poetry in Review* 2, no. 1 (Fall–Winter 1973): 24, reprinted in Gelpi and Gelpi, eds., *Adrienne Rich's Poetry*, 170.

2. Adrienne Rich, *Diving into the Wreck: Poems, 1971–72* (New York: W. W. Norton, 1973), 8 (hereafter cited in the text as *DW*).

3. Statement written by Adrienne Rich, Audre Lorde, and Alice Walker and read at the National Book Award ceremony for *Diving into the Wreck*, in Gelpi and Gelpi, eds., *Adrienne Rich's Poetry*, 204.

4. Alicia Ostriker, "The Thieves of Language: Women Poets and Revisionist Mythmaking," *Signs* 8, no. 1 (Autumn 1982): 72.

5. Vendler, "Ghostlier Demarcations, Keener Sounds," in Gelpi and Gelpi, eds., *Adrienne Rich's Poetry*, 170.

6. Rich, "Anne Sexton: 1928–1974," in *On Lies, Secrets, and Silences*, 122–23; Rich's italics.

7. Jean-Marc Gaspard Itard, *The Wild Boy of Aveyron*, trans. by George and Muriel Humphrey (New York: Appleton-Century-Crofts, 1962), 12.

8. Ibid., 44.

9. "Three Conversations," in Gelpi and Gelpi, eds., *Adrienne Rich's Poetry*, 111.

10. Allen Ginsberg, *The Fall of America: Poems of These States, 1965–1971* (San Francisco: City Lights Books, 1972), 167.

11. Allen Ginsberg, *"The Fall of America" Wins a Prize* (New York: Gotham Book Mart, 1974), unpaged.

12. Allen Ginsberg, *Indian Journals, March 1962–May 1963* (San Francisco: Dave Maselwood Books and City Lights Books, 1970), 61.

13. Allen Ginsberg, *Howl and Other Poems* (San Francisco: City Lights Books, 1956), 21.

14. Allen Ginsberg, "New York to San Fran," in *Airplane Dreams: Compositions from Journals* (Toronto: Anaisi, 1968), 18.

15. Allen Ginsberg, *Gay Sunshine Interview* (Bolinas, Calif.: Grey Fox Press, 1973), 37.

16. Adrienne Rich, *The Dream of a Common Language: Poems, 1974–1977* (New York: W. W. Norton, 1978), 13 (hereafter cited in the text as *DCL*).

17. Allen Ginsberg, *Mind Breaths: Poems, 1972–1977* (San Francisco: City Lights Books, 1977), 46.

18. Adrienne Rich, "From an Old House in America," *Poems: Selected and New, 1950–1975* (New York: W. W. Norton, 1975), 238 (hereafter cited in the text as *PSN*).

19. In her essay, "The Challenge of Women's History," in *The Majority Finds Its Past: Placing Women in History* (New York: Oxford University Press, 1979), 168–80, Gerda Lerner asks for a similar paradigm shift. She suggests that history be woman-centered in order to correct its current distortions: "What would history be like if it were seen through the eyes of women and ordered by the values they define?" (138).

CHAPTER THIRTEEN

1. Rich cites Lynn Sukenick as having coined the term "matrophobia," in Adrienne Rich, "Feeling and Reason in Doris Lessing's Fiction," *Contemporary Literature* 14, no. 4 (no date): 519.

2. In *Themis: A Study of the Social Origins of Greek Religion* (1912; London: Merlin Press, 1963), 208, Jane Harrison observes that in Crete, Asia Minor, Thrace, Macedonia, and Delphi, the mother, child (*kouros*), and sacred bull were

worshiped as embodiments of nature's sacred process. I am indebted to Harrison's discussion of pre-Hellenic civilization and matriarchal values.

3. Ibid., 468.

4. See C. Kerenyi, *Eleusis: Archetypal Image of Mother and Daughter* (New York: Pantheon, 1962). Also see Erich Neumann, *The Great Mother: An Analysis of an Archetype*, Bollingen Series (Princeton: Princeton University Press, 1955).

5. Nancy Chodorow, *The Reproduction of Mothering: Psychoanalysis and the Sociology of Gender* (Berkeley: University of California Press, 1978), 173–90.

6. Ibid., 191–209. In *The Mermaid and the Minotaur: Sexual Arrangements and the Human Malaise* (New York: Harper and Row, 1976), Dorothy Dinnerstein observes that our psychic and social lives would be enriched if nurturing were shared by both women and men.

7. In "Women as Shapers of Human Adaptation," in Frances Dahlberg, ed., *Woman, the Gatherer* (New Haven: Yale University Press, 1981), Adrienne Zihlman observes that females in most primate and hominid societies determine social relationships: "the prolonged physical closeness between mother and offspring results in enduring social and emotional attachments. These are essential for observational learning by the young from mothers and hence for the transmission of behaviors and information vital to individual survival and to the perpetuation of the group and the species" (81). Zihlman also emphasizes that it was females not males who controlled bonding (91). In the same volume, W. C. McGrew, in "The Female Chimpanzee as a Human Evolutionary Prototype," shifts attention from physical size to grooming and food-sharing as factors in social aggression and dominance. Female primates, he points out, bonded with males "only when males were to assist selectively in child-rearing" (54).

Edward O. Wilson, in *Sociobiology: The Abridged Edition* (Cambridge, Mass.: Harvard University Press, 1980), remarks that in primate societies often "the strongest and most enduring bonds are between the mother and her offspring, to an extent that matrilines can be said to be the heart of the society. Mothers are the primary socializing force in early life" (251).

8. Monique Wittig, "One Is Not Born a Woman," *Feminist Issues* 1, no. 2 (Winter 1981): 53.

9. Adrienne Rich, "Compulsory Heterosexuality and Lesbian Existence," *Signs* 5, no. 4 (Summer 1980): 637.

10. Ibid., 641.

11. Ibid., 633.

12. Quoted in Perry Miller, *The New England Mind: From Colony to Province* (Cambridge, Mass.: Harvard University Press, 1953), 190.

CHAPTER FOURTEEN

1. Adrienne Rich, *A Wild Patience Has Taken Me This Far: Poems, 1978–81* (New York: W. W. Norton, 1981) (hereafter cited in the text as *WP*).

2. Adrienne Rich, "Afterword," in Laura Lederer, ed., *Take Back the Night: A*

Collection of Essays on Women and Pornography (New York: William Morrow, 1980).

3. Peggy Reeves Sanday, *Female Power and Male Dominance: On the Origins of Sexual Inequality* (New York: Cambridge University Press, 1981).

4. Rich, *Sources*.

5. Lee Edwards, "The Labors of Psyche: Toward a Theory of Female Heroism," *Critical Inquiry* 6, no. 1 (Fall 1979): 33–49. Edwards applies Victor Turner's methodology and discussion in *Drama, Fields, and Metaphors: Symbolic Action in Human Society* (Ithaca: Cornell University Press, 1974), to the myth of Amor and Psyche. She posits that women are "liminal"—marginal; women's heroic quest is to "liberate love" from "relationships which reinforce existing class, status, and property arrangements" (49).

CHAPTER FIFTEEN

1. Virginia Woolf, *Three Guineas* (New York: Harcourt, Brace, 1966), 63.

2. Mary Douglas and Aaron Wildavsky, *Risk and Culture: An Essay on the Selection of Technologies and Environmental Dangers* (Berkeley: University of California Press, 1982).

3. Johnson, *Wonder-Working Providence of Sions Saviour in New-England* (1653), 231.

4. For example, see Annette Kolodny, "Some Notes on Defining a 'Feminist Literary Criticism,'" *Critical Inquiry* 2 (Autumn 1975): 75–92; Annette Kolodny, "Dancing through the Mine Field: Some Observations on the Theory, Practice, and Politics of a Feminist Literary Criticism," *Feminist Studies* 6, no. 3 (Spring 1980): 1–25; and Jane Marcus, "Storming the Toolshed," *Signs* 7, no. 3 (Spring 1982): 622–40. Objecting to Kolodny's acceptance of a diversity of feminist styles and critical modes as self-indulgent, Marcus observes that Kolodny's pluralism creates the potential for fragmentation of the feminist community. A similar divergence can be seen in Myra Jehlen's advocacy of broadening the base of feminist criticism to include more comparative discussion of female and male texts in "Archimedes and the Paradox of Feminist Criticism," *Signs* 6, no. 4 (Summer 1981): 575–601, and Elaine Showalter's response to Jehlen in the "Letters/Comments" section of *Signs* 8, no. 2 (1982): 160–64, in which she observes that a juxtaposition of male and female texts will lead once again to subordination of female to male modes of discourse.

5. For a feminist analysis of linguistic change, see Helene Cixous, "The Laugh of the Medusa," *Signs* 1, no. 4 (Summer 1976): 875–94.

6. In *The Emerging Goddess: The Creative Process in Art, Science, and Other Fields* (Chicago: University of Chicago Press, 1979), Albert Rothenberg says that creative thinking is characterized by this type of nonpolarized perception.

7. See Carolyn Heilbrun, *Toward a Recognition of Androgyny* (New York: Alfred A. Knopf, 1973), for an extended discussion of androgynous behavior. Also see the special issue devoted to the topic of androgyny in *Women's Studies*, vol. 2 (1974).

8. Thomas Dudley, "Letter to the Countess of Lincoln," in Alexander Young, ed., *Chronicles of the First Planters of the Colony of Massachusetts Bay* (Boston: Charles C. Little and James Brown, 1846), 332.

9. Adrienne Rich, "Racism within Feminism," speech for the Amherst College Colloquium on Sex, Race, and Class, Amherst, Massachusetts, April 24, 1980.

10. Carol Gilligan, *In A Different Voice: Psychological Theory and Women's Development* (Cambridge, Mass.: Harvard University Press, 1982).

Index

Acknowledgments

The author is grateful for permission to reproduce quotations as follows:

EMILY DICKINSON

Reprinted by permission of Little, Brown and Company:

THE COMPLETE POEMS OF EMILY DICKINSON, edited by Thomas H. Johnson. Poems (in whole or in part) nos. 339, 451, 668, 677, 822, 906, 1079, 1295, 1528, 1545, 1684, and 1694. Copyright 1914, 1929, 1935, 1942 by Martha Dickinson Bianchi; © 1957, 1963 by Mary L. Hampson.

Reprinted by permission of the publishers and the Trustees of Amherst College:

THE POEMS OF EMILY DICKINSON, edited by Thomas H. Johnson. Cambridge, Mass.: The Belknap Press of Harvard University Press. Copyright 1951, © 1955, 1979 by the President and Fellows of Harvard College.

ADRIENNE RICH

Reprinted by permission of W. W. Norton & Company, Inc., and Adrienne Rich:

ADRIENNE RICH'S POETRY, A Norton Critical Edition, Selected and Edited by Barbara Charlesworth Gelpi and Albert Gelpi. Copyright © 1975 by W. W. Norton & Company, Inc.

THE DIAMOND CUTTERS and Other Poems by Adrienne Rich. Copyright 1952, 1953, 1954, 1955 by Adrienne Rich Conrad.

DIVING INTO THE WRECK, Poems 1971–1972, by Adrienne Rich. Copyright © 1973 by W. W. Norton & Company, Inc.

THE DREAM OF A COMMON LANGUAGE, Poems 1974–1977, by Adrienne Rich. Copyright © 1978 by W. W. Norton & Company, Inc.

LEAFLETS, Poems, 1965–1968, by Adrienne Rich. Copyright © 1969 by W. W. Norton & Company, Inc.

NECESSITIES OF LIFE, Poems, 1962–1965, by Adrienne Rich. Copyright © 1966 by W. W. Norton & Company, Inc.